THE BEST OF
SAINSBURY'S
WHOLEFOOD
COOKING

THE BEST OF
SAINSBURY'S
WHOLEFOOD
COOKING

CONTENTS

CONTRIBUTORS

Main authors: Carol Bowen, Carole Handslip, Brian Binns

Contributing authors: Julia Roles, Clare Ferguson, Rhona Newman, Carolinc Ellwood, Gwyneth Loveday

Special photography: Clivc Streeter

NOTES

Standard spoon measurements are used in all recipes
1 tablespoon = one 15 ml spoon
1 teaspoon = one 5 ml spoon
All spoon measures are level

Size 3 eggs should be used unless otherwise stated

Ovens should be preheated to the specified temperature

For all the recipes, quantities are given in both metric and imperial measures. Follow either set but not a mixture of both because they are not interchangeable.

If fresh yeast is unobtainable, substitute dried yeast but use only half the recommended quantity and follow the manufacturer's instructions for reconstituting.

Fresh herbs are used unless otherwise stated. If unobtainable substitute a bouquet garni of the equivalent dried herbs or use dried herbs instead but halve the quantities stated.

Published exclusively for
J Sainsbury plc
Stamford House
Stamford Street
London SE1 9LL
by Cathay Books
Michelin House
81 Fulham Road
London SW3 6RB

First published 1986
Reprinted 1991

© Cathay Books 1986
ISBN 0 86178 415 4

Produced by Mandarin Offset
Printed and bound in Hong Kong

INTRODUCTION

Eating the best of fresh foods in season, cooking with care to preserve all essential nutrients and selecting foods that promote good health is the essence of wholefood cooking.

Not to be confused with vegetarian cooking where meat, fish, poultry, dairy produce, and other animal originated foods may be excluded – wholefood cooking is simply healthy cooking using whole foods that have nothing added.

Such philosophy represents food as nature intended it to be before man had a chance to add artificial flavourings, preserving agents, colours and stabilisers and before manufacturing processes take away vital fibre, vitamins, minerals and other trace elements adding in their place extra salt, sugar and often unnecessary flavourings.

Changing to a wholefood diet doesn't mean giving up all the foods you enjoy as the recipes in this book will lavishly show but simply adjusting them to suit a new healthy lifestyle. Start by replacing, gradually at first if wary, wholemeal bread for refined white, brown rice for polished white, honey and unrefined sugars for the pure, white varieties and freshly-cooked vegetables, fruit, wholemeal pasta, cereals, wholegrain, pulses, eggs and cheese for highly-refined processed or convenience foods. Take into account as you select your foods the recommendations of modern day nutritionists who advise reducing fats in general, sugar consumption overall, increasing fibre, cutting down on salt and boosting fruit and vegetable intake in your general diet.

Such a change doesn't mean added expense too – in fact you may count your blessings in more than good health by saving precious pennies if not pounds on basic ingredients. Using dried beans, pulses, rice, vegetables and pasta as main meal anchors will undoubtedly prove cheaper.

Cooking procedures will only need adapting slightly – wholegrains often take a little longer to cook and need more liquid than their processed counterparts; some dried beans, pulses and fruits may need a preliminary soak to ensure tenderness.

New flavours to replace traditional table-added salt, artificial flavourings and flavour enhancers, will come from the clever use of herbs, spices, fragrant oils, vinegars, yeast extract and ground seeds while white sugar can effectively be replaced with molasses, syrups, honey and unrefined sugars of the muscovado or demerara type.

All the recipes in 'The Best of Sainsbury's Wholefood' are designed to bring out the full flavour of natural ingredients, to create tasty, nutritious dishes. Sample some of the recipes for soups and starters, main courses, puddings, desserts and wholegrain baked treats from the pages of this book and you will soon discover that wholefood cooking is both simple and rewarding.

SOUPS AND STARTERS

A herb-scented soup topped with an elegant swirl of soured cream or natural yogurt, a marinated or pickled fish dish sprinkled with a scattering of snipped fresh herbs, a creamy smooth pâté all the better for slicing or spreading on curled wholemeal Melba toast or a mouthwatering dip to savour and scoop with crisp vegetable crudités, crackers or warm bread – such are the delights to enjoy with wholefood soups and starters.

Exploit the best of those healthy wholefood standbys and anchors vegetables, cheese, nuts, beans and grains and you'll find hearty bean soups alongside dainty stuffed mushrooms, light chilled melon cocktails nestled near to baked or coddled eggs and tasty fish kebabs competing with warm and soothing barley and vegetable broths.

Whether you're looking for an impressive dinner party starter or a simple lunchtime appetiser here are recipes to entice. Gain compliments at dinner by serving thinly sliced Gravad Lax with its dill and brandy sauce, an overlapping assembly of avocado slices with its piquant raspberry vinaigrette or creamy layers of aubergine and Mozzarella cheese baked with a fresh tomato sauce.

Many of these wholesome and healthy soups and starters can be made well ahead and reheated, if necessary, just before serving. If you opt to choose such a make-ahead start to a meal then show extra last-minute care by serving imaginative and thoughtful accompaniments like crusty hot bread rolls, crisp and chilled thin julienne strips of vegetables for crudités, sizzling hot and crunchy croûtons or freshly grated cheese for soups and carefully arranged side dishes of salad greenery for marinated fish, vegetable or fruit dishes.

YOGURT AND MINT SOUP

300 g (10 oz)
  natural yogurt
150 ml ($\frac{1}{4}$ pint)
  tomato juice
170 ml (6 fl oz)
  milk
1 clove garlic,
  crushed
1 tablespoon chopped
  mint
$\frac{1}{2}$ cucumber, diced
salt and pepper
mint to garnish

Place the yogurt and tomato juice in a bowl and mix together thoroughly. Stir in the milk, garlic, chopped mint, cucumber and salt and pepper to taste. Transfer to a soup tureen and chill for 2 hours.

Garnish with mint to serve.

Serves 4

LENTIL SOUP

2 tablespoons oil
1 onion, chopped
1 carrot, chopped
1 celery stick,
  chopped
1 clove garlic, crushed
125 g (4 oz) lentils
600 ml (1 pint) stock
salt and pepper
chopped parsley to
  garnish

Heat the oil in a large pan, add the onion, carrot and celery and fry until softened. Add the remaining ingredients, with salt and pepper to taste. Bring to the boil, cover and simmer for 45 minutes, stirring occasionally. Check the seasoning.

Pour into a warmed tureen and sprinkle with the parsley to serve.

Serves 4

Yogurt and Mint Soup; Lentil Soup

SCOTCH BROTH

750 g (1½ lb) neck of
 lamb
900 ml (1½ pints)
 beef stock
1 bouquet garni
salt and pepper
50 g (2 oz) pearl
 barley
250 g (8 oz) carrots,
 sliced
4 celery sticks,
 chopped
2 onions, sliced
2 leeks, sliced
1 turnip, diced
1 small swede, diced
120 ml (4 fl oz) dry
 sherry

Chop the lamb if necessary and discard any fat. Put in a large pan with the stock, bouquet garni, and salt and pepper to taste.

Bring to the boil and remove any scum. Cover and simmer for 1½ hours, skimming occasionally.

Take out the meat and add the pearl barley and vegetables to the pan. Bring to the boil, cover and simmer for 30 minutes. Discard the bouquet garni.

Chop the meat from the bone, and add to the pan with the sherry. Bring to the boil and simmer for 5 minutes.

Remove any fat from the surface with kitchen paper before serving.

Serves 6 to 8

NOTE: For best results, make the soup the day before required. Leave in the refrigerator overnight. Remove the solid fat from the surface, then bring the soup to the boil and heat through.

ADD A GARNISH

Colourful and chunky, velvety-smooth and creamy, or thick and hearty – whatever the soup, you can score points on appearance by adding a complementary garnish. Wholefood alternatives include sprinkling with a few chopped or snipped herbs (parsley, chives, mint, marjoram or thyme for example); a little grated cheese; crispy herb, cheese or garlic-tossed wholemeal bread croûtons; a little chopped watercress; chopped cucumber, spring onions or traffic-light-coloured peppers.

For unashamed luxury add a swirl of cream or natural yogurt; and if appetites are large or the soup is a main course, float with thick slices of toasted wholemeal bread and melted cheese for a meal in one pot.

For special occasions why not make light pastry croûtons from either shortcrust or puff pastry. Cut out shapes from thinly-rolled pastry using canapé cutters, glaze if liked and bake in a hot oven until golden, about 10–15 minutes.

If speed is of the essence, you couldn't opt for anything more elegant than a few thin slices of creamy white mushroom, a paper-thin ring of pepper, a single sprig of a fresh herb or a few strips of vegetable julienne – prepared in a trice.

ADUKI BEAN SOUP

125 g (4 oz) aduki
 beans
2 tablespoons oil
1 onion, chopped
1 celery stick,
 chopped
1 carrot, chopped
1 clove garlic,
 crushed
2 tomatoes, skinned
 and chopped
1 tablespoon tomato
 purée
1 bay leaf
1 teaspoon chopped
 thyme
900 ml (1½ pints)
 stock or water
salt and pepper
chopped parsley

Soak the beans in cold water to cover for 3 hours; drain well.

Heat the oil in a large pan, add the onion, celery and carrot and cook until softened. Add the remaining ingredients, with salt and pepper to taste. Bring to the boil, boil for 10 minutes then simmer for 1 hour.

Pour into a warmed soup tureen and sprinkle with the parsley to serve.

Serves 4

NOTE: Aduki beans are a small type of red kidney bean. If unobtainable, use kidney beans instead.

Aduki Bean Soup

MINESTRONE

2 tablespoons oil
2 onions, chopped
2 carrots, chopped
3 celery sticks
1 leek, sliced
2 cloves garlic
125 g (4 oz) green
  cabbage, shredded
1 bouquet garni
2.5 litres (4 pints)
  water
4 tablespoons tomato
  purée
4 tomatoes, skinned
  and chopped
2 tablespoons parsley
25 g (1 oz)
  wholewheat pasta
salt and pepper
Parmesan cheese

Heat the oil in a large pan, add the onions and fry until softened. Add the chopped carrots, celery, leek and crushed garlic, cover and cook gently for 10 minutes. Add the remaining ingredients, with salt and pepper to taste, and bring to the boil. Cover and simmer gently for 30 to 40 minutes, until all the vegetables are tender. Remove the bouquet garni.

Pour into a warmed soup tureen and serve with grated Parmesan cheese.
Serves 8

BARLEY BROTH

40 g (1½ oz) pot
  barley
2 tablespoons oil
1 onion, chopped
2 celery sticks, sliced
3 carrots, sliced
2 cloves garlic,
  crushed
1 turnip, chopped
75 g (3 oz) French
  beans, cut into
  small pieces
1.5 litres (2½ pints)
  vegetable stock
1 tablespoon soy
  sauce
salt and pepper
4 tomatoes, skinned
  and chopped
2 tablespoons
  chopped parsley

Soak the barley in cold water to cover for 1 hour. Drain well and set aside.

Heat the oil in a pan, add the onion and fry until softened. Add the celery, carrots, garlic and turnip. Cover and cook gently for 10 minutes, shaking the pan occasionally.

Add the barley, French beans, bouquet garni, water or stock, soy sauce and salt and pepper to taste. Cover and simmer for 45 minutes, until tender.

Add the tomatoes and parsley and cook for a further 10 minutes. Check the seasoning and remove the bouquet garni. Pour into a warmed soup tureen to serve.
Serves 6 to 8

LENTIL AND CELERY SOUP

2 tablespoons oil
1 onion, chopped
3 celery sticks, chopped
1 clove garlic, crushed
175 g (6 oz) red lentils
1 litre (1¾ pints) water
salt and pepper

Heat the oil in a large pan, add the onion and fry until softened. Add the remaining ingredients, with salt and pepper to taste. Bring to the boil, cover and simmer for 30 to 35 minutes, stirring occasionally.

Check the seasoning before pouring into a warmed soup tureen to serve.
Serves 6

LEFT: *Minestrone; Barley Broth; Lentil and Celery Soup*
RIGHT: *Pea Soup and Bean Soup*

PEA SOUP

1 tablespoon oil
1 onion, chopped
1 clove garlic,
    crushed
2 celery sticks,
    chopped
250 g (8 oz) dried
    marrowfat peas,
    soaked overnight
1.5 litres (2½ pints)
    water
1 bouquet garni
salt and pepper
mint sprig to garnish

Heat the oil in a large pan, add the onion and cook until softened. Add the garlic and celery and cook for 5 minutes, stirring occasionally.

Drain the peas and add to the pan with the water, bouquet garni, and salt and pepper to taste. Cover and boil rapidly for 10 minutes, then simmer gently for 2 to 3 hours, until the peas are soft. Remove the bouquet garni.

Cool slightly, then place half the soup in an electric blender or food processor and work to a smooth purée. Repeat with the remaining soup. Return to the pan. Reheat the soup gently, adding a little more water if it is too thick. Pour into a warmed soup tureen and garnish.
Serves 4 to 6

BEAN SOUP

250 g (8 oz) haricot
    beans, soaked
    overnight
1.2 litres (2 pints)
    water
salt and pepper
2 tablespoons olive
    oil
1 large onion,
    chopped
2 celery sticks, sliced
2 cloves garlic,
    crushed
chopped parsley to
    garnish

Drain the beans thoroughly, then place in a pan with the water. Cover, bring to the boil and boil rapidly for 10 minutes, then simmer for 1 to 1½ hours until soft, adding a little salt towards the end of cooking. Drain, reserving the cooking liquid.

Heat the oil in a large pan, add the onions, celery and garlic and fry for 5 minutes.

Place half the beans and 600 ml (1 pint) of the reserved liquid in an electric blender or food processor and work to a purée. Add to the onion and celery with remaining beans and bring to the boil. Season to taste and cook for 30 minutes.

Pour into a warmed soup tureen and sprinkle with parsley.
Serves 4 to 6

TOMATO AND CHEESE SOUP

25 g (1 oz) butter
2 large onions,
    chopped
25 g (1 oz) plain
    wholemeal flour
1 kg (2 lb) tomatoes,
    skinned, seeded
    and chopped
1 clove garlic,
    crushed
1 rosemary sprig
1 thyme sprig
600 ml (1 pint)
    chicken stock
salt and pepper
142 ml (5 fl oz)
    double cream
1 egg yolk
125 g (4 oz)
    Gruyère cheese,
    grated

Melt the butter in a pan, add the onions and cook, without browning, for 10 minutes. Stir in the flour and cook for a further minute. Stir in the tomatoes, garlic, herbs, stock, and salt and pepper to taste.

Bring to the boil, cover and simmer for 30 minutes or until the tomatoes are very tender. Cool slightly, then sieve or work in an electric blender until smooth. Return to the pan.

Blend the cream and egg yolk together and stir into the pan. Heat through gently; do not boil or the soup will curdle.

Stir in the cheese and serve immediately.

Serves 6 to 8

CREAM OF CHEDDAR SOUP

40 g (1½ oz) butter
3 large onions, finely
    chopped
900 ml (1½ pints)
    chicken stock
120 ml (4 fl oz) dry
    white wine
1 bouquet garni
salt and pepper
8 slices wholemeal
    French bread,
    1 cm (½ inch)
    thick, toasted
8 slices Gruyère
    cheese, 5 mm
    (¼ inch) thick
3 tablespoons grated
    Parmesan cheese
50 g (2 oz) Cheddar
    cheese, grated

Melt the butter in a pan, add the onions and cook until golden brown; this will take about 30 minutes. Add the stock, wine, bouquet garni, and salt and pepper to taste. Bring to the boil, cover and simmer for 20 minutes. Remove the bouquet garni.

Arrange a layer of toast in the bottom of an ovenproof tureen or deep casserole. Cover with a layer of Gruyère, then sprinkle with Parmesan and Cheddar. Repeat these layers once or twice more, finishing with a layer of cheese.

Pour over the onion-flavoured stock and place in a preheated moderate oven, 180°C (350°F), Gas Mark 4, for 20 minutes, until the cheese has melted.

Serve immediately.

Serves 4 to 6

Tomato and Cheese Soup; Cream of Cheddar Soup

FENNEL SOUP

25 g (1 oz) butter
1 onion, chopped
4 bulbs fennel,
    chopped
1 bouquet garni
900 ml (1½ pints)
    chicken stock
salt and pepper
3 egg yolks
juice of 1 lemon
TO GARNISH:
fennel leaves
croûtons

Melt the butter in a large pan, add the onion and fry for 5 minutes, without browning. Stir in the fennel, then add the bouquet garni, stock and salt and pepper to taste. Bring to the boil, cover and simmer for 30 minutes, until the vegetables are very tender.

Remove the bouquet garni and cool slightly. Sieve or work in an electric blender until smooth, then reheat. Mix the egg yolks and lemon juice together with a few tablespoons of the soup.

Stir the egg mixture into the soup and serve immediately, garnished with fennel leaves and croûtons.
Serves 6

CREAM OF CHICKEN SOUP

1 large onion,
    chopped
2 celery sticks,
    chopped
2 large carrots,
    chopped
1 leek, chopped
1 × 1.25 kg (2½ lb)
    chicken
1 bouquet garni
1 blade mace
grated rind and juice
    of ½ lemon
salt
40 g (1½ oz) butter
40 g (1½ oz) plain
    wholemeal flour
2 egg yolks
142 ml (5 fl oz)
    double cream

Put the vegetables and chicken in a large pan and pour over enough water to cover. Add the bouquet garni, mace, lemon rind and juice, and salt to taste. Bring slowly to the boil, skim, then cover and simmer for 1 hour, until the chicken is tender.

Take out the chicken and cut off about 250 g (8 oz) meat. Dice and set aside. Strain the stock and reserve 1.2 litres (2 pints). Leave to cool, then skim off any fat.

Melt the butter in a pan, stir in the flour and cook for 1 minute, without browning. Gradually stir in the reserved stock. Bring to the boil. Simmer for 2 minutes, then add the diced chicken and heat through.

Blend the egg yolks and cream together. Remove the soup from the heat and stir in the cream mixture. Serve immediately.
Serves 6
NOTE: Use the rest of the chicken for another dish.

Fennel Soup; Cream of Chicken Soup; Artichoke Soup

ARTICHOKE SOUP

1 kg (2 lb)
    Jerusalem
    artichokes
juice of 1 lemon
25 g (1 oz) butter
1 large onion,
    chopped
600 ml (1 pint)
    chicken, stock
300 ml (½ pint) milk
salt
142 ml (5 fl oz)
    single cream
2 tablespoons finely
    chopped parsley

Peel and chop the artichokes. Place in a bowl with the lemon juice and enough water to cover.

Melt the butter in a large pan, add the onion and cook until transparent but not coloured. Drain the artichokes and add to the pan with the stock, milk, and salt to taste. Bring to the boil, cover and simmer for 35 to 40 minutes, until the vegetables are tender. Cool slightly.

Sieve or work in an electric blender until smooth. Return to the pan and reheat. Stir in the cream and parsley and serve immediately.
Serves 4 to 6

CORIANDER YOGURT SOUP

300 g (10 oz)
    natural yogurt
150 ml (¼ pint)
    tomato juice
300 ml (½ pint) milk
1 clove garlic,
    crushed
1 small cucumber,
    peeled and finely
    diced
2 tablespoons
    chopped fresh
    coriander
salt and pepper
coriander sprigs to
    garnish

Place the yogurt and tomato juice in a bowl and mix together thoroughly. Stir in the milk, garlic, cucumber, most of the chopped coriander, and salt and pepper to taste. Chill for 2 hours.

Pour the soup into a tureen, and sprinkle with the remaining coriander. Garnish with coriander sprigs to serve.

Serves 4

CHESTNUT SOUP

1 tablespoon oil
1 onion, chopped
2 celery sticks,
    chopped
600 ml (1 pint)
    water
1 bouquet garni
1 × 439 g (15½ oz)
    can unsweetened
    chestnut purée
300 ml (½ pint) milk
1 teaspoon lemon
    juice
TO SERVE:
4 tablespoons smatana
chopped parsley

Heat the oil in a pan, add the onion and fry until softened. Add the celery, water, bouquet garni, and salt and pepper to taste, cover and simmer gently for 20 minutes. Add the chestnut purée and milk and simmer for 10 minutes. Remove the bouquet garni.

Cool slightly, then place in an electric blender or food processor. Add the lemon juice and blend until smooth. Return to the pan to heat through. Pour into a warmed soup tureen and swirl the smatana on top. Sprinkle with the parsley to serve.

Serves 6

MONKFISH KEBABS

500 g (1 lb)
  monkfish, cubed
2 green peppers,
  cored, seeded and
  cut into 2.5 cm
  (1 inch) squares
250 g (8 oz)
  chopped pineapple
1 tablespoon olive oil
250 g (8 oz) bean
  sprouts
50 ml (2 fl oz)
  orange juice
1 tablespoon soy sauce
salt and pepper
2 spring onions,
  chopped
MARINADE:
150 ml ($\frac{1}{4}$ pint olive
  oil)
1 onion, chopped
2 cloves garlic,
  crushed
1 teaspoon mustard
2 teaspoons cider
  vinegar

Place the monkfish in a shallow dish.
Mix together the marinade
ingredients, pour over the fish and
leave for 1 hour.

Blanch the green pepper in boiling
water for 1 minute.

Thread the fish, green pepper and
pineapple alternately on 8 kebab
skewers. Cook under a preheated
moderate grill for 5 to 6 minutes on
each side, basting with the marinade.

Meanwhile, heat the oil in a large
frying pan, add the bean sprouts and
stir-fry for 1 to 2 minutes. Add the
orange juice, the soy sauce, and salt
and pepper to taste and heat for 1 to
2 minutes. Transfer to a warmed
serving dish and sprinkle with the
spring onions.

Place the kebabs on the bean
sprout mixture and serve
immediately.
Serves 4

HUSS AND WATERCRESS
SOUP

600 ml (1 pint) milk
bouquet garni
2 shallots, chopped
250 g (8 oz) huss,
  chopped
125 g (4 oz)
  watercress
142 ml (5 fl oz)
  single cream
TO GARNISH:
watercress sprigs
  (optional)
croûtons

Place the milk, bouquet garni and
shallots in a saucepan, bring to the
boil, then lower the heat. Add the
huss and watercress and simmer for
8 to 10 minutes, until the fish flakes
when tested with a knife. Place in an
electric blender or food processor
and work until smooth.

Return to the saucepan, stir in the
cream and heat gently; do not boil.

Serve in individual warmed soup
bowls, garnished.
Serves 4

LEFT: *Coriander Yogurt Soup; Chestnut Soup*
RIGHT: *Monkfish Kebabs; Huss and Watercress Soup*

ABOVE: *Iced Cucumber Soup*
RIGHT: *Gravad Lax*

SPAGHETTI WITH GARLIC

500 g (1 lb) fresh wholewheat spaghetti
10 tablespoons olive oil
4 cloves garlic, crushed
25 g (1 oz) butter
3 tablespoons chopped parsley

Cook the spaghetti until *al dente*.

Meanwhile, heat the oil in a pan, add the garlic and fry until golden, stirring constantly.

Drain the spaghetti and turn into a warmed serving dish. Add the butter and toss well. Pour over the oil and garlic and mix well. Stir in the parsley and serve immediately.
Serves 6

RAVIOLI ALLA FIORENTINA

1 kg (2 lb) spinach
125 g (4 oz) butter
25 g (1 oz) plain wholemeal flour
250 g (8 oz) Ricotta or curd cheese
3 egg yolks
pinch of grated nutmeg
salt and pepper
50 g (2 oz) Parmesan cheese, grated
lime or lemon slices to garnish (optional)

Cook the spinach, with just the water clinging to its leaves after washing, for 3 minutes. Drain and cool under cold running water. Drain thoroughly and press well with the hands to remove all the moisture. Chop finely and set aside.

Melt 25 g (1 oz) of the butter in a pan, stir in the flour and cook for 2 minutes, stirring. Add the Ricotta or curd cheese.

Lower the heat and add the spinach, egg yolks, nutmeg, and salt and pepper to taste. Cook, stirring constantly, for 1 minute, taking care not to curdle the egg. Remove from the heat and leave until completely cold.

Roll into pointed sausage shapes about 2.5 cm (1 inch) in length and place on a board to dry for 1 hour.

Cook in batches, in boiling salted water, for about 4 minutes; they are cooked when they rise to the surface. Remove with a slotted spoon and place in a warmed serving dish.

Add the remaining butter and toss well. Sprinkle with the Parmesan. Garnish with lime or lemon slices if liked, and serve immediately.
Serves 6

ICED CUCUMBER SOUP

25 g (1 oz) butter
1 cucumber, chopped
2 shallots, chopped
300 ml (½ pint) milk
2 cloves garlic, crushed
1 bay leaf
salt and pepper
1 tablespoon chopped mint
1 tablespoon chopped chives
250 g (8 oz) prawns
284 ml (10 fl oz) single cream
TO GARNISH:
mint sprigs
cucumber slices
peeled prawns

Melt the butter in a saucepan, add the cucumber and shallots, cover and cook gently for 5 minutes, until softened but not brown.

Add the milk, garlic, bay leaf, and salt and pepper to taste, and simmer for 10 minutes. Remove the bay leaf. Pour the soup into an electric blender or food processor and work until smooth. Pour into a soup tureen and stir in the herbs, prawns and cream. Chill for 2 hours.

Garnish with mint, cucumber slices and prawns to serve.
Serves 4

CHEESE AND HERB MOUSSE

350 g (12 oz)
  cottage cheese,
  sieved
½ cucumber, peeled
  and diced
1 tablespoon chopped
  parsley
1 tablespoon chopped
  chives
1 tablespoon chopped
  thyme
salt and pepper
15 g (½ oz) gelatine,
  soaked in 3
  tablespoons water
150 ml (¼ pint)
  mayonnaise
watercress

Put the cottage cheese in a bowl with the cucumber, herbs, and salt and pepper to taste; mix well.

Place the soaked gelatine in a bowl over a pan of simmering water and stir until dissolved. Cool slightly, then stir into the cheese mixture with the mayonnaise.

Turn into a greased 750 ml (1¼ pint) ring mould and leave to set in the refrigerator.

Turn out onto a serving dish and garnish with watercress to serve.
Serves 6

TAGLIATELLE WITH FOUR CHEESES

50 g (2 oz butter
1 onion, chopped
2–3 cloves garlic,
  crushed
125 g (4 oz) streaky
  bacon, derinded
  and diced
75 g (3 oz) each Bel
  Paese, matured
  Cheddar and
  Gruyère cheese,
  grated
50 g (2 oz) Parmesan
  cheese, grated
284 ml (½ pint)
  double cream
500 g (1 lb) fresh
  wholewheat
  tagliatelle
2 tablespoons each
  chopped parsley
  and chives
1 tablespoon chopped
  basil

Melt half the butter in a saucepan, add the onion and garlic and cook, without browning, for 2 to 3 minutes. Add the bacon and cook for 5 minutes, stirring occasionally. Stir in the cheeses and cream. Remove from the heat.

Cook the pasta until *al dente*. Drain thoroughly and turn into a warmed serving dish. Add the remaining butter and toss well.

Return the sauce to the heat and stir in the herbs. Pour over the pasta and mix well. Serve immediately.
Serves 4 to 6

GRAVAD LAX

750 g–1 kg
  (1½–2 lb) salmon
  tailpiece, scaled
  and filleted
PICKLE:
1 heaped tablespoon
  sea salt
1 tablespoon sugar
1 teaspoon black
  peppercorns,
  crushed
1 tablespoon brandy
1 tablespoon chopped
  dill
TO GARNISH:
dill leaves
lime slices

Mix together the pickle ingredients in a small bowl and transfer approximately a quarter of the mixture to a flat dish.

Place one salmon fillet, skin side down, in the pickle mixture. Spread half of the remaining pickle over the cut side of the salmon. Place the other piece of salmon, skin side up, on top.

Cover with the remaining pickle mixture, rubbing it into the skin. Cover with foil, lay a board on top and weight it down.

Chill for at least 12 hours before serving; it can be left for up to 5 days.

Drain well and slice the salmon either on the bias for smaller slices or parallel to the skin to obtain larger slices. Garnish with dill and lime slices and serve with mustard.
Serves 4 to 6

MELON AND ANCHOVY SALAD

1 medium melon
1 × 49 g (1¾ oz) can
  anchovy fillets
juice of 1 lemon
juice of 1 orange
1 teaspoon light soft
  brown sugar
  (optional)
watercress sprigs to
  garnish

Halve the melon and discard the seeds. Scoop the flesh into a serving dish, using a melon baller (or cut into cubes).

Drain the anchovy fillets, reserving 1 tablespoon of the oil. Cut the anchovies into short slivers and add to the melon.

Mix the lemon and orange juice with the reserved anchovy oil and pour over the salad. Add the light soft brown sugar to taste. Chill before serving, garnished with watercress sprigs.

Serves 4

FETTUCINE WITH CREAM AND MUSHROOM SAUCE

500 g (1 lb) spinach
  noodles
  (fettucine)
salt and pepper
50 g (2 oz) butter
1 clove garlic,
  crushed
175 g (6 oz) button
  mushrooms, sliced
120 ml (4 fl oz)
  double cream
2 egg yolks
grated Parmesan
  cheese to serve

Cook the noodles in boiling salted water for 10 to 15 minutes, until just tender.

Meanwhile, melt the butter in a pan, add the garlic and cook for 1 minute, without browning. Add the mushrooms and fry for 2 minutes. Add the cream and simmer for 10 minutes. Season with salt and pepper to taste. Remove from the heat, leave for 2 minutes, then stir in the egg yolks.

Drain the pasta and add to the sauce; toss well.

Serve immediately, with Parmesan cheese.

Serves 4

BROAD BEANS À LA GRECQUE

2 tablespoons oil
1 clove garlic, thinly
  sliced
1 onion, finely
  chopped
500 g (1 lb) shelled
  broad beans
8 tomatoes, skinned,
  seeded and
  chopped
2 tablespoons dry
  white wine
1 tablespoon chopped
  parsley
1 bay leaf
salt and pepper

Heat the oil in a pan, add the garlic and onion and fry for 4 to 5 minutes, without browning.

Stir in the broad beans and toss well to coat in the oil. Add the remaining ingredients, with salt and pepper to taste. Bring to the boil, cover and simmer for 15 minutes or until the beans are tender. Remove the bay leaf and leave to cool.

Serve chilled, with brown bread.

Serves 4

NOTE: Frozen broad beans can be used: cook the tomato mixture for 10 minutes before adding them.

LEFT: *Melon and Anchovy Salad*
RIGHT: *Avocado with Vinaigrette Dressing; Marinated Kippers; Aubergine Pâté*

AVOCADO WITH VINAIGRETTE DRESSING

2 avocado pears
125 g (4 oz) frozen
  peeled prawns,
  thawed
4 tablespoons
  Vinaigrette
  Dressing
  (see page 93)

Halve the pears and remove the stones. Scoop out the flesh and cut into neat pieces. Place in a bowl with the prawns and dressing.

Mix together carefully and spoon into individual serving dishes. Serve with wholemeal bread and butter.
Serves 4

MARINATED KIPPERS

8 kipper fillets
1 onion, very thinly
  sliced
8 black peppercorns
2 bay leaves
8 tablespoons oil
2 tablespoons cider
  vinegar

Skin the kipper fillets and place in a shallow earthenware or china dish with the onions, peppercorns and bay leaves. Spoon over the oil and vinegar, cover and leave to marinate for 24 hours, turning once or twice.

Serve chilled with wholemeal bread and butter.
Serves 4

AUBERGINE PÂTÉ

2 large aubergines
1 clove garlic,
  crushed
2 teaspoons lemon
  juice
2 tablespoons olive
  oil
salt and pepper
2 tablespoons
  chopped parsley
TO GARNISH:
chopped parsley
lemon wedges

Prick the aubergines all over with a fork, cut in half and place cut side down on a greased baking sheet. Bake in a preheated moderately hot oven, 190°C (375°F), Gas Mark 5, for 30 to 40 minutes until softened.

Peel, then blend the aubergines in an electric blender with the garlic and lemon juice, adding the oil a teaspoon at a time. Alternatively, chop the flesh finely and rub through a sieve, then add the garlic, lemon juice and oil in a steady stream, beating until smooth.

Season with salt and pepper to taste, stir in the parsley and spoon into ramekin dishes. Chill.

Garnish with parsley and lemon wedges. Serve with wholemeal toast.
Serves 4

BUTTER BEAN VINAIGRETTE

250 g (8 oz) butter
   beans, soaked
   overnight
salt
4 tablespoons
   Vinaigrette
   Dressing
   (see page 93)
4 spring onions,
   chopped
1 clove garlic,
   crushed
chopped parsley

Drain the beans, place in a pan and cover with cold water. Bring to the boil and simmer gently for 1 to 1¼ hours, adding a little salt towards the end of cooking; drain.

Mix with the dressing while the beans are still warm. Add the onions and garlic and mix well. Transfer to a serving dish and leave until cold. Sprinkle with the parsley to serve.
Serves 4

Butter Bean Vinaigrette; Melon, Tomato and Grape Vinaigrette

MELON, TOMATO AND GRAPE VINAIGRETTE

2 small Ogen melons
4 tomatoes, skinned
   and quartered
175 g (6 oz) black
   grapes, halved and
   seeded
4 tablespoons Honey
   and Lemon
   Dressing
   (see page 91)
1 tablespoon sesame
   seeds, roasted
4 mint sprigs

Cut the melons in half and discard the seeds. Scoop the flesh into balls, using a melon baller, or cut into cubes; reserve the shells. Place the melon in a bowl with the tomatoes and grapes. Pour over the dressing.

Toss well, then spoon the mixture into the melon shells. Sprinkle with the sesame seeds and garnish with the mint to serve.
Serves 4

CODDLED EGGS

50 g (2 oz) smoked
  salmon, cut into
  small pieces
4 eggs
salt and pepper
4 tablespoons double
  cream
chervil sprigs to
  garnish

Grease 4 ramekin dishes and divide the smoked salmon between them.

Break an egg into each dish, on top of the smoked salmon pieces. Season with salt and pepper to taste and top each dish with 1 tablespoon cream.

Place the dishes in a roasting pan containing enough water to reach half way up the ramekin dishes.

Cook in a preheated moderate oven, 180°C (350°F), Gas Mark 4, for 10 to 15 minutes or until set. Garnish with chervil and serve immediately.
Serves 4

PIQUANT DIP

250 g (8 oz) cottage
  cheese, sieved
150 g (5 oz) natural
  yogurt
$\frac{1}{2}$ red pepper, cored,
  seeded and
  chopped
$\frac{1}{2}$ green pepper,
  cored, seeded and
  chopped
1 tablespoon chopped
  cucumber
50 g (2 oz) ham,
  chopped
$\frac{1}{4}$ teaspoon French
  mustard
dash of Tabasco
  sauce
salt and pepper
TO SERVE:
few carrots, cut into
  strips
few celery sticks, cut
  into strips
1 small cauliflower,
  broken into florets

Place the cottage cheese in a bowl and beat in the yogurt. Add the remaining ingredients with salt and pepper to taste; mix well. Pile into a serving bowl and chill until required.

Serve with the raw vegetables.
Serves 6

Lymeswold Chicken Pots

LYMESWOLD CHICKEN POTS

150 ml ($\frac{1}{4}$ pint) aspic
10–12 basil leaves
125 g (4 oz) cooked
  chicken, diced
75 g (3 oz)
  Lymeswold cheese
$\frac{1}{2}$ teaspoon celery salt
$\frac{1}{2}$ teaspoon paprika

Make up the aspic according to packet directions. Reserve 6 to 8 whole basil leaves and finely chop the remainder.

Using a food processor, electric blender or mincer, work the chicken, cheese, celery salt and paprika together until smooth. Blend in half the aspic and the chopped basil. Pour into small china pots or ramekins, smoothing the tops evenly, and press a reserved basil leaf into each. Pour over the remaining aspic. Chill until set.

Serve with toasted rye bread and unsalted butter.
Serves 6 to 8

KIPPER PÂTÉ

500 g (1 lb) frozen
    kipper fillets
65 g (2½ oz)
    unsalted butter
125 g (4 oz) cottage
    cheese
2 tablespoons lemon
    juice
pepper
TO GARNISH:
lemon and orange
    slices
chervil sprigs

Cook the kipper fillets according to packet instructions. Flake the fish slightly, then place in a food processor or electric blender with 25 g (1 oz) of the butter, the cheese, lemon juice, and pepper to taste. Work until smooth.

Divide the mixture between 4 ramekin dishes and smooth the surface. Melt the remaining butter and pour a little over each ramekin. Chill for at least 2 hours before serving.

Garnish with lemon and orange slices and chervil sprigs. Serve with hot wholemeal toast.
Serves 4 to 6

NEW ENGLAND CHOWDER

50 g (2 oz) butter
2 spring onions,
    chopped
40 g (1½ oz) plain
    flour
pinch of cayenne
    pepper
salt and pepper
600 ml (1 pint) fish
    stock
1 × 175 g (6 oz) can
    clams
125 g (4 oz) frozen
    peeled prawns,
    thawed
198 g (7 oz) can
    sweetcorn, drained
2 potatoes, cubed
142 ml (5 fl oz)
    soured cream
chopped parsley to
    garnish

Melt the butter in a pan, add the spring onions and fry until softened. Stir in the flour, cayenne, and salt and pepper to taste and cook for 1 minute. Gradually add the stock and bring to the boil. Add the clams, prawns, sweetcorn and potatoes and simmer for 15 minutes, or until the potatoes are soft but still hold their shape.

Stir in the soured cream. Sprinkle with the parsley to serve.
Serves 4

ARBROATH PANCAKES

BATTER:
125 g (4 oz)
    wholemeal flour
1 egg
300 ml (½ pint) milk
1 tablespoon
    sunflower oil
FILLING:
350 g (12 oz)
    tomatoes, chopped
4 spring onions,
    chopped
1 teaspoon clear
    honey
pepper
1 Arbroath smokie,
    skinned and flaked
basil leaves to
    garnish

Place the flour in a bowl, add the egg and gradually beat in the milk until a smooth batter is formed.

Heat the oil in a 20 cm (8 inch) frying pan, pour in about 2 tablespoons of the batter and tilt the pan to coat the base evenly. Cook until the batter has set and the edges are golden brown. Turn the pancake over and cook for a further 20 seconds. Turn onto a warmed plate, cover with greaseproof paper and keep warm. Repeat with the remaining batter to make 6 pancakes.

To make the filling, place the tomatoes, spring onions, honey, and pepper to taste in a saucepan, bring to the boil, then simmer for 5 minutes. Stir in the smokie.

Divide the filling between the pancakes and fold up into triangles. Garnish with basil and serve immediately.
Serves 6

MUSSELS WITH HERB BUTTER

2 kg (4 lb) fresh
    mussels
2 glasses dry white
    wine
2 cloves garlic
6 parsley sprigs,
    chopped
6 basil sprigs,
    chopped (optional)
50 g (2 oz) butter,
    softened
2 tablespoons grated
    Parmesan cheese
basil or parsley sprigs
    to garnish

Put the mussels in a pan, pour over the wine and bring to the boil. Cook until the shells have opened discarding any that do not open. Strain the liquor through muslin. Crush the garlic in a mortar, add the herbs and pound. Add the butter and cheese; pound to a smooth paste.

Discard the empty half shell from each mussel. Spread the remaining mussel shell with the herb butter and arrange the shells on individual ovenproof dishes. Moisten with a little of the strained liquor.

Brown under a preheated hot grill. Serve at once, garnished with basil or parsley.
Serves 4

Kipper Pâté; New England Chowder; Arbroath Pancakes

Pears with Curd Cheese

PEARS WITH CURD CHEESE

50 g (2 oz) Stilton
  cheese
150 g (5 oz) natural
  yogurt
125 g (4 oz) curd
  cheese
salt and pepper
2 ripe dessert pears
TO GARNISH:
shredded lettuce
  leaves
1 tablespoon chopped
  chives

Mash the Stilton cheese with
1 tablespoon of the yogurt and set
aside.

Place the curd cheese in a bowl
and beat in the remaining yogurt,
and salt and pepper to taste.

Peel, halve and core the pears.
Place a spoonful of the Stilton filling
in each cavity.

Arrange the lettuce on a serving
dish and place the pears, cut side
down, on top.

Spoon over the yogurt and curd
cheese mixture and sprinkle with the
chives. Serve chilled.
Serves 4

RISOTTO WITH MUSHROOMS

8 dried mushrooms
  (optional)
50 g (2 oz) butter
1 onion, finely
  chopped
1 clove garlic, thinly
  sliced
350 g (12 oz)
  brown rice
250 ml (8 fl oz) dry
  white wine
salt and pepper
300 ml ($\frac{1}{2}$ pint)
  chicken stock
  (approximately)
1 bouquet garni
125 g (4 oz) button
  mushrooms, sliced
pinch of powdered
  saffron
50 g (2 oz) grated
  Parmesan cheese

Soak the dried mushrooms in warm
water for 15 minutes, if using.
Squeeze dry, remove the hard stalks
and chop the mushroom caps. Keep
on one side.

Melt the butter in a pan, add the
onion and garlic and cook for
10 minutes or until lightly browned.
Stir in the rice and wine. Bring to
the boil and boil rapidly until the
wine is reduced by half. Add two
thirds of the stock, bouquet garni
and salt and pepper to taste. Simmer,
uncovered, for 35 to 40 minutes,
until the rice is just tender; add stock
if necessary to prevent the risotto
becoming dry.

Add all the mushrooms and the
saffron; cook for 3 minutes. Remove
the bouquet garni. Sprinkle with the
Parmesan and serve immediately.
Serves 6

CHICKEN LIVER PILAFF

125 g (4 oz) streaky
  bacon
25 g (1 oz) butter
2 cloves garlic, sliced
250 g (8 oz) chicken
  livers, chopped
50 g (2 oz) button
  mushrooms, sliced
250 ml (8 fl oz) dry
  white wine
1 bouquet garni
175 g (6 oz) brown
  rice
salt and pepper
300 ml ($\frac{1}{2}$ pint)
  chicken stock
3 tablespoons single
  cream
2 tablespoons
  chopped parsley

Remove the rinds from the bacon
and cut into small pieces.

Melt the butter in a pan, add the
bacon and sauté gently for 2
minutes. Add the garlic and chicken
livers and cook for 5 minutes,
stirring occasionally. Add the
mushrooms, wine, bouquet garni,
rice and salt and pepper to taste. Stir
in the stock, bring to the boil, cover
and simmer for 40 minutes.

Remove the lid, increase the heat,
and stir until the rice is just tender
and all the liquid has been absorbed.
Discard the bouquet garni.

Just before serving, stir in the
cream and parsley. Serve
immediately, garnished with lemon
twists.
Serves 4 to 6

AVOCADO WITH RASPBERRIES

2 avocado pears
1 tablespoon lemon
   juice
125 g (4 oz)
   raspberries
2 tablespoons olive
   oil
1 tablespoon wine
   vinegar
½ teaspoon honey
salt and pepper
fennel leaves

Peel, halve and stone each avocado and place cut side down on a serving plate. Slice lengthways, then separate the slices slightly. Brush lightly with the lemon juice.

Press the raspberries through a nylon sieve to remove the seeds, then mix with the oil, vinegar, honey and salt and pepper to taste. Spoon around each avocado and serve immediately, garnished with fennel.
Serves 4

STUFFED MUSHROOMS

500 g (1 lb)
   mushrooms
2 tablespoons oil
2 cloves garlic,
   crushed
1 tablespoon each
   chopped chives
   and parsley
1 egg yolk
2 tablespoons single
   cream
50 g (2 oz)
   wholemeal
   breadcrumbs
SAUCE:
25 g (1 oz) margarine
25 g (1 oz)
   wholemeal flour
300 ml (½ pint) milk
50 g (2 oz) Cheddar
   cheese, grated
TO FINISH:
1 tablespoon grated
   Parmesan cheese
1 tablespoon toasted
   wholemeal
   breadcrumbs

Remove the stalks from 16 of the mushrooms. Heat the oil in a frying pan, add the mushroom caps, rounded side down, and fry for 1 to 2 minutes to soften. Place rounded side down on 4 ovenproof dishes.

Chop the stalks and remaining mushrooms and mix with the remaining ingredients. Place a spoonful in each mushroom cap.

To make the sauce, melt the margarine in a small pan and stir in the flour. Remove from the heat and stir in the milk until blended. Cook gently, stirring constantly, until thickened. Add salt and pepper to taste, then stir in the Cheddar cheese. Spoon over the mushrooms.

Mix the Parmesan cheese and breadcrumbs together, then sprinkle over the mushrooms. Cook in a preheated moderate oven, 180°C (350°F), Gas Mark 4, for 20 minutes, until golden. Garnish with thyme sprigs.
Serves 4

Avocado with Raspberries; Stuffed Mushrooms

MOZZARELLA SALAD

3 large tomatoes
¼ cucumber
1 red and 1 green
  pepper, cored and
  seeded
2–3 young courgettes
250 g (8 oz)
  Mozzarella cheese
4 spring onions,
  chopped
6 tablespoons olive
  oil
3–4 tablespoons lime
  juice
1–2 cloves garlic,
  crushed
1 teaspoon each
  honey and French
  mustard
1 tablespoon each
  chopped parsley
  and basil
salt
basil sprigs

Thinly slice the tomatoes, cucumber, peppers, courgettes and cheese and arrange on a flat serving platter, as illustrated. Sprinkle with the spring onions.

Mix the remaining ingredients together, seasoning with salt to taste. Spoon over the salad, cover and chill for 30 minutes. Remove from the refrigerator 15 minutes before required.

Garnish with basil sprigs to serve.

Serves 4 to 6

PEANUT DIP WITH CRUDITÉS

2 tablespoons
  sunflower oil
1 onion, chopped
2 cloves garlic,
  crushed
½ teaspoon chilli
  powder
1 teaspoon ground
  cumin
1 teaspoon ground
  coriander
6 tablespoons crunchy
  peanut butter
120 ml (4 fl oz)
  water
1 teaspoon soy sauce
1 teaspoon lemon
  juice
CRUDITÉS:
1 small cauliflower
1 bunch of radishes
1 red pepper
6 carrots

Heat the oil in a pan, add the onion and fry until softened. Add the garlic and spices, stir and cook for 1 minute. Mix in the peanut butter, then gradually blend in the water, stirring until thickened. Add the soy sauce and lemon juice and leave to cool.

Break the cauliflower into florets and halve the radishes if large. Cut the remaining vegetables into long thin pieces.

Turn the dip into a dish, place on a large plate and surround with the vegetables.

Serves 6

FLAGEOLET VINAIGRETTE

250 g (8 oz)
  flageolet beans,
  soaked overnight
salt
6 tablespoons French
  Dressing (see
  page 91)
1 red pepper, cored,
  seeded and chopped
4 spring onions,
  chopped
1 tablespoon chopped
  mixed herbs
2 celery sticks, sliced

Drain the beans, place in a pan and cover with cold water. Bring to the boil and boil rapidly for 10 minutes. Cover and simmer for about 1 hour, until tender, adding a little salt towards the end of cooking. Drain thoroughly and place in a bowl.

Pour over the dressing while still warm and mix well. Leave to cool, then add the remaining ingredients. Toss thoroughly and transfer to a shallow dish to serve.

Serves 4

LEFT: *Mozzarella Salad*
RIGHT: *Hummous; Tzatsiki; Flageolet Vinaigrette*

HUMMOUS

250 g (8 oz) chick
    peas, soaked
    overnight
150 ml (¼ pint)
    tahini
3 cloves garlic
juice of 1–2 lemons
salt and pepper
TO FINISH:
1 tablespoon olive oil
    blended with
    1 teaspoon
    paprika
1 teaspoon chopped
    parsley

Drain the chick peas, place in a pan and cover with cold water. Bring to the boil, cover and boil rapidly for 10 minutes, then simmer gently for 1½ to 2 hours, until soft; the time will vary depending on the age and quality of the peas. Drain, reserving 300 ml (½ pint) of the liquid.

Place the chick peas in an electric blender or food processor and add the remaining ingredients, seasoning with salt and pepper to taste, and enough of the reserved liquid to blend to a soft creamy paste.

Turn into a shallow serving dish, dribble over the blended oil and sprinkle with the parsley.
Serves 8 to 10
NOTE: This will keep for up to 1 week, covered in the refrigerator.

TZATSIKI

500 g (1 lb) natural
    yogurt (preferably
    Greek)
1 cucumber, peeled
    and grated
3 cloves garlic,
    crushed
salt and pepper
1 tablespoon chopped
    mint

Mix the yogurt with a fork until smooth. Drain the cucumber, then add the yogurt with the garlic, and salt and pepper to taste. Chill for 2 hours, then turn into a serving bowl and sprinkle with the mint. Serve with wholemeal pitta bread.
Serves 6

SAUTÉ OF AUBERGINES

500 g (1 lb)
    aubergines
salt
3 tablespoons oil
2 cloves garlic thinly
    sliced
2 tablespoons
    chopped parsley

Cut the aubergines into 1 cm (½ inch) pieces. Put into a colander, sprinkle with salt and leave for 3 minutes. Rinse well. Heat the olive oil in a large frying pan, add the aubergines and fry until golden. Stir in the garlic and parsley and cook for a further 2 minutes.
Serves 4 to 6

Leek Soufflé

LEEK SOUFFLÉ

50 g (2 oz) butter
500 g (1 lb) leeks,
    thinly sliced
25 g (1 oz) plain
    wholemeal flour
150 ml (¼ pint) milk
125 g (4 oz)
    matured Cheddar
    cheese, grated
1 tablespoon grated
    Parmesan cheese
1 teaspoon made
    mustard
salt and pepper
6 eggs, separated

Melt half the butter in a pan, add the leeks and toss until coated in butter. Cook for approximately 5 to 7 minutes until soft.

Melt the remaining butter in another pan, stir in the flour and cook for 1 minute. Gradually add the milk, stirring constantly. Cook, stirring, for 1 minute then add the cheeses, mustard, and salt and pepper to taste. Stir until the cheeses have melted. Remove from the heat and leave to cool for 5 minutes, then beat in the egg yolks. Drain the leeks, then stir into the sauce.

Whisk the egg whites until very stiff, then gradually fold into the leek mixture. Turn into a greased 1.2 litre (2 pint) soufflé dish and bake in a preheated moderate oven, 180°C (350°F), Gas Mark 4, for 45 minutes, until well risen and golden brown.

Serve immediately.

Serves 4 to 6

AUBERGINE BAKE

500 g (1 lb)
    aubergines, sliced
salt and pepper
3 tablespoons oil
250 g (8 oz) Mozza-
    rella cheese, sliced
1 tablespoon grated
    Parmesan cheese
2 tablespoons
    wholemeal
    breadcrumbs
TOMATO SAUCE:
1 tablespoon oil
1 clove garlic, crushed
1 large onion,
    chopped
500 g (1 lb)
    tomatoes, skinned,
    seeded and
    chopped
1 bouquet garni
3 tablespoons dry
    white wine
1 tablespoon tomato
    purée

Sprinkle the aubergines with salt, place in a colander and leave for 1 hour. Rinse in cold water and dry on kitchen paper.

Meanwhile, make the sauce. Heat the oil in a pan, add the garlic and onion and sauté until soft. Add the tomatoes and cook for 2 minutes. Add the remaining ingredients, with salt and pepper to taste. Simmer, uncovered, for 45 minutes, until thickened. Remove bouquet garni.

Heat the oil in a frying pan, add the aubergine slices and fry until golden. Drain on kitchen paper.

Fill a shallow ovenproof dish with alternate layers of aubergines, Mozzarella and tomato sauce, finishing with cheese. Sprinkle with Parmesan and breadcrumbs.

Bake in a preheated moderately hot oven, 200°C (400°F), Gas Mark 6, for 30 minutes. Serve hot or cold.
Serves 6 to 8

AVOCADO MOUSSE

2 avocado pears
150 g (5 oz) natural
    yogurt
150 ml (¼ pint) milk
15 g (½ oz) gelatine
150 ml (¼ pint)
    boiling water
1 teaspoon finely
    chopped onion
1 teaspoon lemon
    juice
salt and pepper
150 ml (¼ pint)
    double cream,
    whipped
watercress sprigs to
    garnish

Peel the avocados, halve and remove the stones. Cut the avocados into chunks and place in the blender with the yogurt and milk.

Soak the gelatine in 2 tablespoons cold water to soften. Pour the boiling water onto the gelatine and stir until dissolved, then pour into the blender. Add the onion, lemon juice and salt and pepper to taste. Blend on maximum speed for 30 seconds.

Turn into a basin and leave to cool. When just beginning to thicken, fold in the cream and pour into a greased 1.2 litre (2 pint) mould. Chill until set. Garnish with watercress before serving.
Serves 6

FALAFEL

250 g (8 oz) chick
  peas, soaked
  overnight
4 spring onions,
  chopped
2 cloves garlic,
  chopped
3 tablespoons water
4 large parsley sprigs
½ teaspoon ground
  cumin
1 teaspoon ground
  coriander
salt and pepper
oil for deep-frying

Drain the peas and place in an electric blender or food processor with the spring onions, garlic, water and parsley. Work to a purée, scraping down the sides when necessary. Stir in the remaining ingredients, with salt and pepper to taste, then turn into a bowl and leave for 1 to 2 hours and dry out slightly.

Form the mixture into walnut-sized balls and flatten slightly. Heat the oil in a deep-fryer, add the falafel, a few at a time, and fry for about 4 minutes, until golden. Drain.

Serve hot with Tomato Mayonnaise (see page 93).
Serves 6

BABA GHANOUSH

2 large aubergines
2 cloves garlic,
  crushed
4 tablespoons tahini
juice of 1 lemon
½ teaspoon ground
  cumin
2 tablespoons
  chopped parsley
salt and pepper
TO GARNISH:
2 black olives,
  halved and stoned

Prick the aubergines all over with a fork, cut in half and place, cut side down, on a grill pan rack. Place under a preheated low grill until the skins are black and start to blister and the flesh feels soft. Peel and wash the aubergines and squeeze out as much of the juice as possible, as this is rather bitter.

Chop the aubergine flesh, place in an electric blender or food processor with the garlic and blend to a purée. Add the tahini and lemon juice alternately, blending between each addition. Turn into a bowl and stir in the cumin, parsley, and salt and pepper to taste.

Turn into a shallow serving dish and garnish with the olives. Serve with wholemeal pitta bread.
Serves 6
NOTE: Tahini is a sesame seed paste. It is available from healthfood stores and delicatessens.

Falafel; Baba Ghanoush

Steamed Chicken Creams

STEAMED CHICKEN CREAMS

These unusual flavoured cream chicken mixtures make a pleasant starter, or light lunch or supper dish.

350 g (12 oz)
  boneless chicken
  breast, skinned
  and chopped
$\frac{1}{2}$ teaspoon salt
$\frac{1}{4}$ teaspoon ground
  white pepper
4 tablespoons dry
  vermouth
2 egg whites
142 ml (5 fl oz)
  double cream,
  lightly whipped
GARLIC AND
  MUSHROOM:
15 g ($\frac{1}{2}$ oz) butter
1 clove garlic,
  crushed
50 g (2 oz) flat
  mushrooms, diced
PRAWN AND DILL:
50 g (2 oz) cooked
  Pacific prawns,
  shelled and
  chopped
1 teaspoon chopped
  dill
CHICKEN AND
  GHERKIN:
50 g (2 oz) cooked
  chicken, diced
1 tablespoon diced
  gherkin
CHICKEN LIVER AND
  TOMATO:
2 teaspoons oil
2 chicken livers,
  halved and
  trimmed
1 teaspoon tomato
  purée

Put the chicken breast into a food processor or electric blender and work until smooth. Add the salt, pepper and vermouth and process again.

Whisk the egg whites to the soft foam stage and add to the chicken mixture. Process again briefly or stir until evenly blended.

Fold in the whipped cream and chill in the refrigerator while preparing the flavourings:

Garlic and Mushroom: Melt the butter in a small pan, add the garlic and mushrooms and sauté for 2 to 3 minutes. Stir into a quarter of the chicken cream mixture.

Prawn and Dill: Mix the prawns and dill together and stir into a quarter of the chicken cream mixture.

Chicken and Gherkin: Mix the chicken and gherkin together and stir into a quarter of the chicken cream mixture.

Chicken Liver and Tomato: Heat the oil in a small pan, add the chicken livers and sauté for 2 minutes. Chop and mix with the tomato purée. Stir into a quarter of the chicken cream mixture.

To cook: Lightly oil four 150 ml ($\frac{1}{4}$ pint) ramekins, moulds or cups. Line the base of each with a piece of foil cut to fit exactly; oil again.

Spoon the mixtures into the containers, cover each with foil and place on a rack or trivet over 2 cm ($\frac{3}{4}$ inch) of boiling water in a saucepan, or place in a steamer. Cover securely and steam for 12 minutes or until firm.

Leave to cool for 1 minute then turn out, removing the foil. Slice each into 4 or 8.

CHEESE-FILLED AVOCADO

1 avocado pear
1 teaspoon lemon
  juice
50 g (2 oz) Danish
  blue cheese
2 tablespoons curd
  cheese
salt and pepper
parsley sprigs to
  garnish

Halve the avocado, remove the stone and scoop out some of the flesh, leaving 1 cm ($\frac{1}{2}$ inch) thick shells. Reserve the shells.

Place the avocado flesh and lemon juice in a bowl and mash, using a fork. Blend in the cheeses and salt and pepper to taste.

Pile the mixture into the shells. Serve chilled, garnished with parsley.
Serves 2

MUSHROOM AND EMMENTHAL SALAD

125 g (4 oz)
  Emmenthal cheese
250 g (8 oz) button
  mushrooms, sliced
250 ml (8 fl oz)
  single cream
juice of 2 lemons
salt and pepper
chopped parsley to
  garnish

Cut the cheese into thin strips and mix with the mushrooms and cream.

Add the lemon juice and salt and pepper to taste; toss well.

Spoon into a serving dish and sprinkle with parsley.

Serves 4

SPINACH AND CREAM CHEESE PÂTÉ

250 g (8 oz) cream
  cheese
125 g (4 oz) frozen
  chopped spinach,
  thawed
juice of ½ lemon
grated nutmeg
salt and pepper
4 lemon twists to
  garnish

Beat the cream cheese until soft. Drain the spinach thoroughly, then gradually add to the cream cheese, beating constantly.

Add the lemon juice and nutmeg, salt and pepper to taste. Continue beating until the pâté is thoroughly blended. Spoon into individual dishes and chill well.

Garnish each portion with a lemon twist. Serve with buttered wholemeal toast.

Serves 4

NOTE: Cooked fresh, or canned spinach may be used.

QUICK AND EASY

There are so many starters that use peeled tomatoes and avocado, either halved, sliced or diced, that it is well worth knowing a couple of speedy tips to ensure they can be prepared quickly.

You can peel tomatoes in no time at all if you slit the skins with a pointed knife, then cover with boiling water for 45–60 seconds. Drain, and the skins will slip away.

Avocados, which tend to discolour quickly upon exposure to the air, will stay pale green and fresh for 1–2 hours if you brush the flesh with, or toss it in a little lemon juice after peeling.

POTTED SHRIMPS

750 g (1½ lb)
  shrimps in shells,
  or 500 g (1 lb)
  shelled shrimps
250 g (8 oz)
  unsalted butter,
  clarified (see
  below)
¼ teaspoon cayenne
  pepper
½ teaspoon ground
  mace
½ teaspoon grated
  nutmeg
salt
TO GARNISH:
lemon slices
chervil sprigs

Shell the shrimps if necessary. Drain the shrimps well and dry with kitchen paper.

Put two thirds of the clarified butter into a saucepan with the spices, and salt to taste. Add the shrimps and heat gently for a few minutes. Divide between 4 to 6 cocotte or ramekin dishes and pack down tightly. Chill until set.

Heat the remaining clarified butter until just melted, then pour evenly over the shrimp mixture to make an airtight seal. Cover and keep in the refrigerator for at least a day to develop the flavour.

Garnish each dish with a lemon slice and chervil sprig. Serve with hot wholemeal toast.

Serves 4 to 6

TO CLARIFY BUTTER: Melt the butter, leave to settle, then strain through muslin.

Potted Shrimps

EGGS AND CHEESE

Whether you choose a heaven-bound light-as-air soufflé, a fluffy and creamy omelette, a mouth-watering flan, quiche or tart, a stuffed and rolled crêpe or pancake, a lavishly coated saucy vegetable, a bubbling pizza or creamy mousse for a starter, main course, supper dish or snack you'll agree there are few foods quite so versatile as eggs and cheese. These magnificent storecupboard standbys, almost virtuous in their simplicity, can take on a whole host of guises to surprise even the most jaded of appetites.

Few can resist cracking an egg to make a simple folded omelette with snipped herb, chopped vegetable or grated cheese filling; whisking the same to make a golden-crowned soufflé flavoured with spinach, garlic and cream cheese or sun-baked olive and tomato mixture; choosing cheese to encase in pastry for a jalousie, layering on ratatouille for a golden grilled gratin or placing on pizza for a melting mouthful.

For repeated success use eggs and cheese in recipes when they are at their best and freshest – eggs will keep for up to 3 weeks in a cool larder or refrigerator but do remember to store round-end up. Store separated eggs in airtight containers in the refrigerator.

Contrary to belief, once matured, cheese does not improve upon keeping so only buy enough for weekly requirements and store, wrapped tightly in cling film or foil, in the refrigerator. Freeze excess or cheese bargains (except cottage and cream cheese) carefully freezer-wrapped for up to 3 months and thaw at room temperature for 2–3 hours or overnight in the refrigerator.

CHIVES AND SOURED CREAM FILLING:

2 egg yolks
142 ml (5 fl oz)
    soured cream
2 tablespoons
    chopped chives
salt and pepper
spring onions to
    garnish

Remove the baked potatoes from the oven, cut in half lengthways, scoop out the flesh and mash until smooth. Beat in the filling ingredients, adding salt and pepper to taste. Spoon the mixture back into the potato shells. Place on a baking sheet and return to the oven for 15 to 20 minutes, until hot and golden brown.

Garnish with spring onions and serve immediately.
Serves 4

BACON AND SALAMI FILLING:

50 g (2 oz) butter
1 large onion, finely
    chopped
4 rashers streaky
    bacon, derinded
    and diced
salt and pepper
25 g (1 oz) garlic
    sausage, diced
1 tablespoon chopped
    parsley
25 g (1 oz) grated
    Parmesan cheese
mustard and cress to
    garnish

Remove the baked potatoes from the oven, cut in half lengthways, scoop out the flesh and mash until smooth.

Melt the butter in a pan, add the onion and cook until golden brown. Add the bacon and cook for 2 minutes, then stir into the mashed potato. Season well with salt and pepper, stir in the garlic sausage and parsley and mix well.

Spoon the mixture back into the potato shells and sprinkle with the cheese. Bake as above.

Garnish with mustard and cress and serve immediately.
Serves 4

SOUFFLÉ CHEESE FILLING:

2 eggs, separated
125 g (4 oz)
    matured Cheddar
    cheese, grated
1 teaspoon English
    mustard
salt and pepper
1 tablespoon grated
    Parmesan cheese
rosemary or parsley
    sprigs to garnish

Remove the baked potatoes from the oven, cut in half lengthways, scoop out the flesh and mash until smooth. Beat in the egg yolks, Cheddar cheese, mustard and salt and pepper to taste.

Whisk the the egg whites until very stiff and fold into the mixture. Spoon into the potato shells and sprinkle with the Parmesan and bake as opposite.

Garnish with rosemary or parsley and serve immediately.
Serves 4

JACKET POTATOES

4 large potatoes
oil for brushing
butter to serve

Brush the potatoes all over with oil and cook in a preheated moderately hot oven, 200°C (400°F), Gas Mark 6, for about 1 hour or until soft.

Cut a large deep cross in one side, fill generously with butter and serve immediately, or use any of the following fillings.
Serves 4

LEFT: *Jacket Potatoes*
RIGHT: *Watercress Flan*

CHEESE AND ONION PUDDING

50 g (2 oz) butter
6 thin slices
 wholemeal bread
175 g (6 oz)
 Cheddar cheese,
 grated
1 onion, chopped
4 eggs
284 ml (½ pint)
 single or half
 cream
300 ml (½ pint) milk
½ teaspoon dried
 mustard
salt and pepper

Spread most of the butter onto the bread. Cut each slice into 16 squares. Use remaining butter to grease a 1.5 litre (2½ pint) casserole.

Layer the bread, cheese and onion in the dish, finishing with a layer of cheese. Whisk eggs with remaining ingredients, adding salt and pepper to taste. Pour into the dish and set aside for 10 minutes.

Bake on the top shelf of a preheated moderately hot oven, 200°C (400°F), Gas Mark 6, for 30 minutes, or until set and golden brown and slightly puffed up.
Serves 4

MUSHROOM GOUGÈRE

CHOUX PASTRY:
50 g (2 oz)
 margarine
150 ml (¼ pint)
 water
65 g (2½ oz)
 wholemeal flour
2 eggs
50 g (2 oz) Cheddar
 cheese, grated
FILLING:
2 tablespoons oil
1 onion, chopped
250 g (8 oz)
 mushrooms, sliced
2 cloves garlic,
 crushed
1 tablespoon
 wholemeal flour
150 ml (¼ pint)
 vegetable stock
75 g (3 oz) walnuts,
 roughly chopped
2 tablespoons
 chopped parsley
salt and pepper

Melt the margarine in a large pan, add the water and bring to the boil. Add the flour all at once and beat until the mixture leaves the side of the pan. Cool slightly, then add the eggs one at a time, beating vigorously until glossy. Beat in the cheese. Spoon the pastry around the edge of a greased 1.2 litre (2 pint) ovenproof dish.

To make the filling, heat the oil in a pan, add the onion and fry until softened. Add the mushrooms and garlic and fry for 2 minutes. Stir in the flour, then add the stock and bring to the boil, stirring. Cook for 3 minutes, until thickened. Stir in all but 2 tablespoons of the walnuts, the parsley, and salt and pepper to taste.

Pour the filling into the centre of the dish and sprinkle with walnuts.

Bake in a preheated moderately hot oven, 200°C (400°F), Gas Mark 6, for 40 to 45 minutes, until the pastry is golden brown.
Serves 4

WATERCRESS FLAN

175 g (6 oz)
 wholemeal flour
pinch of salt
75 g (3 oz)
 margarine
2 tablespoons grated
 Parmesan cheese
1 egg yolk
iced water to mix
FILLING:
25 g (1 oz) butter
1 bunch spring
 onions, chopped
1 bunch watercress,
 finely chopped
3 eggs
142 ml (5 fl oz)
 soured cream
125 g (4 oz)
 Cheddar cheese,
 grated
salt and pepper
TO GARNISH:
watercress sprigs

Place the flour and salt in a bowl and rub in the fat until the mixture resembles fine breadcrumbs. Stir in the Parmesan and egg yolk and add a little water to make a firm dough. Turn onto a floured surface and knead lightly. Roll out and use to line a 20 cm (8 inch) flan ring placed on a baking sheet. Prick all over and chill for 30 minutes. Bake blind as for Broccoli and Cheese Flan (see page 38).

Melt the butter in a pan, add the onions and cook, without browning, for 5 minutes. Stir in the watercress and cook for 2 minutes, until soft.

Beat the eggs and soured cream together, stir in the cheese and season well with salt and pepper.

Spoon the onion and watercress into the flan case. Pour over the egg mixture and return to the oven for 20 to 25 minutes, until golden.

Serve hot or cold, garnished.
Serves 4 to 6

BRITTANY CRÊPES

BATTER:
250 g (8 oz)
  wholemeal flour
good pinch of salt
2 eggs
300 ml (½ pint) milk
150 ml (¼ pint)
  water
oil for frying
FILLING:
1 tablespoon oil
2 cloves garlic, thinly
  sliced
1 large onion, sliced
1 green pepper,
  cored, seeded and
  sliced
1 aubergine, chopped
350 g (12 oz)
  tomatoes, skinned
  and sliced
1 teaspoon dried
  mixed herbs
1 tablespoon chopped
  parsley
salt and pepper
2 tablespoons grated
  Parmesan cheese

Put the flour and salt in a bowl, make a well in the centre and add the eggs, milk and water. Beat to make a smooth batter. Leave for 30 minutes.

Heat a little oil in a 15 cm (6 inch) heavy-based frying pan and pour in just enough batter to cover the base. Cook for 2 to 3 minutes until the underside is brown; turn and cook the other side until golden. Place on a piece of greaseproof paper and cover with a tea-towel. Repeat with remaining batter.

To make the filling, heat the oil in a pan, add the garlic and onion and cook gently for 5 minutes. Add the remaining ingredients, except the Parmesan, seasoning well with salt and pepper. Cook for 15 to 20 minutes. Stir in the Parmesan.

Divide the filling between the crêpes and roll up, tucking under the ends. Place on a greased baking sheet and bake in a preheated moderately hot oven, 200°C (400°F), Gas Mark 6, for 30 to 35 minutes, until crisp.
Makes 10 to 12

CHEESE AND HERB SOUFFLÉ

40 g (1½ oz) butter
40 g (1½ oz) plain
  wholemeal flour
284 ml (½ pint) half
  cream or milk
3 eggs (size 1),
  separated
1 × 150 g (5 oz)
  packet full fat soft
  cheese with garlic
  and herbs,
  crumbled
salt and pepper

Melt the butter in a pan, add the flour and cook, stirring, for 1 minute. Remove from the heat and gradually stir in the cream or milk, mixing well. Bring to the boil, stirring until thickened.

Remove from the heat and beat in the egg yolks, one at a time. Add the cheese and stir until melted. Season with a little salt and pepper. Leave to cool.

Whisk the egg whites until just stiff enough to stand in peaks. Mix about 2 tablespoons into the cheese mixture, making it soft and 'slack'. Carefully fold the egg whites and cheese mixture together.

Turn into a buttered 1.2 litre (2 pint) soufflé dish, placed on a baking sheet. Bake immediately in a preheated moderately hot oven, 190°C (375°F), Gas Mark 5, for 35 to 40 minutes, until well risen and golden brown. Serve immediately.
Serves 3 to 4

LAYERED CHEESE AND TOMATO SOUFFLÉ

25 g (1 oz) butter
1 clove garlic,
  crushed
1 onion, chopped
350 g (12 oz)
  tomatoes, skinned
  and chopped
6–8 black olives,
  stoned and
  chopped
salt and pepper
Cheese and herb
  soufflé mixture
  (see recipe)

Melt the butter in a pan, add the garlic, onion and tomatoes and fry lightly for 3 to 4 minutes. Add the olives, and seasoning. Cool.

Prepare the soufflé mixture (see above). Spread the tomato mixture in a buttered 1.5 litre (2½ pint) soufflé dish placed on a baking sheet and cover with the soufflé mixture. Bake immediately in a preheated moderately hot oven, 190°C (375°F), Gas Mark 5, for 35 to 40 minutes, until well risen and golden brown.
Serves 4

LEFT: *Brittany Crêpes*
RIGHT: *Spinach Lattice Flan; Provençale Pancakes*

SPINACH LATTICE FLAN

2 tablespoons oil
1 large onion,
    chopped
2 cloves garlic,
    crushed
500 g (1 lb) frozen
    chopped spinach,
    thawed and
    drained
2 eggs
½ teaspoon ground
    nutmeg
250 g (8 oz) Ricotta
    or curd cheese
50 g (2 oz)
    Parmesan cheese,
    grated
salt and pepper
WHOLEMEAL
    SHORTCRUST
    PASTRY:
350 g (12 oz)
    wholemeal flour
175 g (6 oz)
    margarine
iced water
beaten egg to glaze

Heat the oil in a pan and fry the onion until softened. Add the garlic and spinach and cook gently for 10 minutes, stirring occasionally. Cool slightly then beat in the eggs, nutmeg, cheeses, and salt and pepper.

To make the pastry, place the flours in a mixing bowl and rub in the margarine until the mixture resembles breadcrumbs. Add enough water to mix to a firm dough, then turn onto a floured surface and knead lightly until smooth. Cut off two thirds of the pastry, roll out thinly and use to line a 23 cm (9 inch) flan dish, leaving it overlapping the side.

Spread the filling evenly in the pastry case. Moisten pastry edge. Roll out remaining pastry and cut into 5 mm (¼ inch) strips. Arrange in a lattice design over the filling and press the edges to secure. Brush with egg and bake in a preheated moderately hot oven. 200°C (400°F), Gas Mark 6, for 45 to 50 minutes, until golden. Serve warm or cold.
Serves 6

PROVENÇALE PANCAKES

50 g (2 oz)
    buckwheat flour
50 g (2 oz) plain
    wholemeal flour
pinch of salt
1 egg, beaten
300 ml (½ pint) milk
1 tablespoon olive oil
FILLING:
2 tablespoons olive
    oil
1 onion, chopped
2 cloves garlic,
    crushed
1 green pepper,
    cored, seeded and
    chopped
1 small aubergine
4 large tomatoes,
    skinned and
    chopped
1 tablespoon tomato
    purée
TO FINISH:
25 g (1 oz)
    margarine
2 tablespoons grated
    Parmesan cheese

Place the flours and salt in a bowl and make a well in the centre. Add the egg, then gradually stir in half the milk and the oil. Beat until smooth. Add the remaining milk.

Heat a 15 cm (6 inch) omelette pan and add a few drops of oil. Pour in 1 tablespoon of the batter, lifting the pan to coat the bottom evenly. Cook until the underside is brown, then turn over and cook for 10 seconds. Turn onto a warmed plate. Repeat with the remaining batter.

For the filling, heat the oil in a pan and cook the onion until softened. Add the garlic, pepper and chopped aubergine and fry for 10 minutes, stirring. Add remaining ingredients, cover and cook for 15 minutes.

Divide filling between pancakes, roll up and place in an oiled shallow ovenproof dish. Top with the melted margarine and cheese. Bake in a preheated moderately hot oven, 190°C (375°F), Gas Mark 5, for 15 minutes. Serve immediately.
Serves 4

BROCCOLI AND CHEESE FLAN

CHEESE PASTRY:
175 g (6 oz)
   wholemeal flour
75 g (3 oz)
   margarine
50 g (2 oz) matured
   Cheddar cheese,
   grated
½ teaspoon mixed
   herbs
1 egg yolk
iced water to mix
FILLING:
250 g (8 oz) broccoli
2 eggs, beaten
150 ml (¼ pint) milk
125 g (4 oz)
   Cheddar cheese,
   grated
1 teaspoon dry
   mustard
salt and pepper

Place the flour in a bowl and rub in the margarine until the mixture resembles fine breadcrumbs. Stir in the cheese and herbs. Make a well in the centre and add the egg yolk and enough water to mix to a firm dough. Roll out and use to line a 20 cm (8 inch) flan dish. Bake 'blind' in a moderately hot oven, 200°C (400°F), Gas Mark 6, for 10 minutes.

Meanwhile, cook the broccoli in boiling salted water for 5 to 6 minutes. Rinse in cold water, drain thoroughly, then chop roughly.

Mix the beaten eggs with the milk, three quarters of the cheese, the mustard, and salt and pepper to taste.

Arrange the broccoli in the flan case and pour over the egg mixture. Sprinkle with remaining cheese and return to the oven for 35 minutes, until set and golden.
Serves 4

ABOVE: *Broccoli and Cheese Flan; Spinach Pancakes*

SPINACH PANCAKES

PANCAKE BATTER:
125 g (4 oz)
   wholemeal flour
1 egg, beaten
300 ml (½ pint) milk
FILLING:
350 g (12 oz) frozen,
   chopped spinach
175 g (6 oz) Ricotta
   cheese
2 tablespoons grated
   Parmesan cheese
1 egg
grated nutmeg
SAUCE:
2 tablespoons oil
2 tablespoons
   wholemeal flour
300 ml (½ pint) milk
50 g (2 oz) Cheddar
   cheese, grated
TO FINISH:
1 tablespoon grated
   Parmesan cheese
1 tablespoon
   wholemeal
   breadcrumbs

Make and cook the pancakes as for Provençale Pancakes (page 37).

Place the spinach in a pan and heat gently until completely thawed. Cook for 2 minutes, then pour off any liquid. Beat in the cheeses, egg, and salt, pepper and nutmeg to taste.

Divide the filling between the pancakes, roll up and place in an oiled shallow ovenproof dish.

To make the sauce, heat the oil in a pan, remove from the heat and stir in the flour. Stir in the milk until blended, return to the heat and bring to the boil, stirring, until thickened. Remove from the heat and stir in the cheese.

Spoon the sauce over the pancakes, then sprinkle with the Parmesan cheese and breadcrumbs. Cook in a preheated moderately hot oven, 190°C (375°F), Gas Mark 5, for 15 to 20 minutes, until golden.
Serves 4

SPINACH SOUFFLÉ

25 g (1 oz)
    margarine
25 g (1 oz)
    wholemeal flour
150 ml ($\frac{1}{4}$ pint) milk
3 eggs, separated
125 g (4 oz) frozen
    spinach purée,
    thawed
50 g (2 oz) Cheddar
    cheese, grated
$\frac{1}{4}$ teaspoon grated
    nutmeg
salt and pepper
2 tablespoons grated
    Parmesan cheese

Tie a double band of foil around a greased 1.2 litre (2 pint) soufflé dish, to come 5 cm (2 inches) above rim.

Melt the margarine in a pan and stir in the flour. Remove from the heat and stir in the milk. Return to the heat and slowly bring to the boil, stirring. Cook for 3 minutes, then add the egg yolks, spinach, Cheddar cheese, nutmeg, and salt and pepper to taste. Mix thoroughly.

Whisk the egg whites until fairly stiff, then carefully fold into the spinach mixture using a metal spoon.

Turn into the prepared dish, sprinkle with the Parmesan cheese and cook in a preheated moderately hot oven, 190°C (375°F), Gas Mark 5, for 30 to 35 minutes, until risen and golden. Serve immediately.
Serves 4

Spanish Eggs

VEGETABLE GRATIN

2 tablespoons oil
2 onions, sliced
1 clove garlic, crushed
350 g (12 oz)
    courgettes, sliced
1 tablespoon chopped
    parsley
1 teaspoon chopped
    thyme
salt and pepper
4 large tomatoes,
    skinned and sliced
25 g (1 oz)
    margarine
25 g (1 oz)
    wholemeal flour
300 ml ($\frac{1}{2}$ pint) milk
125 g (4 oz)
    Cheddar cheese,
    grated
1 tablespoon fresh
    wholemeal
    breadcrumbs

Heat the oil in a pan, add the onions and fry gently until softened. Add the garlic, courgettes, herbs, and salt and pepper to taste, and cook for 5 minutes, stirring occasionally.

Put half the mixture in a 1.5 litre (2$\frac{1}{2}$ pint) pie dish and cover with the tomatoes. Top with remaining mixture.

Melt the margarine in a saucepan, stir in the flour, remove from the heat and blend in the milk. Bring to the boil, stirring constantly, until the sauce thickens. Add half of the cheese, and salt and pepper to taste and pour over the courgettes.

Sprinkle with the breadcrumbs then the remaining cheese. Bake in a preheated moderate oven, 180°C (350°F), Gas Mark 4, for 30 minutes, until golden.
Serves 4

SPANISH EGGS

4 tablespoons oil
2 slices stale
    wholemeal bread,
    cubed
2 large potatoes,
    diced
1 onion, chopped
125 g (4 oz) bacon,
    derinded and
    chopped
50 g (2 oz) French
    beans, cut into
    lengths
6 tomatoes, skinned,
    seeded and
    chopped
2 courgettes, sliced
8 thin slices garlic
    sausage, diced
4 eggs
1 tablespoon chopped
    parsley to garnish

Heat the oil in a large frying pan, add the bread cubes and fry until browned. Remove and drain on kitchen paper.

Add the potatoes to the pan, toss in the oil and cook for 15 minutes, until browned on all sides. Add the onion and bacon and cook for 2 minutes. Stir in the beans, tomatoes and courgettes and cook for 5 to 7 minutes. Stir in the garlic sausage.

Transfer to a large shallow ovenproof dish and make 4 hollows in the mixture with the back of a spoon; break an egg into each. Bake in a preheated moderate oven, 180°C (350°F), Gas Mark 4, for 12 minutes. Sprinkle over the fried bread and return to the oven for 3 minutes.

Sprinkle with the parsley and serve immediately.
Serves 4

FARMHOUSE OMELETTE

30 g (1 oz) butter
1 onion, diced
1 potato, diced
30 g (1 oz) streaky bacon, derinded and chopped
30 g (1 oz) mushrooms, chopped
2 eggs
2 tablespoons milk
¼ teaspoon dried mixed herbs
salt and pepper
½ cup grated Cheddar cheese
chopped parsley to garnish

Melt the butter in a frying pan, add the onion, potato and bacon and cook gently, turning occasionally, until soft. Add the mushrooms, increase the heat and cook until the vegetables begin to brown.

Beat together the eggs, milk and herbs with salt and pepper to taste. Pour over the vegetables, tilting the pan to spread the mixture evenly. Cook over a moderate heat until the omelette starts to set.

Sprinkle with the cheese and place the frying pan under a preheated hot grill until the cheese is bubbling and golden brown.

Sprinkle with parsley and cut the omelette in half. Lift onto warmed serving plates and serve immediately.

RATATOUILLE AU GRATIN

6 tablespoons olive oil
1 small aubergine, sliced
2 cloves garlic, crushed
350 g (12 oz) courgettes, sliced
1 red pepper, cored, seeded and sliced
350 g (12 oz) tomatoes, skinned and sliced
1 tablespoon chopped basil
salt and pepper
500 g (1 lb) potatoes, boiled and sliced
250 g (8 oz) Mozzarella cheese, thinly sliced

Heat half the oil in a frying pan, add the aubergine and fry on both sides until just beginning to brown, adding more oil if necessary. Remove from the pan and drain on kitchen paper.

Add the remaining oil to the pan and fry the garlic, courgettes and red pepper for 8 to 10 minutes, until softened, stirring occasionally. Add the tomatoes, basil, aubergine, and salt and pepper to taste and simmer for 10 minutes.

Place the potatoes in a shallow ovenproof dish and cover with the ratatouille. Spread evenly to the edges and arrange the cheese slices over the top. Bake in a preheated moderately hot oven, 190°C (375°F), Gas Mark 5, for 15 to 20 minutes, until the cheese begins to melt. Serve immediately.
Serves 4

Frittata Verde; Ratatouille au Gratin; Spanish Omelet

FRITTATA VERDE

350 g (12 oz) fresh spinach
3 tablespoons oil
1 onion, chopped
6 eggs
2 tablespoons grated Parmesan cheese
½ teaspoon grated nutmeg
salt and pepper

Cook the spinach with just the water clinging to its leaves after washing, for 6 to 8 minutes. Drain well, squeeze dry, then chop finely.

Heat 1 tablespoon of the oil in a pan, add the onion and fry until softened. Mix with the spinach.

Break the eggs into a bowl, add the cheese, spinach mixture, nutmeg, and salt and pepper to taste.

Heat the remaining oil in a 23 cm (9 inch) frying pan, add the egg mixture and stir lightly until beginning to set. Cook for about 5 minutes, until the underneath is set, then invert a large plate over the pan, turn the pan over and ease the frittata onto the plate. Add a little more oil to the pan, heat it then slide the frittata back into the pan and cook until the other side is set.

Cut into wedges and serve with salad and wholemeal bread.

SPANISH OMELETTE

3 tablespoons olive oil
2 onions, chopped
2 cloves garlic, crushed
1 red pepper, cored, seeded and chopped
4 eggs
salt and pepper
2 large potatoes, boiled and chopped
2 tablespoons chopped parsley

Heat 2 tablespoons of the oil in a 25 cm (10 inch) frying pan, add the onions and cook until softened. Add the garlic and red pepper; cook for 8 to 10 minutes, stirring occasionally.

Whisk the eggs, with salt and pepper to taste, in a bowl, then stir in the potatoes, parsley and fried vegetables.

Heat the remaining oil in the pan, pour in the egg mixture and spread evenly to the edge. Cook for about 5 minutes, shaking the pan to prevent the omelette sticking, until it comes away from the side of the pan.

Place the pan under a preheated moderate grill for about 3 minutes to cook the top. Slide the omelette onto a warmed serving plate.
Serves 4

TOMATO AND CHEESE TOASTIE

4 slices brown bread
butter for spreading
4 large tomatoes,
  skinned and sliced
salt and pepper
4 basil sprigs, chopped
75 g (3 oz) matured
  Cheddar cheese,
  grated
4 rashers bacon,
  derinded and
  halved

Toast the bread on both sides and spread one side with butter. Arrange the tomatoes on the buttered side and season with salt and pepper to taste. Sprinkle with the basil and cheese, and top with 2 bacon pieces.

Cook under a preheated hot grill for 5 to 7 minutes, until the bacon is cooked and the cheese bubbling. Serve immediately.
Serves 4

COURGETTE ROULADE

25 g (1 oz)
  margarine
500 g (1 lb)
  courgettes, grated
4 eggs, separated
1 teaspoon chopped
  savory
1 tablespoon chopped
  parsley
salt and pepper
2 tablespoons grated
  Parmesan cheese
FILLING:
2 tablespoons oil
1 onion, chopped
175 g (6 oz)
  mushrooms, sliced
1 tablespoon
  wholemeal flour
120 ml (4 fl oz)
  milk

Melt the margarine in a pan, add the courgettes and fry for 7 minutes.

Place in a bowl with the egg yolks, herbs, and salt and pepper to taste and mix well. Whisk the egg whites until fairly stiff, fold 2 tablespoons into the courgette mixture to lighten it, then carefully fold in the rest.

Turn the mixture into a lined and greased 30 × 20 cm (12 × 8 inch) Swiss roll tin and spread evenly. Cook in a preheated moderately hot oven, 200°C (400°F), Gas Mark 6, for 10 to 15 minutes, until risen.

Meanwhile, prepare the filling. Heat the oil in a pan, add the onion and fry until softened. Add the mushrooms and fry for 3 minutes. Stir in the flour, then gradually stir in the milk. Add salt and pepper to taste and simmer for 3 minutes.

Sprinkle the Parmesan cheese on a sheet of greaseproof paper. Turn the roulade out onto the paper and peel off the lining paper. Spread with the filling and roll up like a Swiss roll.
Serves 4

WHOLEMEAL PIZZA

DOUGH:
250 g (8 oz)
  wholemeal flour
$\frac{1}{2}$ teaspoon salt
7 g ($\frac{1}{4}$ oz) fresh
  yeast
150 ml ($\frac{1}{4}$ pint)
  warm water
1 tablespoon olive oil
TOPPING:
1 tablespoon olive oil
1 large onion, sliced
500 g (1 lb)
  tomatoes, skinned
  and chopped
1 tablespoon chopped
  marjoram
salt and pepper
2 tablespoons tomato
  purée
250 g (8 oz)
  Mozzarella or
  Bel Paese cheese,
  thinly sliced
1 × 49 g (1$\frac{3}{4}$ oz) can
  anchovy fillets,
  halved lengthways
8 black olives,
  halved and stoned

Mix the flour and salt together in a bowl. Cream the yeast with a little of the water and leave until frothy. Add to the flour with the remaining water and the oil and mix to a dough.

Turn onto a floured surface and knead for 10 minutes until smooth and elastic. Place in a clean bowl, cover with a damp cloth and leave to rise in a warm place for about 1$\frac{1}{2}$ hours, until doubled in size.

Meanwhile, heat the oil in a pan, add the onion and fry until softened. Add the tomatoes, marjoram, and salt and pepper to taste and cook for 5 minutes.

Turn the dough onto a floured surface and knead for a few minutes. Divide in half and roll each piece out to a 20 cm (8 inch) circle. Place on greased baking sheets and spread with the tomato purée. Spoon over the tomato mixture and cover with the cheese. Top with the anchovies and olives.

Bake in a preheated moderately hot oven, 200°C (400°F), Gas Mark 6, for 15 to 20 minutes. Serve immediately cut into wedges.
Serves 4

STILTON CAULIFLOWER

1 small cauliflower,
   divided into florets
salt and pepper
15 g (½ oz) butter
2 tablespoons plain
   wholemeal flour
150 ml (¼ pint) milk
40 g (1½ oz) blue
   Stilton cheese,
   crumbled
1 tablespoon dry
   wholemeal
   breadcrumbs

Cook the cauliflower in boiling salted water for about 12 minutes until tender. Drain and transfer to a warmed ovenproof serving dish.

Melt the butter in a saucepan, stir in the flour and continue cooking for 1 minute. Gradually blend in the milk and heat, stirring, until thickened.

Stir in the cheese and heat gently, stirring, until melted. Add salt and pepper to taste.

Pour the sauce over the cauliflower and top with the breadcrumbs. Place under a preheated medium grill until the topping is golden brown. Serve hot.
Serves 2

CHEESE AND ONION OAT FLAN

OAT PASTRY:
125 g (4 oz)
   wholemeal flour
125 g (4 oz)
   medium oatmeal
pinch of salt
125 g (4 oz)
   margarine
2–3 tablespoons
   water
FILLING:
2 tablespoons oil
2 onions, chopped
2 eggs
150 ml (¼ pint) milk
250 g (8 oz)
   Cheddar cheese,
   grated
salt and pepper

Place the flour, oatmeal and salt in a mixing bowl and rub in the margarine until the mixture resembles breadcrumbs. Add the water and mix to a firm dough. Turn onto a floured surface and knead lightly until smooth. Roll out and use to line a 20 cm (8 inch) flan dish. Chill for 15 minutes.

Meanwhile, make the filling. Heat the oil in a pan, add the onions and fry gently until transparent. Mix the eggs and milk together, then stir in the cheese, onions, and salt and pepper to taste.

Pour into the flan case and bake in a preheated moderately hot oven, 190°C (375°F), Gas Mark 5, for 35 to 40 minutes. Serve hot or cold, with salad.
Serves 4

LEFT: *Courgette Roulade*
RIGHT: *Provençale Tartlets*

PROVENÇALE TARTLETS

wholemeal shortcrust
   pastry made with
   250 g (8 oz)
   flour (see Spinach
   Lattice Flan,
   page 37)
1 tablespoon olive oil
1 onion, chopped
1 clove garlic, crushed
1 red pepper, cored,
   seeded and sliced
175 g (6 oz)
   courgettes, sliced
4 tomatoes, skinned
   and chopped
1 tablespoon chopped
   marjoram
1 tablespoon chopped
   basil
salt and pepper
1 egg
75 ml (3 fl oz)
   single cream
50 g (2 oz) Gruyère
   cheese, grated

Roll out the pastry on a lightly floured surface and use to line six 11 cm (4½ inch) individual flan tins. Pick the base of each and chill for 20 minutes.

Bake 'blind' in a preheated moderately hot oven, 200°C (400°F), Gas Mark 6, for 10 minutes. Remove the foil and beans.

Heat the oil in a pan, add the onion and fry until softened. Add the garlic, remaining vegetables, herbs, and salt and pepper to taste, cover and simmer for 15 minutes, then spoon into the pastry cases.

Beat the egg, cream and cheese together, seasoning with a little salt and pepper, and pour over the filling. Lower the oven temperature to 190°C (375°F), Gas Mark 5, and cook the tartlets for 15 to 20 minutes, until set.
Makes 6

MAIN COURSE DISHES

Take a trip around the world with this sumptuous selection of main course dishes based on meat, fish and poultry. Dip into the warm aromatic flavours of Southern France with Lamb Cutlets Provençale, Boeuf à la Bourguignonne and Fish Boulangère; sample a slice of Scandinavia with Soused Herrings and Scandinavian Mackerel; bask in the best of the Mediterranean with Poussins with Herb Sauce, Mediterranean Fish Stew or Mullet Mornay; enjoy the warm-blooded offerings of the Italians with Veal Escalopes, Prawn Risotto and Italian Veal Casserole; a taste of the Orient with Honey Curry Chicken, Stir-fried Shredded Beef with Ginger and Kashmiri Chicken; then return home for the best of traditional British Somerset Lamb Chops, Rabbit with Mustard Sauce and Somerset Pork Casserole.

High on flavour, rich in nutrients and based on the best of fresh ingredients, these recipes show how imaginative and healthy main course wholefood eating can be – and not a convenience food in sight. By definition, a wholefood is an unrefined food, to which nothing has been added or taken away. It contains no artificial flavourings, colourings, preservatives or other additives. Essentially, wholefoods are used as close as possible to their original state.

This chapter successfully illustrates that you don't have to be vegetarian to enjoy wholefoods at their best – there is ample meat, fish, poultry, eggs and cheese to satisfy the heartiest of appetites but they have been cleverly combined with fresh vegetables and aromatic herbs, given a nutritious crunchy topping or coating of wholegrains and cereals or 'stretched' with a spicy or fruity stuffing.

TANDOORI SOLE

½ teaspoon chilli
    powder
½ teaspoon turmeric
½ teaspoon ground
    coriander
½ teaspoon ground
    cumin
1 teaspoon ground
    ginger
½ teaspoon garam
    masala
¼ teaspoon salt
300 g (10 oz)
    natural yogurt
2 cloves garlic, crushed
2 lemon sole, skinned
    and filleted
TO GARNISH:
coriander leaves
lime wedges

Mix all the spices together. Add to the yogurt with the garlic and stir until well mixed. Pour into a large bowl, add the fish, turn to coat thoroughly and leave to marinate for 1 hour.

Pour boiling water into a roasting pan to come halfway up the sides. Put a grill rack in the pan and place the marinated fish on the rack. Pour any remaining marinade over the fish.

Cook in a preheated moderate oven, 180°C (350°F), Gas Mark 4, for 15 minutes.

Garnish with coriander and lime wedges and serve immediately.

Serves 2

NOTE: To serve 4 people, just add 2 more fish to the marinade.

STIR-FRIED FISH

500 g (1 lb) cod
    fillet, skinned
1 teaspoon salt
1 tablespoon oil
2 rashers back bacon,
    derinded and
    shredded
50 g (2 oz) frozen
    peas, cooked
50 g (2 oz) frozen
    sweetcorn, cooked
6 tablespoons chicken
    stock or water
2 teaspoons dry
    sherry
2 teaspoons soy sauce
1 teaspoon sugar
1 teaspoon cornflour,
    blended with 1
    teaspoon water
spring onion fans to
    garnish (see right)

Cut the fish fillet into 2.5 cm (1 inch) wide strips, sprinkle with the salt, leave for 15 minutes.

Heat the oil in a frying pan, add the fish and bacon and stir-fry for 3 minutes. Add the remaining ingredients, except the blended cornflour, and bring to the boil. Stir in the blended cornflour and cook for 1 minute.

Garnish with spring onion fans and serve immediately.

Serves 4

TO MAKE SPRING ONION FANS: Trim the tops off the spring onions and remove the root base. Shred carefully, leaving 2.5 cm (1 inch) attached. Immerse in iced water until the spring onions open out and curl.

SCANDINAVIAN MACKEREL

*3 tablespoons cider
   vinegar*
*300 ml (½ pint)
   water*
1 onion, sliced
1 bay leaf
1 parsley sprig
1 thyme sprig
6 peppercorns
½ teaspoon salt
4 mackerel, cleaned
SAUCE:
*150 g (5 oz) natural
   yogurt*
1 tablespoon mustard
*1 teaspoon
   muscovado sugar*
*1 tablespoon cider
   vinegar*
*1 tablespoon chopped
   fennel*
lemon wedges

Put the vinegar, water, onion, herbs, peppercorns and salt in a pan. Bring to the boil and simmer for 20 minutes.

Place the mackerel in a shallow ovenproof dish and pour over the infused liquid. Cover and cook in a preheated moderate oven, 180°C (350°F), Gas Mark 4, for 20 to 25 minutes. Transfer the fish to a warmed serving dish and keep hot.

Put all the sauce ingredients in a small bowl and place over a pan of simmering water. Stir until blended and heated through.

Pour over the fish, garnish with lemon wedges and serve immediately.
Serves 4

BAKED MACKEREL
IN CIDER

*1 kg (2 lb) cooking
   apples, peeled,
   cored and thinly
   sliced*
*5 tablespoons dry
   cider*
*150 g (5 oz) natural
   yogurt*
*2 tablespoons Dijon
   mustard*
salt and pepper
4 mackerel, filleted
TO GARNISH:
lemon slices
parsley sprigs

Spread the apples in a large buttered gratin dish.

Heat the cider gently and pour over the apples. Cover with foil and cook in a preheated moderately hot oven, 200°C (400°F), Gas Mark 6, for 15 minutes. Lower the temperature to 180°C (350°F), Gas Mark 4.

Meanwhile, mix the yogurt with the mustard, and salt and pepper.

Arrange the mackerel in the dish and pour over the yogurt mixture. Return to the oven and cook for 30 minutes.

Garnish before serving.
Serves 4

HADDOCK WITH SOUR
CREAM
AND MUSHROOMS

*300 g (10 oz)
   haddock fillet*
salt and pepper
knob of butter
4 tablespoons water
SAUCE:
15 g (½ oz) butter
*50 g (2 oz) button
   mushrooms, sliced*
*120 ml (4 fl oz)
   fresh sour cream*
¼ teaspoon paprika
*chopped parsley, to
   garnish*

Place the haddock in a shallow 600 ml (1 pint) ovenproof dish. Sprinkle with salt and pepper, dot with the butter and add the water. Cover with foil and cook in a preheated moderate oven, 160°C (325°F), Gas Mark 3, for 20 minutes.

Make the sauce: Melt the butter in a saucepan and fry the mushrooms for 1 minute. Stir in the sour cream, paprika and salt and pepper to taste. Heat through gently.

Drain the fish, pour over the sauce and garnish with parsley.
Serves 2

LEFT: *Tandoori Sole; Stir-Fried Fish*
RIGHT: *Baked Mackerel in Cider*

MEDITERRANEAN FISH STEW

3 tablespoons olive oil

2 onions, sliced

2 cloves garlic, crushed

4 large tomatoes, skinned and chopped

150 ml ($\frac{1}{4}$ pint) water

150 ml ($\frac{1}{4}$ pint) white wine

1 bay leaf

1 teaspoon salt

$\frac{1}{2}$ teaspoon pepper

750 g (1$\frac{1}{2}$ lb) cod fillet, skinned and boned

600 ml (1 pint) mussels

175 g (6 oz) frozen peeled prawns, thawed

1 tablespoon chopped parsley

Heat the oil in a pan, add the onions and fry until softened. Add the garlic, tomatoes, half the water, the wine, bay leaf, salt and pepper. Simmer for 15 minutes.

Cut the cod into 5 cm (2 inch) squares, add to the pan and simmer for 15 minutes.

Scrub the mussels thoroughly, pulling off the beard. Discard any which are open and will not close when tapped. Put them into a heavy pan with the remaining water, cover and cook over a high heat for 5 minutes until they have opened; discard any that do not.

Discard the top shell from each mussel. Add the mussels with their liquid and the prawns to the stew. Cook for a further 3 minutes.

Turn into a warmed serving dish and sprinkle with the parsley. Serve with crusty wholemeal bread.

Serves 4 to 6

MARINER'S PIE

450 ml ($\frac{3}{4}$ pint) milk

1 bay leaf

2 lemon slices

salt and pepper

500 g (1 lb) whiting fillets

50 g (2 oz) butter

125 g (4 oz) button mushrooms, quartered

25 g (1 oz) plain wholemeal flour

3 tablespoons yogurt or soured cream

2 tablespoons chopped parsley

2 hard-boiled eggs, chopped

500 g (1 lb) potatoes, boiled and sliced

50 g (2 oz) Cheddar cheese, grated

parsley sprigs to garnish

Put the milk, bay leaf, lemon slices, and salt and pepper to taste in a saucepan and bring to the boil. Add the fish and simmer for 10 to 15 minutes, until tender. Remove with a slotted spoon. Strain and reserve the liquid. Flake the fish, removing any skin or bones.

Melt the butter in a pan, add the mushrooms and cook for 2 minutes. Stir in the flour, cook for 1 minute, then gradually stir in the reserved liquid and bring to the boil.

Remove from the heat and stir in the fish, yogurt or soured cream, parsley and chopped egg. Check the seasoning and pour into a 1.2 litre (2 pint) pie dish. Arrange the potato on top, then sprinkle with the cheese.

Cook under a preheated moderate grill for 5 minutes, or in a preheated moderate oven, 180°C (350°F), Gas Mark 4, for 10 to 15 minutes.

Garnish with the parsley and serve immediately.

Serves 4

COD IN TOMATO SAUCE

4 cod steaks, fresh or frozen

TOMATO SAUCE:

4 tablespoons olive oil

500 g (1 lb) tomatoes, skinned and chopped

1 clove garlic, crushed

1 tablespoon chopped parsley

4 tablespoons white wine

salt and pepper

First make the tomato sauce. Heat the oil in a pan, add the tomatoes, garlic, parsley, wine, and salt and pepper to taste. Simmer for 7 to 10 minutes, stirring occasionally.

Pour half the sauce into a shallow casserole dish, lay the fish on top and cover with the remaining sauce. Cover and cook in a preheated moderately hot oven, 190°C (375°F), Gas Mark 5, for 20 to 25 minutes until cooked. Turn onto a warmed dish and serve immediately.

Serves 4

PRAWN RISOTTO

4 tablespoons oil

1 onion, chopped

250 g (8 oz) brown rice

600 ml (1 pint) water

salt and pepper

1 red pepper, cored, seeded and chopped

1 clove garlic, crushed

50 g (2 oz) flaked almonds

350 g (12 oz) frozen peeled prawns, thawed

1 tablespoon chopped parsley

Heat half the oil in a pan, add the onion and fry until softened. Add the rice and cook for 2 minutes, stirring. Add the water and 1 teaspoon salt and bring to the boil. Simmer for 40 to 45 minutes.

Heat the remaining oil in a pan, add the pepper and fry for 3 minutes. Add the garlic, almonds and prawns. Fry for a further 2 minutes, until the almonds are browned and the prawns heated through.

Stir into the cooked rice, add pepper to taste and more salt if necessary. Transfer to a warmed dish and sprinkle with the parsley.

Serves 4

Mediterranean Fish Stew; Cod in Tomato Sauce; Prawn Risotto

MULLET MORNAY

500 g (1 lb) spinach
salt and pepper
50 g (2 oz) butter
125 g (4 oz)
    mushrooms, sliced
750 g–1 kg
    (1½–2 lb) mullet
    or other fish
    fillets, skinned
25 g (1 oz) plain
    wholemeal flour
450 ml (¾ pint) milk
grated nutmeg
50 g (2 oz) Gruyère
    cheese, grated
50 g (2 oz) Cheddar
    cheese, grated
parsley sprigs to
    garnish

Cook the spinach, with only the water clinging to the leaves after washing, until tender. Drain well, pressing out all excess water, then chop. Season with salt and pepper to taste and stir in 15 g (½ oz) of the butter. Spread the spinach over the bottom of a greased casserole. Cover with the mushrooms and arrange the fish fillets on top.

Melt the remaining butter in a saucepan. Add the flour and cook, stirring, for 1 minute. Gradually stir in the milk and bring to the boil. Simmer, stirring, until thickened. Season to taste with salt, pepper and nutmeg, then stir in all but 2 tablespoons of the cheese.

Pour the cheese sauce over the fish and sprinkle the reserved cheese on top. Cook in a preheated moderate oven, 180°C (350°F), Gas Mark 4, for about 30 minutes or until the fish is tender. Garnish with parsley.
Serves 4

MACKEREL WITH GOOSEBERRIES

2 mackerel, filleted
1 tablespoon fine
    oatmeal
salt and pepper
knob of butter
SAUCE:
125 g (4 oz)
    gooseberries
1 tablespoon water
1 teaspoon light soft
    brown sugar
pinch of grated
    nutmeg

Rinse and dry the mackerel fillets. Season the oatmeal with salt and pepper to taste and sprinkle over the mackerel. Dot with butter and cook under a preheated medium grill for 15 to 20 minutes.

To make the sauce: Put all the ingredients in a saucepan. Cover and simmer for 10 to 15 minutes until the fruit is soft.

Cool slightly, then rub through a sieve or work in an electric blender until smooth and strain.

Place the mackerel on a warmed serving dish. Pour over the sauce. Serve immediately.
Serves 2

SOUSED HERRINGS

150 ml (¼ pint) wine
    vinegar
150 ml (¼ pint)
    white wine
150 ml (¼ pint) water
1 tablespoon pickling
    spice
8 peppercorns
1 bay leaf
1 onion, thinly sliced
1 tablespoon
    muscovado sugar
6 boned herrings

Put all the ingredients, except the fish, into a pan. Bring to the boil then leave to cool.

Place the herrings in a shallow ovenproof dish and pour over the liquid. Cover and cook in a preheated moderate oven, 160°C (325°F), Gas Mark 3, for 1 hour. Allow to cool, then chill in the refrigerator overnight.

Serve with salad and crusty wholemeal bread.
Serves 6

WHOLEMEAL FISH CRUMBLE

750 g (1½ lb) halibut
300 ml (½ pint) milk
bouquet garni
1 celery heart, cut
    into pieces
1 fennel bulb, diced
2 leeks, sliced
1 carrot, sliced
juice of ½ lemon
1 teaspoon grated
    lemon rind
150 ml (¼ pint) water
40 g (1½ oz)
    unsalted butter
25 g (1 oz) plain
    wholemeal flour
3 tablespoons crème
    fraîche
2 tablespoons
    chopped parsley
1 teaspoon chopped
    fennel leaves
TOPPING:
50 g (2 oz) unsalted
    butter
125 g (4 oz)
    wholemeal flour
75 g (3 oz) Cheddar
    cheese, grated
½ teaspoon cayenne
    pepper

Put the fish in a saucepan with the milk, bouquet garni, and salt and pepper to taste, cover and simmer for 10 to 15 minutes, until the fish flakes away from the skin. Remove with a slotted spoon, reserving the cooking liquid. Remove any skin and bones and flake the fish.

Place the vegetables in a saucepan with the lemon rind, juice and water. Bring to the boil, then cover and simmer for 5 minutes, until just tender. Drain, reserving the cooking liquid, and set aside.

Melt the butter in a pan, stir in the flour and cook for 1 minute. Gradually stir in the reserved cooking liquids, bring to the boil and boil for 1 minute. Remove from the heat and stir in the crème fraîche, parsley, fennel leaves, fish and vegetables. Pour into a 1.2 litre (2 pint) pie dish.

Rub the butter into the flour until the mixture resembles breadcrumbs. Stir in the cheese and cayenne and sprinkle over the fish mixture.

Cook in a preheated moderately hot oven, 200°C (400°F), Gas Mark 6, for 20 minutes. Serve hot.
Serves 4 to 6

FISH BOULANGÈRE

500 g (1 lb) potatoes
salt and pepper
50 g (2 oz) butter
1 clove garlic, very
* finely chopped*
750 g (1½ lb) white
* fish fillets, skinned*
* and cut into*
* chunks*
1 large onion, thinly
* sliced*

Parcook the potatoes in boiling salted water for 10 minutes. Drain and slice thinly.

Cream half the butter with the garlic and spread over the bottom of a casserole. Arrange the fish chunks on top and sprinkle with salt and pepper. Cover with the onion and then the potato slices. Dot with the remaining butter.

Cook in a preheated moderate oven, 180°C (350°F), Gas Mark 4, for about 40 minutes or until the fish and potatoes are tender.

Serves 4

HADDOCK WITH GRAPEFRUIT AND MUSHROOMS

4 haddock fillets,
* skinned*
50 g (2 oz) butter
3 spring onions,
* chopped*
salt and pepper
2 grapefruit
125 g (4 oz)
* mushrooms, sliced*

Arrange the haddock fillets in a greased casserole. Mash the butter with the spring onions and salt and pepper to taste. Grate the rind from the grapefruit and beat into the butter. Spread this over the haddock fillets. Cover with the mushrooms.

Squeeze the juice from one grapefruit and peel and segment the other. Pour the grapefruit juice over the mushrooms and place the grapefruit segments on top.

Cover and cook in a preheated moderate oven, 180°C (350°F), Gas Mark 4, for about 30 minutes or until the fish is cooked.

Serves 4

Fish Boulangère; Haddock with Grapefruit and Mushrooms

Beef with Orange

BEEF WITH ORANGE

1½ tablespoons plain
  wholemeal flour
salt and pepper
350 g (12 oz) chuck
  steak, cubed
15 g (½ oz) butter
1 small onion,
  chopped
½ green pepper,
  cored, seeded and
  chopped
grated rind and juice
  of 2 small oranges
200 ml (⅓ pint) beef
  stock
chopped parsley to
  garnish

Season the flour with salt and pepper
and use to coat the meat. Melt the
butter in a pan, add the onion and
pepper and fry until soft. Add the
meat and fry, turning, until evenly
browned. Transfer to a 900 ml
(1½ pint) casserole dish.

Stir in the orange rind and juice,
stock and salt and pepper to taste.
Cover and cook in a preheated
moderate oven, 160°C (325°F), Gas
Mark 3, for 1 to 1¼ hours. Serve hot,
garnished with parsley.
Serves 2

BEEF CRUMBLE

250 g (8 oz) minced
  beef
1 small onion, finely
  chopped
1 celery stick,
  chopped
25 g (1 oz)
  mushrooms,
  chopped
1 small carrot, grated
1 teaspoon plain
  wholemeal flour
150 ml (¼ pint) beef
  stock
salt and pepper
TOPPING:
75 g (3 oz)
  wholemeal flour
25 g (1 oz) porridge
  oats
25 g (1 oz) butter
40 g (1½ oz)
  Cheddar cheese,
  grated
½ teaspoon dried
  mixed herbs
parsley sprigs, to
  garnish

Place a frying pan over moderate
heat. Add the minced beef and fry in
its own fat, turning, until evenly
browned. Add the onion, celery,
mushrooms and carrot and fry for
5 minutes. Stir in the flour and cook
for 1 minute. Add the stock and salt
and pepper to taste. Bring to the
boil, stirring. Cover and simmer for
30 to 40 minutes.

To make the topping: Place the
flour and oats in a bowl. Rub in the
butter until the mixture resembles
coarse breadcrumbs. Stir in the
cheese, herbs and salt and pepper to
taste.

Transfer the meat to a greased
600 ml (1 pint) ovenproof dish and
spoon the topping over. Cook in a
preheated moderately hot oven,
190°C (375°F), Gas Mark 5, for 20 to
30 minutes. Serve hot, garnished
with parsley.
Serves 2

┌─────── MEAT ───────┐

Meat is the basis of thousands of wonderful dishes and
plays a major role in most people's diets. It is an excellent
source of protein, vitamins and minerals. If used in
conjunction with pulses or vegetables, meat can be
economical and at the same time very nutritious.

The most healthy way to prepare and cook meat is to
eliminate as much fat as possible. Choose lean cuts and
trim off all the visible fat before cooking. Cut down on
the amount of oil used when frying cubed meat for
casseroles, and remember that poultry contains less fat than
red meat especially if you remove the skin before cooking.

Italian Veal Casserole; Veal Escalopes

ITALIAN VEAL CASSEROLE

1 tablespoon oil
350 g (12 oz) lean
    veal, cubed
1 clove garlic,
    crushed
1 small onion, sliced
½ green pepper,
    cored, seeded and
    chopped
125 g (4 oz)
    tomatoes, skinned
    and chopped
200 ml (⅓ pint) light
    stock
salt and pepper
1 bouquet garni
chopped parsley to
    garnish

Heat the oil in a frying pan, add the veal and fry, turning, until golden brown all over. Add the garlic and onion and cook until they are soft.

Stir in the green pepper, tomatoes, stock and salt and pepper to taste. Transfer to a 1.2 litre (2 pint) casserole dish. Add the bouquet garni. Cover and cook in a preheated moderate oven, 180°C (350°F), Gas Mark 4, for 1 to 1½ hours.

Remove the bouquet garni and skin off any excess fat. Serve hot, garnished with parsley.
Serves 2

VEAL ESCALOPES

2 × 150 g (5 oz)
    veal escalopes
15 g (½ oz) butter
1 teaspoon oil
½ small onion, sliced
50 g (2 oz) button
    mushrooms
2 tablespoons dry
    sherry
4 tablespoons double
    cream
salt and pepper
paprika
TO GARNISH:
2 lemon twists
1 teaspoon chopped
    parsley

Trim the escalopes into neat shapes and snip the edges to prevent the meat from curling up.

Heat the butter and oil in a frying pan, add the onion and fry for 2 to 3 minutes. Add the veal and mushrooms and cook for 8 to 10 minutes, turning the escalopes once, until golden brown.

Stir in the sherry and bring to the boil. Add the cream and heat through, stirring. Season to taste.

Lift the veal escalopes onto a warmed serving dish and spoon the sauce over. Sprinkle with paprika to taste. Garnish each escalope with a lemon twist and chopped parsley.
Serves 2

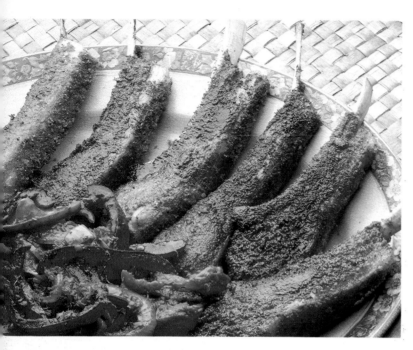

Lamb Cutlets Provençale

LAMB CUTLETS PROVENÇALE

4 tablespoons
   wholemeal
   breadcrumbs
salt and pepper
8 lamb cutlets,
   trimmed
1 egg, beaten
oil for shallow frying
PROVENÇALE SAUCE:
2 tablespoons olive
   oil
1 onion, sliced
1 red and 1 green
   pepper, cored,
   seeded and sliced
4 tomatoes, skinned
1 clove garlic, crushed
1 teaspoon tomato
   purée
1 teaspoon chopped
   thyme
chopped parsley

Mix the breadcrumbs with the salt and pepper. Brush the cutlets with the egg and roll in the breadcrumbs, pressing on well with a palette knife.

To make the sauce: heat the oil in a pan, add the onion and peppers and fry until softened. Cut the tomatoes into eighths and add to the pan. Add the remaining ingredients, with salt and pepper to taste. Cover and simmer for 7 to 8 minutes.

Pour the oil into a frying pan to a depth of 5 mm ($\frac{1}{4}$ inch) and place over moderate heat. When the oil is hot, add the chops and fry for 4 to 5 minutes on each side until tender and golden brown; drain.

Arrange the cutlets along one side of a warmed serving dish and spoon the sauce on the other side. Sprinkle with the parsley before serving.
Serves 4

BOEUF À LA BOURGUIGNONNE

175 g (6 oz) streaky
   bacon, derinded
   and chopped
2 large onions,
   chopped
1.2 kg (2$\frac{1}{2}$ lb) piece
   boned and rolled
   topside or sirloin
   of beef
1 bouquet garni
3 tablespoons olive
   oil
300 ml ($\frac{1}{2}$ pint) dry
   red wine
1 tablespoon olive oil
1$\frac{1}{2}$ tablespoons plain
   wholemeal flour
2 cloves garlic,
   crushed
salt and pepper
250 g (8 oz) button
   mushrooms
12 baby onions
1 tablespoon chopped
   parsley to garnish

Put the bacon, chopped onions and beef in a dish. Add the bouquet garni, oil and wine and stir well. Leave to marinate for 4 hours.

Remove the bacon, onions, meat and bouquet garni and drain well. Strain the marinade and set aside.

Heat the oil in a flameproof casserole. Add the bacon and onion and fry gently for 5 minutes; remove.

Add the meat to the fat remaining in the casserole and brown well on all sides. Stir in the flour and cook for 1 minute. Stir in the marinade and bring to the boil. Add the bouquet garni, garlic, and salt and pepper to taste. Cover and cook in a preheated moderate oven, 160°C (325°F), Gas Mark 3, for 1$\frac{1}{2}$ to 2 hours.

Return the bacon and onion to the casserole, add the mushrooms and whole onions and cook for 1 hour. Remove the bouquet garni. Garnish.
Serves 6

LAMB HOTPOT

500 g (1 lb) middle
   neck of lamb
250 g (8 oz)
   potatoes, sliced
salt and pepper
1 onion, sliced
2 carrots, sliced
1 celery stick,
   chopped
$\frac{1}{2}$ teaspoon dried
   mixed herbs
200 ml ($\frac{1}{3}$ pint) stock
15 g ($\frac{1}{2}$ oz) butter,
   melted

Divide the lamb into cutlets.

Cover the base of a 1.2 litre (2 pint) casserole dish with half the potatoes. Arrange the lamb on top and sprinkle with salt and pepper.

Mix together the onion, carrots, celery and herbs, with salt and pepper to taste. Spread over the lamb. Pour over the stock. Arrange the remaining potatoes in circles on top and brush with the butter.

Cover and cook in a preheated moderate oven, 180°C (350°F), Gas Mark 4, for 1$\frac{1}{2}$ hours. Remove the lid and continue to cook for 20 to 30 minutes until browned.
Serves 2

KIDNEY AND BACON KEBABS

12 rashers streaky
    bacon, derinded
2 green peppers,
    cored and seeded
12 lambs' kidneys
6 onions, quartered
2 tablespoons olive oil
1 tablespoon chopped
    thyme
PILAFF:
2 tablespoons olive
    oil
1 onion, chopped
1 red pepper, cored,
    seeded and chopped
1 clove garlic, crushed
250 g (8 oz) brown
    rice
600 ml (1 pint) stock
1 bay leaf
salt and pepper
50 g (2 oz) raisins
chopped parsley

First, prepare the pilaff. Heat the oil in a pan, add the onion and cook until softened. Add the pepper, garlic and rice and cook for a further 2 minutes, stirring. Add the stock, bay leaf, and salt and pepper to taste. Bring to the boil, stirring. Cover and simmer for 35 minutes. Add the raisins and cook for about 7 minutes.

Cut the bacon rashers in half and roll up. Cut the peppers into pieces. Skin, core and halve the kidneys.

Thread the kidney, bacon, onion and pepper alternately onto 8 skewers. Mix the oil and thyme with $\frac{1}{2}$ teaspoon salt and $\frac{1}{4}$ teaspoon pepper; brush over the kebabs. Cook under a preheated hot grill for 8 minutes, turning and basting with oil.

Stir the parsley into the pilaff and serve with the kebabs.
Serves 4

LIVER WITH HERBS

2 tablespoons
    wholemeal flour
500 g (1 lb) lambs'
    liver, sliced
2 tablespoons oil
2 onions, chopped
150 ml ($\frac{1}{4}$ pint) red
    wine
150 ml ($\frac{1}{4}$ pint) stock
2 tablespoons tomato
    purée
1 teaspoon chopped
    thyme
2 tomatoes, skinned,
    seeded and sliced
chopped parsley

Season the flour with salt and pepper and use to coat the liver. Heat the oil in a pan, add the liver and fry gently for 2 minutes on each side. Remove.

Add the onions to the pan and fry gently until softened. Stir in the wine, stock, tomato purée, thyme, and salt and pepper to taste. Bring to the boil. Return the liver to the pan, cover and simmer for 15 minutes. Add the tomatoes and cook for a further 5 minutes or until tender.

Arrange the liver on a warmed serving dish. Pour the sauce over the liver. Sprinkle with parsley and serve.
Serves 4

Kidney and Bacon Kebabs; Liver with Herbs

PORK WITH ORANGE AND APRICOTS

15 g (½ oz) butter
2 pork chops
grated rind and juice of ½ orange
salt and pepper
1 small onion, finely chopped
½ green pepper, cored, seeded and chopped
200 ml (⅓ pint) stock
1 teaspoon cornflour
pinch of light soft brown sugar
50 g (2 oz) dried apricots
watercress sprigs to garnish

Melt the butter in a frying pan. Add the chops and fry on both sides until evenly browned.

Transfer to a shallow ovenproof dish, using a slotted spoon. Sprinkle with the orange rind and season.

Add the onion and pepper to the fat remaining in the pan and fry until soft. Stir in the stock. Blend the cornflour with the orange juice and add to the pan. Heat, stirring, until the sauce thickens. Add the sugar and salt and pepper to taste.

Arrange the apricots on top of the pork and pour over the sauce. Cover with foil and cook in a preheated moderate oven, 180°C (350°F), Gas Mark 4, for 1 to 1¼ hours. Garnish.
Serves 2

WINTER FAMILY CASSEROLE

1 kg (2 lb) stewing steak
3 tablespoons oil
25 g (1 oz) wholemeal flour
750 ml (1¼ pints) beef stock
4 onions, chopped
250 g (8 oz) carrots, sliced
1 turnip, diced
salt and pepper
grated nutmeg
2 bay leaves
4 medium potatoes, sliced

Cut the meat into 2.5 cm (1 inch) cubes. Heat the oil in a flameproof casserole, add the meat in batches and quickly brown on all sides, moving the meat cubes to the side of the casserole as they brown.

Sprinkle in the flour and cook, stirring, for 1 minute. Gradually add the stock and bring to the boil, stirring constantly. Lower the heat to simmering point and add the onion, carrot and turnip.

Season to taste with salt, pepper and nutmeg and add the bay leaves. Cover and cook in a preheated moderate oven, 160°C (325°F), Gas Mark 3, for 1½ hours.

Add the potatoes and return to the oven for a further 1 hour. Remove the bay leaves before serving.
Serves 4 to 6

STIR-FRIED SHREDDED BEEF WITH GINGER

500 g (1 lb) rump steak, shredded
1 teaspoon salt
2 tablespoons oil
2 cloves garlic, sliced
4 × 2.5 cm (1 inch) pieces of fresh root ginger, shredded
4 tablespoons soy sauce
2 tablespoons dry sherry
4 spring onions, shredded
shredded root ginger and spring onion to garnish

Sprinkle the steak with the salt. Heat the oil in a wok or deep frying pan, add the garlic and fry quickly until browned. Add the meat and ginger and stir-fry for 2 minutes. Stir in the soy sauce and sherry and cook for 1 minute. Stir in the spring onions.

Spoon onto a warmed serving dish and sprinkle with the ginger and spring onions. Serve immediately.
Serves 4 to 6

STUFFED LEG OF LAMB

1.5 kg (3 lb) boned leg of lamb
2 cloves garlic
2–3 large rosemary sprigs, broken into pieces
2 teaspoons chopped sage
8 tablespoons chopped parsley
1 tablespoon chopped thyme
2 teaspoons chopped rosemary
4 shallots, finely chopped
¼ teaspoon ground ginger
salt and pepper

Lay the lamb, skin side down, on a board. Slice 1 garlic clove and crush the other. Put half the rosemary in a roasting pan.

Put the crushed garlic, chopped herbs, shallots, ginger, and salt and pepper to taste in a bowl and mix well. Spread over the lamb and roll up, enclosing the stuffing completely. Secure with string. Make small incisions in the surface of the lamb and insert the garlic slices. Lay the remaining rosemary on top.

Cook in a preheated moderate oven, 180°C (350°F), Gas Mark 4, for 1½ hours; the meat should be pink inside.

Serve with sautéed potatoes, tossed in parsley.
Serves 6 to 8

Stuffed Leg of Lamb

Moussaka

MOUSSAKA

2 medium
    aubergines, sliced
salt and pepper
6 tablespoons olive
    oil
    (approximately)
1 large onion,
    chopped
1 clove garlic, finely
    chopped
750 g (1½ lb) cooked
    lamb, finely
    chopped
250 g (8 oz)
    tomatoes, skinned
    and chopped
2 tablespoons
    chopped parsley
grated nutmeg
25 g (1 oz) butter
25 g (1 oz) plain
    wholemeal flour
300 ml (½ pint) milk
1 egg yolk
parsley sprigs to
    garnish

Sprinkle the aubergine slices with salt and leave to drain for 30 minutes. Rinse and pat dry with kitchen paper. Heat a little of the olive oil in a frying pan. Fry the aubergine slices, in batches, until golden brown on both sides, adding more oil as necessary.

Add the onion and garlic to the pan, with more oil if necessary, and fry until softened. Stir in the lamb, tomatoes, parsley, salt, pepper and nutmeg to taste. Cook for 5 minutes.

Make alternate layers of aubergine and lamb in a casserole, beginning and ending with aubergine slices.

Melt the butter in a saucepan. Add the flour and cook, stirring, for 1 minute. Gradually stir in the milk and bring to the boil. Simmer, stirring, until thickened. Season with salt, pepper and nutmeg to taste. Cool slightly, then beat in the egg yolk.

Pour the sauce over the aubergine slices. Cook in a preheated moderate oven, 180°C (350°F), Gas Mark 4, for 45 minutes. Garnish with parsley.
Serves 4

KIDNEY RAGOÛT

3 tablespoons plain
    wholemeal flour
salt and pepper
25 g (1 oz) butter
250 g (8 oz)
    unsmoked streaky
    bacon rashers,
    derinded and diced
12 lambs' kidneys,
    sliced
1 large onion, finely
    chopped
1 clove garlic,
    crushed
1 red pepper, cored,
    seeded and diced
2 tomatoes, skinned,
    seeded and
    chopped
150 ml (¼ pint) beef
    stock
6 tablespoons red
    wine
triangles of fried
    wholemeal bread
    to garnish

Season the flour and use to coat the kidney slices. Melt the butter in a frying pan and fry the bacon until crisp. Remove with a slotted spoon and place in a casserole.

Add the kidney slices to the frying pan and brown on all sides. Transfer to the casserole.

Add the onion, garlic and red pepper to the frying pan and fry until the onion is softened. Stir in the tomatoes, stock and wine and bring to the boil, then pour into the casserole and mix well. Cover and cook in a preheated moderate oven, 180°C (350°F), Gas Mark 4, for 30 minutes or until the kidneys are tender. Garnish with triangles of fried bread before serving.
Serves 4

OXTAIL CASSEROLE

25 g (1 oz) plain
    wholemeal flour
salt and pepper
2 oxtails, chopped
    into pieces
3 tablespoons brandy
1 onion, chopped
2 carrots, chopped
1 bouquet garni
300 ml (½ pint) red
    wine
    (approximately)
450 ml (¾ pint) beef
    stock or water
    (approximately)

Season the flour and use to coat the oxtail pieces. Place in a casserole and cook in a preheated hot oven, 230°C (450°F), Gas Mark 8, for 30 minutes, turning frequently.

Pour off all the fat from the casserole. Warm the brandy, pour over the oxtail pieces and set alight. When the flames have died down, add the onion, carrots, bouquet garni, wine and stock or water.

Lower the oven temperature to moderate, 180°C (350°F), Gas Mark 4, and cook for 4 hours or until the oxtail is tender. Stir during cooking and add more liquid as necessary. Discard the bouquet garni.
Serves 4 to 6

SOMERSET LAMB CHOPS

25 g (1 oz) butter
1 tablespoon oil
1 large onion, thinly
  sliced
2 large cooking
  apples, peeled,
  cored and sliced
2 tablespoons raisins
2 tablespoons light
  soft brown sugar
salt and pepper
8 or 12 lamb chops
150 ml (¼ pint) dry
  cider

Melt the butter with the oil in a frying pan. Add the onion and fry until softened. Remove the onion from the pan with a slotted spoon and spread half over the bottom of a casserole. Cover with half the apple slices and sprinkle with half the raisins, half the sugar and salt and pepper to taste.

Put the chops in the frying pan and brown on both sides. Drain the chops and place in the casserole. Cover with the rest of the onion and apples and sprinkle with the remaining raisins, sugar, salt and pepper. Pour in the cider.

Cover the casserole and cook in a preheated moderate oven, 180°C (350°F), Gas Mark 4, for 1½ hours or until the chops are very tender.
Serves 4

LAMB, PORK AND POTATO CASSEROLE

25 g (1 oz) butter
750 g (1½ lb)
  potatoes, sliced
500 g (1 lb) boned
  shoulder of lamb,
  cubed
500 g (1 lb) boned
  shoulder of pork,
  cubed
2 onions, chopped
salt and pepper
150 ml (¼ pint) dry
  white wine

Grease a casserole with half the butter. Make a layer of half the potato slices on the bottom, then add the lamb, pork and onions in layers, sprinkling each layer with a little salt and pepper. Pour over the wine. Arrange the remaining potato slices on top and dot with the remaining butter. Cover and cook in a preheated moderately hot oven, 190°C (375°F), Gas Mark 5, for 1½ hours.

Uncover the casserole and continue cooking for 30 minutes or until the potato topping is golden brown.
Serves 4

Somerset Lamb Chops; Lamb, Pork and Potato Casserole

BEEF, PEPPER AND MUSHROOM CASSEROLE

1 kg (2 lb) braising steak
3 tablespoons plain wholemeal flour
salt and pepper
3 tablespoons oil
3 onions, chopped
1 large green pepper, cored, seeded and chopped
600 ml (1 pint) stock (or a mixture of stock and red wine)
1 bouquet garni
250 g (8 oz) mushrooms, sliced

Cut the meat into 2.5 cm (1 inch) cubes. Season the flour with salt and pepper and use to coat the meat.

Heat the oil in a flameproof casserole, add the meat in batches and quickly brown on all sides. Remove from the casserole.

Add the onion and pepper to the fat remaining in the casserole and fry until softened. Return the meat to the casserole, sprinkle in any remaining seasoned flour and cook, stirring, for 1 minute.

Gradually add the stock (or stock and wine) and bring to the boil, stirring constantly. Add the bouquet garni, cover and cook in a preheated moderate oven, 160°C (325°F), Gas Mark 3, for 2 hours.

Add the mushrooms, adjust the seasoning if necessary and cook for 30 minutes. Remove the bouquet garni.

Serves 4 to 6

BELGIAN STEAK

3 tablespoons oil
2 large onions, sliced
125 g (4 oz) mushrooms, halved
750 g (1½ lb) blade or chuck steak, cut into 4 pieces
salt and pepper
2 tablespoons plain wholemeal flour
300 ml (½ pint) lager
1 clove garlic, crushed
1 tablespoon brown sugar

Heat the oil in a pan, add the onions and fry until just coloured. Place in a casserole with the mushrooms.

Sprinkle the steaks with salt and pepper and coat with flour. Fry in the oil in the pan until browned then place in the casserole.

Sprinkle any leftover flour into the pan and blend into the fat; cook, stirring, until well browned, then remove from the heat and stir in the lager. Add the garlic, sugar and salt and pepper to taste and bring to the boil. Pour over the beef, cover and cook in a preheated moderate oven, 160°C (325°F), Gas Mark 3, for 2 to 2½ hours or until tender.

Serves 4

BEEF AND SPINACH BAKE

750 g (1½ lb) fresh spinach
1 tablespoon oil
1 large onion, finely chopped
500 g (1 lb) minced beef
250 g (8 oz) mushrooms, sliced
142 ml (5 fl oz) fresh sour cream
½ teaspoon dried oregano
½ teaspoon dried basil
½ teaspoon dried thyme
125 g (4 oz) Cheddar cheese, grated
125 g (4 oz) Parmesan cheese, grated
salt and pepper

Cook the spinach, with just the water clinging to the leaves after washing, until tender. Drain well, pressing out all excess water. Chop the spinach.

Heat the oil in a frying pan. Add the onion and fry until softened. Add the beef and fry until well browned. Stir in the mushrooms and fry for a further 5 minutes. Remove from the heat and drain off all the fat from the pan. Add the chopped spinach, cream, herbs, half the Cheddar and half the Parmesan. Mix well, adding salt and pepper to taste, then turn into a casserole.

Sprinkle the remaining cheeses over the top. Bake in a preheated moderate oven, 180°C (350°F), Gas Mark 4, for 25 minutes.

Serves 4

Beef and Spinach Bake

LEMON-PEAR PORK CHOPS

5 tablespoons oil
6 pork chops
1 onion, chopped
150 ml ($\frac{1}{4}$ pint)
    orange juice
salt and pepper
3 firm pears, peeled,
    cored and halved
2 tablespoons light
    soft brown sugar
6 thin lemon slices
whole cloves
2 teaspoons cornflour

Heat the oil in a frying pan. Add the chops and brown on both sides. Arrange in a baking dish, in one layer.

Add the onion to the pan and fry until softened. Spoon around the chops and pour over the orange juice. Add salt and pepper to taste. Cover and cook in a preheated moderately hot oven, 190°C (375°F), Gas Mark 5, for 45 to 50 minutes or until the chops are cooked through.

Fill each pear half with a little brown sugar and place a lemon slice on each, securing with cloves. Place a pear on each pork chop and bake, uncovered, for 10 minutes.

Transfer the chops and pears to a warmed serving dish and keep hot. Skim the fat from the cooking liquid and strain into a measuring jug. Make up to 170 ml (6 fl oz) with water and pour into a saucepan. Dissolve the cornflour in a little water and add to the pan. Cook, stirring, until thickened. Pour over the chops before serving.
Serves 6

Hunter's Casserole

HUNTER'S CASSEROLE

300 ml ($\frac{1}{2}$ pint) dry
    red wine
4 tablespoons olive
    oil
1 clove garlic,
    crushed
1 bay leaf
salt and pepper
1 kg (2 lb) boneless
    hare, cut into
    cubes
25 g (1 oz) butter
2 large carrots, sliced
150 ml ($\frac{1}{4}$ pint) beef
    stock
250 g (8 oz) baby
    onions
250 g (8 oz) button
    mushrooms

Mix together the wine, oil, garlic, bay leaf and salt and pepper in a shallow dish. Add the hare and leave to marinate overnight.

Drain the hare, reserving the marinade, and pat dry with kitchen paper. Melt the butter in a flameproof casserole. Add the hare cubes and brown on all sides. Stir in the reserved marinade, carrots and stock and bring to the boil. Cover and cook in a preheated moderate oven, 180°C (350°F), Gas Mark 4, for 2 hours.

Meanwhile, blanch the onions in boiling water for 5 minutes, then drain and peel, when cool enough to handle.

Add the onions and mushrooms to the casserole and stir well. Cook, uncovered, for a further 30 minutes or until the hare is tender. Discard the bay leaf before serving.
Serves 4

SOMERSET PORK CASSEROLE

25 g (1 oz) butter
2 cooking apples,
    peeled and sliced
1 onion, chopped
2 teaspoons light soft
    brown sugar
2 teaspoons dried
    sage
4 or 8 pork chops
125 g (4 oz)
    mushrooms, sliced
150 ml ($\frac{1}{4}$ pint) dry
    cider
50 g (2 oz) fresh
    wholemeal
    breadcrumbs
50 g (2 oz) Cheddar
    cheese, grated

Grease a shallow baking dish with half the butter. Place half the apple slices in the dish and sprinkle with half the onion, sugar and sage. Arrange the chops on top, season with salt and pepper to taste and cover with the mushrooms. Add the remaining apples, onion, sugar and sage. Pour in the cider.

Mix together the breadcrumbs and cheese and sprinkle over the top. Dot with the remaining butter. Cook in a preheated moderately hot oven, 200°C (400°F), Gas Mark 6, for 45 minutes or until the chops are cooked and the top is browned.
Serves 4

RABBIT WITH MUSTARD SAUCE

4 rabbit quarters
1 tablespoon vinegar
25 g (1 oz) butter
250 g (8 oz)
    unsmoked streaky
    bacon, derinded
    and diced
2 onions, chopped
15 g ($\frac{1}{2}$ oz) plain
    wholemeal flour
450 ml ($\frac{3}{4}$ pint)
    chicken stock
salt and pepper
1 bouquet garni
142 ml (5 fl oz)
    double cream
2 tablespoons French
    mustard
chopped parsley to
    garnish

Soak the rabbit quarters overnight in water with the vinegar added. Drain, rinse and pat dry with kitchen paper.

Melt the butter in a flameproof casserole. Add the rabbit quarters and brown on all sides, then remove.

Add the bacon and onions to the casserole and fry until golden brown. Sprinkle over the flour and cook, stirring, for 2 minutes. Gradually stir in the stock and bring to the boil. Season, then return the rabbit to the casserole and add the bouquet garni.

Cover and cook in a preheated moderate oven, 180°C (350°F), Gas Mark 4, for 1½ hours.

Remove the rabbit from the casserole. Discard the bouquet garni. Mix the cream with the mustard and stir into the cooking liquid. Heat, stirring, on top of the stove; do not boil. Return the rabbit and reheat. Serve garnished with parsley.
Serves 4

CRUMBED VENISON CUTLETS

8 venison best end
    cutlets
1 clove garlic, halved
4 tablespoons olive
    oil
wholemeal flour for
    coating
salt and pepper
2 eggs, beaten
250 g (8 oz) fresh
    wholemeal
    breadcrumbs
4 tablespoons grated
    Parmesan cheese
1 teaspoon ground
    coriander
1 teaspoon paprika
40 g (1½ oz) butter

Rub the venison with the cut garlic. Place the oil in a large flat dish, add the venison and leave for 15 minutes, turning once. Drain well, reserving the oil, and pat dry with kitchen paper. Season the flour with salt and pepper and use to coat the meat, then dip the cutlets in the egg.

Mix the breadcrumbs, Parmesan, coriander and paprika together and use to coat the cutlets, pressing on firmly. Chill for 5 minutes.

Heat the reserved oil and the butter in a roasting pan. Remove from the heat and add the cutlets, turning them over carefully so that both sides are coated in oil. Cook in a preheated hot oven, 220°C (425°F), Gas Mark 7, for 15 to 20 minutes.
Serves 4

BUTTERFLY VENISON STEAKS

4 × 125 g (4 oz)
    venison fillet
    steaks
salt and white pepper
40 g (1½ oz) butter
1 tablespoon olive oil
2 tablespoons brandy
HORSERADISH
    BUTTER:
25 g (1 oz) butter,
    softened
2 tablespoons
    chopped chives
2 teaspoons grated
    horseradish

First, make the horseradish butter: mix all the ingredients together and shape into a roll. Chill until firm, then slice and cut into shapes.

Cut the venison steaks almost in half horizontally and open out flat to form a 'butterfly' shape; press with the hand to flatten. Sprinkle each with salt and pepper.

Heat the butter and oil in a heavy-based frying pan, add the steaks and fry for 15 seconds on each side, pressing down firmly. Transfer to a warmed serving dish and keep hot.

Remove the pan from the heat and pour in the brandy, stirring to dissolve the sediment. Pour over the steaks and top with a portion of horseradish butter.
Serves 4

PIGEONS IN HONEY

1 teaspoon coriander
  seeds, lightly
  crushed
2 tablespoons honey
2 onions, sliced
300 ml ($\frac{1}{2}$ pint) dry
  cider
300 ml ($\frac{1}{2}$ pint)
  chilli vinegar
4 oven-ready wood
  pigeons, halved
  lengthwise
salt and pepper
25 g (1 oz) butter
2 tablespoons oil
chopped parsley to
  garnish

Mix the coriander, honey, onion, cider and vinegar in a large non-metal bowl. Add the pigeons and leave to marinate for 8 hours or overnight. Drain, reserving marinade, dry well.

Heat the butter and oil in a large flameproof casserole, add the pigeons in 2 batches, seasoning them with salt and pepper, and brown on both sides. Put all the birds in the casserole and pour over the marinade. Cover and cook in a preheated moderate oven, 160°C (325°F), Gas Mark 3, for 1 to 1$\frac{1}{4}$ hours, until tender.

Serve garnished with parsley, and accompanied by sautéed mushrooms and a celery julienne.

Serves 4

Venison Loaf

MARINATED GRILLED DUCK

4 duck breast and
  wing portions
MARINADE:
1 teaspoon soy sauce
150 ml ($\frac{1}{4}$ pint) red
  wine vinegar
1 onion, chopped
12 juniper berries,
  crushed
2 teaspoons fennel
  seeds
1 clove garlic,
  crushed
SAUCE:
150 g (5.2 oz)
  natural yogurt
salt and pepper
watercress sprigs to
  garnish

Put the duck portions in a large clear plastic bag. Add marinade ingredients, exclude any air and seal. Leave for 8 hours, turning occasionally.

Drain, reserving the marinade, and place, skin side down, in a roasting pan. Cook in a preheated hot oven, 220°C (425°F), Gas Mark 7, for 30 minutes, basting once with the marinade. Turn and cook for a further 30 minutes, basting again. Transfer to a warmed dish; keep hot.

Place 6 tablespoons of the reserved marinade in a small pan, cover and heat gently for 5 minutes. Strain, whisk into the yogurt and season with salt and pepper to taste.

Serve the duck on a bed of brown rice, garnished with watercress and topped with the sauce.

Serves 4

VENISON LOAF

250 g (8 oz) streaky
  bacon derinded
625 g (1$\frac{1}{4}$ lb) pie
  venison, minced
salt and pepper
1 egg, beaten
250 g (8 oz) fresh
  wholemeal
  breadcrumbs
finely grated or
  shredded rind of
  1 lemon
25 g (1 oz) parsley,
  coarsely chopped
75 g (3 oz) stoned
  black olives

Line the base and sides of a 500 g (1 lb) loaf tin with bacon rashers, stretching them to fit if necessary; chop the remainder and set aside.

Place the venison in a bowl, season with salt and pepper to taste and bind with half the egg. Spread half this mixture over the bacon.

Mix the breadcrumbs, remaining egg, lemon rind, parsley and chopped bacon together and spread half on top of the venison. Press the olives into the mixture. Spread the remaining venison on top and cover with the remaining breadcrumb mixture.

Cover loosely with foil and bake in a preheated moderately hot oven, 190°C (375°F), Gas Mark 5, for 1 hour. Allow to stand for 3 to 4 minutes, then pour off and reserve the juices. Turn out the terrine onto a serving dish and serve sliced.

Serves 4

RABBIT CASSEROLE

750 g (1½ lb) rabbit
  joints
300 ml (½ pint) red
  wine
rind of 1 lemon
2 cloves garlic, crushed
bouquet garni
250 g (8 oz) cooked
  ham, cubed
250 g (8 oz) onion,
  sliced
250 g (8 oz) carrots,
  thinly sliced
125 g (4 oz) button
  mushrooms, halved
15 g (½ oz) butter
1 tablespoon
  wholemeal flour
¼ teaspoon cayenne
1 tablespoon
  redcurrant jelly

Put the rabbit, wine, lemon rind, garlic, herbs, ham, onion, carrot and salt in a flameproof casserole. Bring to simmering point, cover and cook in a preheated moderate oven, 180°C (350°F), Gas Mark 4, for 35 minutes.

Add the mushrooms and cook for 15 minutes or until the rabbit and vegetables are tender. Using a slotted spoon, transfer meat and vegetables to a warmed serving dish; keep hot.

Soften the butter and mix with the flour to form a paste, then drop small pieces into the liquid in the casserole. Cook, stirring over moderate heat, until thickened.

Add the cayenne and redcurrant jelly and cook for 3 to 4 minutes, until syrupy. Pour over the meat and vegetables. Serve with dumplings.
Serves 4

CLASSIC GROUSE CASSEROLE

2 oven-ready
  casserole grouse
salt and pepper
1 small onion,
  chopped
40 g (1½ oz) butter
1 teaspoon thyme
  leaves
2 juniper berries,
  crushed
150 ml (¼ pint)
  game stock or dry
  cider
2 tablespoons
  rowanberry jelly

Season the grouse inside and out with salt and pepper and place half the onion inside each body cavity. Mix the butter, thyme and juniper berries together and spread all over the grouse. Place in a roasting pan and cook in a preheated moderate oven, 180°C (350°F), Gas Mark 4, for 20 minutes.

Cut the grouse in half lengthways and place in a casserole dish. Add the stock or cider and jelly, cover and return to the oven for 30 minutes.

Serve with puréed carrot and leeks.
Serves 2

SALMIS OF PARTRIDGE

2 slices Parma or
  raw smoked ham,
  halved
2 oven-ready
  partridges
pepper
1 tablespoon olive oil
40 g (1½ oz) butter
4 shallots or 1 small
  onion, chopped
bunch of mixed
  parsley, thyme
  and winter savory
4 tablespoons game
  stock or water
6 tablespoons red
  wine
2 tablespoons port

Place a half ham slice in the cavity of each partridge. Sprinkle with pepper and truss securely.

Heat the oil and butter in a frying pan, add the partridges and fry for 15 to 20 minutes, until browned. Remove from the pan; cool slightly.

Using a sharp knife or poultry shears, cut off and reserve the wing, leg and breast portions. Cut up the carcasses and put in a saucepan with the shallots or onion and herbs.

Pour the stock or water into the frying pan and stir well to dissolve the sediment. Add to the saucepan with the wine. Cover and cook gently for 1 hour. Strain, then add the port.

Shred the remaining ham and put into a clean pan with the partridge portions. Pour in the sauce and heat gently for 20 to 25 minutes.

Transfer the partridge to a warmed serving dish and pour the sauce around them.
Serves 2

GUINEA FOWL WITH GRAPES

50 g (2 oz) butter
2 tablespoons oil
2 guinea fowl, each
cut into 4 pieces
8 shallots
500 g (1 lb) seedless
black grapes
450 ml (¾ pint)
grape juice
(unsweetened)
300 ml (½ pint) dry
white wine
350 g (12 oz)
brown rice
3 tablespoons
chopped tarragon

Heat half the butter and the oil in a large flameproof casserole. Sauté the guinea fowl until well browned.

Add the shallots, 350 g (12 oz) of the grapes, the grape juice, wine, and salt and pepper to taste.

Cover and cook in a preheated moderate oven, 160°C (325°F), Gas Mark 3, for 20 minutes.

Stir in the rice and cook for 35 to 40 minutes or until the birds are tender and the rice is cooked. Stir in the remaining butter and tarragon.

Garnish with the remaining grapes and serve with a watercress salad.
Serves 8

GUINEA FOWL WITH RASPBERRIES

1 oven-ready guinea
fowl
salt and pepper
25 g (1 oz) butter
2 rosemary sprigs
175 g (6 oz) fresh
raspberries
1 tablespoon oil
4 tablespoons
raspberry vinegar
4 tablespoons double
cream
TO GARNISH:
50 g (2 oz) fresh
raspberries
parsley sprigs
bay leaves

Season the guinea fowl well inside and out. Put half the butter, the rosemary and 50 g (2 oz) of the raspberries in the body cavity.

Heat the remaining butter and the oil in a pan, add the guinea fowl and brown on all sides. Add the vinegar.

Lay the guinea fowl on its side and cook for 20 to 25 minutes, then turn onto the other side and cook for a further 20 to 25 minutes. Transfer to a warmed serving dish; keep warm.

Add the cream, and salt and pepper to taste to the pan, stirring well to dissolve the sediment, then add the remaining raspberries and heat through, without stirring.

Spoon the raspberry sauce around the guinea fowl. Garnish with the raspberries and herbs.
Serves 2 or 4

LEFT: *Rabbit Casserole*
ABOVE: *Partridge with Quince*

PARTRIDGE WITH QUINCE

2 oven-ready young
partridges
salt and pepper
2 teaspoons butter
2 cloves garlic
2 parsley sprigs
4 rashers streaky
bacon, derinded
1 ripe quince, peeled,
cored and cut
into 8
150 ml (¼ pint) dry
vermouth
1 teaspoon cornflour
4 tablespoons double
cream
1 bunch watercress to
garnish

Season the partridges inside and out with salt and pepper. Put 1 teaspoon butter, 1 garlic clove and a parsley sprig inside each body cavity. Wrap 2 bacon rashers around each partridge, securing underneath with wooden cocktail sticks. Place in a roasting pan and cook in a preheated hot oven, 220°C (425°F), Gas Mark 7, for 15 minutes. Add the quince, turning to coat in the pan juices, and return to the oven for 20 minutes, or until the partridges are tender. Transfer the partridges and quince to a warmed serving dish; keep hot.

Pour the vermouth into the pan and stir well to dissolve the sediment. Stir the cornflour into a little of the cream, add the remaining cream, then pour into the pan. Cook gently, stirring, for 2 to 3 minutes until smooth and thickened.

Garnish with watercress.
Serves 2

Turkey Fricassée

TURKEY FRICASSÉE

25 g (1 oz) streaky
  bacon, derinded
  and chopped
1 small onion,
  chopped
1 small carrot, grated
1 celery stick,
  chopped
150 ml ($\frac{1}{4}$ pint) light
  stock
1 bouquet garni
salt and pepper
150 ml ($\frac{1}{4}$ pint) milk
  (approximately)
15 g ($\frac{1}{2}$ oz) butter
2 tablespoons plain
  wholemeal flour
grated nutmeg
250 g (8 oz) cooked
  turkey meat,
  chopped
1 tablespoon single
  cream
chopped parsley to
  garnish

Place the bacon, onion, carrot, celery, stock and bouquet garni in a saucepan. Add salt and pepper to taste. Bring to the boil, cover and simmer for 15 minutes.

Strain the stock into a measuring jug and add enough milk to make 300 ml ($\frac{1}{2}$ pint) liquor.

Melt the butter in a clean saucepan, stir in the flour and cook for 1 minute. Gradually blend in the liquor and heat, stirring, until thickened. Add nutmeg, salt and pepper to taste.

Stir in the vegetables and turkey meat. Cover and simmer for 15 minutes. Remove from the heat and stir in the cream.

Transfer to a warmed serving dish and sprinkle with parsley. Serve immediately.
Serves 2

TURKEY BREASTS COLOMBIAN

2 × 250 g (8 oz)
  turkey breast
  fillets
salt and pepper
25 g (1 oz) butter
2 tablespoons olive
  oil
1 lemon, halved
SAUCE:
1 avocado, peeled,
  stoned and cubed
4 spring onions,
  sliced
$\frac{1}{2}$ green pepper,
  cored, seeded and
  cubed
142 ml (5 fl oz)
  soured cream
TO GARNISH:
$\frac{1}{2}$ green pepper,
  cored, seeded and
  sliced into rings

Holding the turkey fillets firmly and using a sharp knife, cut through horizontally to give 4 thin slices. Place in one layer between 2 sheets of waxed paper and beat with a rolling pin or wooden mallet to flatten. Season liberally.

Heat the butter and oil in a pan. Add the fillets, two at a time, and sauté for 2 minutes on each side. Return all fillets to the pan, lower the heat, squeeze over the juice from $\frac{1}{2}$ lemon and keep warm.

To make the sauce, mash the avocado to a paste with the juice of the remaining lemon half. Add the spring onions, green pepper and salt to taste, then fold in the cream.

Arrange the turkey on a warmed serving dish and trickle over the sauce. Garnish with the pepper rings.
Serves 4

SCRAMBLED TURKEY LIVERS WITH BASIL

6 eggs
2 tablespoons double
  cream
salt and pepper
50 g (2 oz) butter
225 g (8 oz) turkey
  livers, trimmed
  and quartered
6–8 basil leaves
8 thin slices
  wholemeal French
  bread, toasted

Place the eggs and cream in a small bowl with salt and pepper to taste and beat lightly with a fork.

Melt half the butter in a small frying pan, add the livers and sauté until golden on the outside but still pink inside. Turn the heat to low.

Melt the remaining butter in another pan until foaming, add the eggs and scramble until creamy, stirring only enough to prevent sticking. Pile the egg onto a warmed serving dish and spoon the livers on top. Chop half the basil and sprinkle over all.

Garnish with the remaining basil and serve immediately with the toast.
Serves 4

CHICKEN WITH HONEY

3 tablespoons clear honey
1 teaspoon dry mustard
1 teaspoon salt
½ teaspoon pepper
2 teaspoons soy sauce
1 × 1.5 kg (3 lb) oven-ready chicken
150 ml (¼ pint) chicken stock
150 ml (¼ pint) white wine
125 g (4 oz) green grapes, halved and seeded
150 g (5 oz) natural yogurt

Place the honey, mustard, salt, pepper and soy sauce in a small basin and mix well. Spread the mixture over the chicken, place in a roasting pan and pour in the stock.

Roast in a preheated moderately hot oven, 200°C (400°F), Gas Mark 6, for 1 to 1¼ hours, basting occasionally. Carve and arrange on a warmed serving dish; keep hot.

Pour the wine into the roasting pan and stir to mix in the juices. Bring to the boil, add the grapes and check the seasoning. Stir in the yogurt. Pour over the chicken to serve.

Serves 4

POUSSINS WITH HERB SAUCE

2 tablespoons oil
4 × 400 g (14 oz) poussins (young chicken)
grated rind and juice of 1 lemon
2 tablespoons chicken stock
salt and pepper
2 tablespoons chopped mixed herbs (parsley, chives, thyme and marjoram)
142 ml (5 fl oz) double cream
watercress to garnish

Heat the oil in a large pan, add the poussins and brown lightly all over. Add the lemon rind and juice, stock, and salt and pepper to taste.

Cover and simmer for 20 to 25 minutes until tender. Place on a warmed serving dish and keep hot.

Add the herbs and cream to the pan and heat gently. Check the seasoning. Pour the sauce around the poussins and garnish with watercress to serve.

Serves 4

Chicken with Honey; Poussins with Herb Sauce

CURRIED CHICKEN CASSEROLE

50 g (2 oz) butter
2 large onions, finely
  chopped
1 clove garlic, crushed
1 green chilli, seeded
  and finely chopped
2.5 cm (1 inch) piece
  of fresh root
  ginger, peeled and
  finely chopped
1 teaspoon turmeric
½ teaspoon ground
  cardamom
1 teaspoon ground
  coriander
1 teaspoon ground
  cumin
1 teaspoon salt
450 ml (¾ pint)
  natural yogurt
4 chicken quarters,
  skinned

Melt the butter in a flameproof casserole, add the onions and fry until softened. Stir in the garlic, chilli, ginger, turmeric, cardamom, coriander, cumin and salt and cook, stirring, for 5 minutes. Stir in the yogurt, then add the chicken pieces to the casserole and spoon the spice mixture over them. Cover and cook in a preheated moderate oven, 160°C (325°F), Gas Mark 3, for 1½ hours or until the chicken is tender.
Serves 4

BAKER'S CHICKEN

1 × 2.25 kg (5 lb)
  roasting chicken
  with giblets
50 g (2 oz) butter
4 rosemary sprigs
750 g (1½ lb)
  potatoes, thickly
  sliced
500 g (1 lb) onions,
  thickly sliced
salt and white pepper
450–600 ml (¾–1
  pint) chicken stock

Remove the giblets from the chicken and chop. Spread a little butter inside the chicken cavity, then add 2 rosemary sprigs. Truss securely.

Spread half the remaining butter over the base of a roasting pan or casserole. Place the chicken in the centre, with the giblets at one end, and surround with the potato and onion slices. Add the remaining rosemary and season with salt and pepper to taste.

Pour over 450 ml (¾ pint) of the stock and dot the chicken with the remaining butter. Cook in a preheated moderate oven, 180°C (350°F), Gas Mark 4, for 1¾ to 2 hours until tender; add extra stock if necessary to keep the potatoes and onions moist.

Transfer the chicken and vegetables to a warmed serving dish. Serve with green beans and carrots.
Serves 6 to 8

ORANGE BAKED CHICKEN

2 eggs, beaten
6 tablespoons orange
  juice
50 g (2 oz) fresh
  wholemeal
  breadcrumbs
1½ teaspoon grated
  orange rind
1 teaspoon paprika
salt and pepper
6 chicken quarters
75 g (3 oz) butter,
  melted
orange wedges and
  watercress to
  garnish

Mix together the eggs and orange juice in a shallow dish. Combine the breadcrumbs, orange rind, paprika and salt and pepper to taste on a sheet of greaseproof paper. Dip the chicken quarters in the egg mixture, then coat with the breadcrumb mixture.

Pour half the melted butter into a roasting pan. Arrange the chicken quarters in the pan in one layer and drizzle over the remaining butter. Bake in a preheated moderately hot oven, 190°C (375°F), Gas Mark 5, for 1 hour or until the chicken is cooked through, turning the chicken quarters halfway through cooking.

Serve garnished with orange wedges and watercress.
Serves 6

CHICKEN AND MUSHROOM PIE

PASTRY:
250 g (8 oz)
    wholemeal flour
pinch of salt
125 g (4 oz)
    margarine or
    butter
2–3 tablespoons
    water
beaten egg to glaze
FILLING:
2 tablespoons oil
1 onion, chopped
1 clove garlic,
    crushed
125 g (4 oz)
    mushrooms, sliced
1 tablespoon
    wholemeal flour
300 ml (½ pint)
    chicken stock
500 g (1 lb) cooked
    chicken, diced
1 tablespoon chopped
    parsley
salt and pepper

Make the pastry as for Spinach Lattice Flan (see page 37); chill.

Meanwhile, heat the oil in a pan, add the onion and fry until softened. Add the garlic and mushrooms and cook for 2 minutes. Remove from the heat and stir in the flour; add the stock and stir until blended. Return to the heat and bring to the boil, stirring until thickened. Add the remaining ingredients. Mix, then transfer to a 1.2 litre (2 pint) pie dish.

Roll out the pastry to a shape larger than the dish. Cut off a narrow strip all round and place on the dampened edge of the dish. Moisten the strip, then cover with the pastry, pressing the edges firmly.

Trim and flute the edges, decorate with pastry leaves made from the trimmings, and make a hole in the centre. Brush with beaten egg and bake in a preheated moderately hot oven, 200°C (400°F), Gas Mark 6, for 30 minutes until golden.
Serves 4

HONEY CURRY CHICKEN

75 g (3 oz) butter
175 g (6 oz) clear
    honey
1½ teaspoon mild
    curry powder
6 tablespoons
    German mustard
salt and pepper
8 chicken breasts,
    skinned

Melt the butter in a saucepan and stir in the honey, curry powder, mustard and season. Cook, until blended.

Arrange the chicken breasts in a roasting tin in one layer and pour over the honey mixture. Turn the chicken breasts to coat on all sides.

Roast in a preheated moderately hot oven, 190°C (375°F), Gas Mark 5, for 1 hour or until the chicken is cooked through, turning the chicken over halfway through cooking.
Serves 4

SPICED ROTISSERIE CHICKEN

2 cloves garlic,
    halved
10 black peppercorns,
    roughly crushed
salt
1 × 1.75 kg (4 lb)
    roasting chicken
1 teaspoon cumin
1 teaspoon turmeric
1 teaspoon paprika
2 tablespoons oil
1 tablespoon white
    wine or vinegar

Put the garlic, peppercorns, and salt to taste inside the cavity of the chicken. Place it on the rotisserie skewer and secure with the two-pronged 'forks' at either end. Switch on the rotisserie and check that the bird is centred well, then switch off.

Mix the 3 spices, ½ teaspoon salt and the oil to a thick paste and spread half all over the bird. Leave for 2 hours.

Switch on the rotisserie and cook for 50 minutes on high heat and 15 minutes on low heat. Stir the wine or vinegar into the remaining paste and use to baste the chicken occasionally. Remove and transfer to a warmed serving dish.

Serve with shredded raw courgette, mint and yogurt salad.
Serves 4 to 6

LEFT: *Baker's Chicken*
RIGHT: *Spiced Rotisserie Chicken*

KASHMIRI CHICKEN

125 g (4 oz) butter
3 large onions, finely
 sliced
10 peppercorns
10 cardamom, split
5 cm (2 inch) piece
 of cinnamon stick
5 cm (2 inch) piece
 of fresh root
 ginger, chopped
2 cloves garlic, finely
 chopped
1 teaspoon chilli
 powder
2 teaspoons paprika
salt
1.5 kg (3 lb) chicken
 pieces, skinned
250 g (8 oz) natural
 yogurt

Melt the butter in a deep, lidded frying pan. Add the onions, peppercorns, cardamom and cinnamon and fry until the onions are golden. Add the ginger, garlic, chilli powder, paprika and salt to taste and fry for 2 minutes, stirring occasionally. Add the chicken pieces and fry until browned. Gradually add the yogurt, stirring constantly. Cover and cook gently for about 30 minutes.
Serves 6

CHICKEN MINCEUR WITH MELON

1 × 1.5 kg (3 lb)
 roasting chicken
 with giblets
finely grated rind and
 juice of 2 limes
2 tarragon sprigs
450 ml (¾ pint) hot
 chicken stock
salt and pepper
TO SERVE:
1 charentais melon,
 sliced
¼ head of curly
 endive
lime slices to garnish

Use the chicken trimmings and giblets to make stock if wished; keep on one side. Truss the chicken.

Place the lime rind and juice, the tarragon and the simmering stock in a flameproof casserole. Add the chicken, breast side down, cover and simmer for 1¾ to 2 hours, until the juices run clear yellow, turning the chicken halfway through cooking. Cut into quarters and leave to cool.

Boil the cooking liquid rapidly on top of the stove until reduced by half; leave to cool.

Arrange the melon and endive on a serving dish and lay the chicken on top. Spoon over some of the sauce and hand the rest separately. Garnish.
Serves 4

LEMON POUSSINS PERSILLADES

75 g (3 oz) butter,
 softened
finely grated rind and
 juice of 2 lemons
4 poussins
4 tablespoons
 chopped parsley
2 shallots, chopped
salt and pepper
4 tablespoons dry
 white wine
TO GARNISH:
parsley sprigs
lemon twists

Place the butter, lemon rind and juice in a small bowl and beat until well blended. Spread all over the poussins and inside the cavities. Mix the parsley and shallots together and place a spoonful inside each poussin. Sprinkle with salt and pepper to taste, place in a roasting pan and pour a tablespoon of wine over each poussin.

Roast in a preheated moderate oven, 180°C (350°F), Gas Mark 4, for 30 minutes, basting occasionally. Increase the heat to 200°C (400°F), Gas Mark 6, and cook for a further 10 minutes or until well browned.

Transfer to a warmed serving dish and garnish with parsley and lemon twists. Serve with sauté potatoes and green beans tossed with toasted almonds.
Serves 4

CHICKEN WITH CHICK PEAS

250 g (8 oz) chick
    peas
15 g (½ oz) butter
2 tablespoons olive
    oil
1.5 kg (3½ lb)
    roasting chicken
pinch of powdered
    saffron
¼ teaspoon cayenne
    pepper
2 teaspoons tomato
    purée
2 onions, quartered
finely grated rind and
    juice of 1 orange
1 tablespoon orange
    flower water
300 ml (½ pint)
    chicken stock
salt and pepper
parsley to garnish

Soak the chick peas in cold water to cover for 8 hours; drain well.

Heat the butter and oil in a heavy-based pan, add the chicken and cook, turning occasionally, for about 10 minutes, until brown all over. Add the remaining ingredients, with salt and pepper to taste, cover and simmer for 1½ to 2 hours, until the juices run clear yellow; add more stock or water if necessary to keep the chick peas covered.

Transfer to a warmed serving dish and sprinkle with parsley to serve.
Serves 4 to 6

GRAPEFRUIT CHICKEN

8 chicken breasts,
    skinned
salt and pepper
25 g (1 oz) butter
1 tablespoon oil
1 large onion, sliced
1 teaspoon grated
    grapefruit rind
175 ml (6 fl oz)
    fresh grapefruit
    juice
3 tablespoons honey
grapefruit segments to
    garnish

Rub the chicken breasts with salt and pepper. Melt the butter with the oil in a frying pan and fry the chicken pieces until browned on all sides. Transfer to a casserole.

Add the onion to the fat remaining in the pan and fry until softened. Arrange over the chicken.

Mix together the grapefruit rind and juice, honey and salt and pepper to taste, then pour over the chicken pieces. Cover and cook in a preheated moderate oven, 180°C (350°F), Gas Mark 4, for 1¼ to 1½ hours or until the chicken is cooked through. Garnish before serving.
Serves 4

LEFT: *Chicken Minceur with Melon*
RIGHT: *Surprise Spring Chicken*

SURPRISE SPRING CHICKEN

2 limes
1 small onion, cut
    into 8 slices
1 × 1–1.25 kg
    (2–2½ lb) spring
    chicken
25 g (1 oz) raisins
2 tablespoons olive
    oil
pinch of chilli
    powder
sea salt
lime and onion slices
    to garnish

Slash one lime almost through in 8 places and insert an onion slice in each cut. Place inside the chicken cavity with the raisins.

Squeeze the juice from the remaining lime and mix with the oil, chilli powder and salt to taste. Pour over the chicken and leave to marinate for 1 hour.

Truss securely and place in a roasting pan. Cook in a preheated moderately hot oven, 190°C (375°F), Gas Mark 5, for 1½ hours, basting twice, until the juices run clear yellow.

Serve the chicken, with its juices, on a bed of noodles tossed in a herb-flavoured butter. Garnish with lime and onion slices.
Serves 2 to 4

SALADS AND DRESSINGS

Carefully arranged, casually tossed, piled high, layered in aspic or gelatine or displayed with bistro charm – the range of salads available to make throughout the year sinks the myth of tedious rabbit food.

No longer are we confronted with the inevitable lettuce, celery, cucumber and tomato for colour. Salads today can include traffic-light coloured peppers in hues from rich red to mellow yellow, creamy white or seductive shiny black; fruit as exotic as kiwi and watermelon; foreign specialities like bamboo shoots, water chestnuts and sprouted beans; not forgetting main course salads with their assortment of eggs, cheese, nuts and pulses like black-eyed beans, chick peas and lentils.

If the salad choice is wide then the dressing selection is even greater – choose from light clear vinaigrette dressings of oil and vinegar spiked with lemon, garlic or herbs for variation, to creamy smooth mayonnaises, cheesy coatings, piquant flavoured yogurt mixtures and exotic Chinese soy-sauce inspired flavourings. Carefully shaken, beaten, or mixed they can lift a simple salad into the luxury class.

Ring the changes with basic vinaigrettes by varying the oil from sunflower to sesame or walnut, the vinegar from wine to cider or tarragon and the flavouring from herb to lemon or the distinctive if delicate flavour of a salad ingredient.

However, use dressings sparingly, they should never drown a salad. Store them carefully in bulk in a screw-topped jar or lidded container in a cool place or in the refrigerator.

GAZPACHO RING

1 × 397 g (14 oz)
  can tomatoes
2 cloves garlic,
  chopped
150 ml (¼ pint)
  water
1 bouquet garni
½–1 teaspoon sugar
salt and pepper
1 tablespoon gelatine,
  soaked in 4
  tablespoons water
6 tablespoons French
  Dressing (see
  page 91)
SALAD:
4 tomatoes, skinned,
  seeded and diced
¼ cucumber, diced
½ green pepper,
  cored, seeded and
  diced
½ onion, chopped

Place the tomatoes, with their juice, in a pan with the garlic, water and bouquet garni. Add sugar, salt and pepper to taste. Bring slowly to the boil, then simmer for 5 minutes. Discard the bouquet garni.

Place the mixture in an electric blender or food processor. Add the soaked gelatine and blend on maximum speed for 30 seconds. Leave to cool.

Add 4 tablespoons of the dressing and half the salad ingredients and stir well. Turn into a 750 ml (1¼ pint) non-stick ring mould and chill in the refrigerator for about 3 hours, or until set.

Mix the remaining salads ingredients with the remaining French Dressing. Turn out the tomato ring onto a serving plate and place the salad in the centre.
Serves 6

CASHEW COLESLAW

250 g (8 oz) firm
  white cabbage,
  shredded
3 celery sticks, sliced
3 red-skinned eating
  apples, cored and
  thinly sliced
4 spring onions,
  sliced
50 g (2 oz) cashew
  nuts, toasted and
  split
2 tablespoons
  chopped parsley
150 ml (¼ pint)
  Quick Mayonnaise
  (see page 93)
2 tablespoons natural
  yogurt

Place the cabbage, celery, apples, spring onions, cashews and parsley in a mixing bowl.

Mix the mayonnaise and yogurt together, then pour over the salad and toss thoroughly. Transfer to a salad bowl to serve.
Serves 6 to 8

RED BEAN
AND BEANSHOOT SALAD

1 cup red kidney
  beans, soaked
  overnight
salt
125 g (4 oz)
  mushrooms, sliced
5 tablespoons
  Vinaigrette
  Dressing (see
  page 93)
250 g (8 oz) bean-
  shoots
1 red pepper, cored,
  seeded and sliced
2 tablespoons toasted
  sunflower seeds
2 tablespoons
  chopped parsley

Drain the beans, place in a pan and cover with cold water. Bring to the boil, cover and boil rapidly for 10 minutes, then simmer for 45 minutes to 1 hour, until tender; add a little salt towards the end of cooking.

Drain the beans and place in a bowl with the mushrooms. Pour over the dressing and mix thoroughly. Leave to cool.

Add the remaining ingredients and toss well. Transfer to a shallow dish to serve.
Serves 6

LEFT: *Gazpacho Ring*
RIGHT: *Salade de Pissenlits; Spring Green Salad; Spinach and Roquefort Salad*

SALADE DE PISSENLITS

125 g (4 oz)
  dandelion leaves
2 hard-boiled eggs,
  chopped
125 g (4 oz) streaky
  bacon, derinded
  and chopped
1 clove garlic,
  crushed
2 tablespoons cider
  vinegar
pepper

Trim the dandelion leaves, wash
them well and dry thoroughly. Place
in a salad bowl with the eggs.
  Fry the bacon in its own fat until
golden, then add the garlic and fry
until the bacon is crisp. Pour the hot
bacon and fat over the dandelion
leaves and toss well.
  Add the cider vinegar to the pan,
stir to dissolve any juices and pour
over the salad. Add plenty of pepper
and toss thoroughly.
Serves 4

SPRING GREEN SALAD

250 g (8 oz) spring
  greens
4 tablespoons olive
  oil
2 teaspoons soy sauce
1 tablespoon lemon
  juice
2 cloves garlic,
  crushed
salt and pepper
3 celery sticks
$\frac{1}{2}$ × 198 g (7 oz) can
  sweetcorn, drained
2 tablespoons
  chopped parsley

Shred the spring greens finely and
place in a mixing bowl. Mix
together the oil, soy sauce, lemon
juice, garlic, and salt and pepper to
taste and pour over the greens. Mix
thoroughly and leave to marinate for
1 hour.
  Slice the celery and add to the
salad with the sweetcorn and parsley.
Mix thoroughly, then transfer to a
serving dish.
Serves 6

SPINACH AND ROQUEFORT
SALAD

250 g (8 oz) young
  spinach leaves
50 g (2 oz) walnuts,
  roughly chopped
250 ml (8 fl oz)
  Roquefort
  Dressing (see
  page 91)

Trim the stalks from the spinach,
wash and dry thoroughly, then tear
into pieces. Place in a salad bowl
with the walnuts and pour over the
dressing. Toss thoroughly before
serving.
Serves 6

Frisée aux Lardons

CELERIAC AND EGG SALAD

500 g (1 lb) celeriac
4 tablespoons
  Vinaigrette
  Dressing (see
  page 91)
2 hard-boiled eggs
1 tablespoon chopped
  parsley

Grate the celeriac finely and place in a mixing bowl. Pour over the dressing, toss thoroughly and leave for 1 hour.

Shred the egg whites finely and mix with the celeriac. Place in a shallow serving dish and sieve the egg yolks over the top. Sprinkle with the parsley to serve.
Serves 4

CHICORY AND SESAME SALAD

3 heads of chicory
2 oranges
1 bunch of watercress
$\frac{1}{4}$ cup sesame seeds,
  toasted
3 tablespoons olive
  oil
1 tablespoon lemon
  juice
salt and pepper

Cut the chicory diagonally into 1 cm ($\frac{1}{2}$ inch) slices and place in a bowl. Remove the peel and pith from the oranges and cut the flesh into segments, holding the fruit over the bowl so that any juice is included.

Divide the watercress into sprigs and add to the bowl with the sesame seeds.

Whisk together the oil, lemon juice, and salt and pepper to taste, then pour over the salad and toss thoroughly. Transfer to a salad bowl to serve.
Serves 4 to 6

FRISÉE AUX LARDONS

3 slices wholemeal
  bread, crusts
  removed
4 tablespoons oil
125 g (4 oz) streaky
  bacon, sliced
  5 mm ($\frac{1}{4}$ inch)
  thick
$\frac{1}{2}$ head curly endive
6 tablespoons
  Vinaigrette
  Dressing (see
  page 93)
3 hard-boiled eggs,
  sliced

Cut the bread into 5 mm ($\frac{1}{4}$ inch) cubes. Heat the oil in a pan, add the bread cubes and fry until golden; drain on kitchen paper.

Cut the bacon into 5 mm ($\frac{1}{4}$ inch) strips, add to the pan and fry until golden brown.

Tear the endive into pieces and place in a salad bowl. Pour over half the vinaigrette dressing and toss well. Arrange the eggs in a circle on top, leaving a border of endive.

Place the croûtons in the centre and sprinkle with the bacon. Pour over the remaining dressing just before serving.
Serves 4 to 6

WHOLEWHEAT SALAD

250 g (8 oz)
  wholewheat,
  soaked overnight
6 tablespoons Soy
  Sauce Dressing
  (see page 91)
1 red pepper, cored,
  seeded and
  chopped
50 g (2 oz) raisins
2 celery sticks, diced
chopped parsley

Drain the wheat thoroughly. Place in a pan, cover with water, bring to the boil and simmer for 1 to 1$\frac{1}{2}$ hours; drain well. Mix with the dressing while still warm, then leave to cool.

Add the remaining ingredients, toss well, then transfer to a shallow dish to serve.
Serves 4 to 6

BULGAR WHEAT VINAIGRETTE

75 g (3 oz) bulgar
    wheat
4 tomatoes, chopped
50 g (2 oz) black
    olives, halved and
    stoned
1 celery stick, thinly
    sliced
4 spring onions,
    chopped
2 tablespoons
    chopped parsley
2 tablespoons toasted
    sunflower seeds
3 tablespoons French
    Dressing (see
    page 91)

Soak the bulgar wheat in cold water for 1 hour. Line a sieve with muslin and tip the wheat into it. Lift out the muslin and squeeze out as much moisture as possible.

Place the wheat in a bowl, add the remaining ingredients and mix well. Transfer to a shallow dish to serve.
Serves 4
NOTE: Bulgar wheat is available from healthfood stores and Greek delicatessens.

BROWN RICE AND HAZELNUT SALAD

175 g (6 oz) brown
    rice
75 g (3 oz)
    hazelnuts,
    chopped and
    toasted
1 red pepper, cored,
    seeded and diced
6 spring onions,
    sliced
3 celery sticks,
    chopped
60 g (2 oz) button
    mushrooms, sliced
4 tablespoons French
    Dressing (see
    page 91)
3 tablespoons
    chopped parsley

Cook the rice in boiling water for 30 to 40 minutes, until tender. Rinse and drain well.

Place in a bowl with the remaining ingredients and toss thoroughly. Transfer to a shallow dish to serve.
Serves 6 to 8

Brown Rice and Hazelnut Salad; Bulgar Wheat Vinaigrette; Wholewheat Salad

Carrot, Turnip and Sesame Seed Salad

JERUSALEM ARTICHOKE SALAD

500 g (1 lb)
  Jerusalem
  artichokes,
  scrubbed
salt and pepper
3 tablespoons olive
  oil
2 teaspoons lemon
  juice
1 tablespoon chopped
  parsley

Cut the artichokes into small even-sized pieces and place in a pan of salted water. Bring to the boil, cover and simmer for 12 to 15 minutes, until just tender. Drain and leave to cool in a mixing bowl.

Mix the remaining ingredients together, adding salt and pepper to taste, pour over the artichokes and toss well. Transfer to a serving dish.
Serves 4 to 6

CAROTTES RÂPÉES

750 g (1½ lb) carrots
2 tablespoons
  chopped parsley
5 tablespoons French
  Dressing (see
  page 91)

Grate the carrots finely and place them in a bowl with the chopped parsley.

Pour over the dressing and toss thoroughly.

Transfer the salad to a serving dish and chill lightly before serving if preferred.
Serves 4 to 6

Variation: Use young turnips, when they are in season, instead of carrots. Add 2 tablespoons Meaux mustard to the French Dressing to make a piquant dressing, before adding to the salad.

CARROT, TURNIP AND SESAME SEED SALAD

350 g (12 oz) carrots
175 g (6 oz) turnip
50 g (2 oz) seedless
  raisins
2 tablespoons sesame
  seeds, toasted
2 tablespoons snipped
  chives
4 tablespoons Honey
  and Lemon
  Dressing (see
  page 91)

Grate the carrot and turnip finely and place in a salad bowl. Add the raisins, sesame seed and chives and pour over the dressing. Toss well.
Serves 4 to 6

SPROUTING BEANS

Sprouted beans with their crispy, crunchy texture are welcome additions to any salad. To sprout your own at home, start with the simplest bean to sprout – the mung bean. Wash the beans thoroughly, place about 2 tablespoons in a wide-necked jar and fill up with warm water. Leave to stand overnight, then drain. Cover the top of the jar with a piece of muslin, secure with an elastic band, turn upside down to drain in a warm place. Every night and morning for about 4 days, rinse the beans in warm water, shake gently, then turn upside down to drain. Use when about 4 cm/1½ inches long.

POTATO AND MUSTARD SALAD

500 g (1 lb) baby
  new potatoes
salt
2 tablespoons Meaux
  mustard
142 ml (5 fl oz)
  double cream

Cook the potatoes, in their skins, in boiling salted water until tender. Drain well and leave to cool in a mixing bowl. Halve the potatoes if necessary. Stir the mustard into the cream, pour over the potatoes and toss well. Transfer to a serving dish.
Serves 4

WARM POTATO SALAD

500 g (1 lb) new
  potatoes
salt
3 tablespoons French
  Dressing (see
  page 91)
3 tablespoons
  chopped mint

Cook the potatoes, in their skins, in boiling salted water until tender. Drain well and mix with the dressing and mint while warm. Transfer to a serving dish and serve immediately.
Serves 4

POTATO MAYONNAISE

750 g (1½ lb) new
  potatoes, scraped
salt
2 tablespoons French
  Dressing (see
  page 91)
1–2 tablespoons
  snipped chives
4 tablespoons Quick
  Mayonnaise (see
  page 93)
2 tablespoons natural
  yogurt

Cook the potatoes in boiling salted water until tender. Drain well, chop roughly and place in a mixing bowl. Add the dressing and most of the chives while still warm and toss well.

Transfer to a serving dish and leave to cool.

Mix the mayonnaise with the yogurt and spoon over the potatoes. Sprinkle with the remaining chives.
Serves 6

Potato and Mustard Salad; Warm Potato Salad; Potato Mayonnaise

BEETROOT AND YOGURT SALAD

350 g (12 oz)
    cooked beetroot
2 dill cucumbers
2 tablespoons wine
    vinegar
4 tablespoons natural
    yogurt
salt and pepper
1 tablespoon chopped
    dill or fennel

Cut the beetroot and dill cucumbers into 1 cm (½ inch) dice and place in a mixing bowl.

Mix together the vinegar, yogurt, and salt and pepper to taste. Pour over the beetroot and cucumber and mix thoroughly.

Turn into a shallow serving dish and sprinkle with the dill or fennel to serve.
Serves 4

Variation: To turn this into a more substantial salad add 500 g (1 lb) cooked and diced potatoes. Increase the vinegar to 3 tablespoons and the yogurt to 8 tablespoons.

CELERIAC RÉMOULADE

500 g (1 lb) celeriac
3 tablespoons Meaux
    mustard
3 tablespoons Quick
    Mayonnaise
    (see page 93)
2 tablespoons single
    cream
2 tablespoons natural
    yogurt
1 tablespoon chopped
    parsley

Peel and cut the celeriac into julienne strips and blanch in boiling water for 2 minutes. Drain well and leave to cool.

Mix the mustard with the mayonnaise, cream and yogurt. Toss the celeriac in the mayonnaise mixture and spoon into a serving dish. Sprinkle with the parsley and serve.
Serves 4

ABOVE: *Beetroot and Yogurt Salad; Celeriac Rémoulade*
RIGHT: *Mushroom Salad; Tomatoes with Avocado; Cauliflower with Egg; Mangetout Salad*

MUSHROOM SALAD

500 g (1 lb) button
  mushrooms
120 ml (4 fl oz)
  French Dressing
  (see page 91)
125 g (4 oz) smoked
  streaky bacon,
  derinded and
  chopped
3 tablespoons
  chopped parsley

Trim the mushroom stalks level with the caps. Wipe the mushrooms with a damp cloth, place in a bowl with the dressing and toss well. Leave to stand, stirring occasionally.

Fry the bacon in its own fat until crisp. Add to the mushrooms with the parsley. Toss thoroughly and transfer to a serving dish.
Serves 4 to 6

TOMATOES WITH AVOCADO

500 g (1 lb) baby
  tomatoes, skinned
150 ml ($\frac{1}{4}$ pint)
  Avocado Dressing
  (see page 93)
chopped parsley

Pile the tomatoes onto a shallow serving dish. Pour over the dressing and sprinkle with the parsley.
Serves 4

CAULIFLOWER WITH EGG

1 small cauliflower,
  broken into florets
3 hard-boiled eggs,
  chopped
150 ml ($\frac{1}{4}$ pint)
  Roquefort Dressing
  (see page 91)
chopped chives

Blanch the cauliflower in boiling water for 2 to 3 minutes; drain and leave to cool completely.

Place in a bowl, add the eggs and dressing and toss thoroughly. Transfer to a serving dish and sprinkle with the chives.
Serves 6

MANGETOUT SALAD

250 g (8 oz)
  mangetout
1 red pepper, cored,
  seeded and sliced
1 tablespoon sesame
  seeds, toasted
4 tablespoons French
  Dressing (see
  page 91)

Top and tail the mangetout and, if large, cut in half diagonally. Place in a bowl with the remaining ingredients and toss thoroughly. Turn into a shallow serving dish.
Serves 4

MIXED BEAN SALAD

125 g (4 oz) red
kidney beans,
soaked overnight
125 g (4 oz) haricot
beans, soaked
overnight
salt
125 g (4 oz) French
beans
125 g (4 oz) shelled
broad beans
6 tablespoons Garlic
Dressing (see
page 91)
2 tablespoons
chopped parsley

Drain the kidney beans and haricot beans. Place in separate pans, cover with cold water, bring to the boil, boil for 10 minutes then simmer for 1 to 1½ hours, until tender, adding a little salt towards the end of cooking. Drain and place in a bowl.

Cut the French beans into 2.5 cm (1 inch) lengths. Cook the broad beans and French beans in boiling salted water for 7 to 8 minutes, until just tender. Drain and add to the bowl. Pour over the dressing while still warm and mix well. Cool, then stir in the parsley. Transfer to a serving dish.
Serves 8

CAULIFLOWER AND MUSHROOM SALAD

250 g (8 oz)
cauliflower,
broken into florets
125 g (4 oz) button
mushrooms, sliced
1 large avocado pear,
halved, stoned,
peeled and sliced
50 g (2 oz) flaked
almonds, roasted
DRESSING:
4 tablespoons Quick
Mayonnaise (see
page 93)
4 tablespoons soured
cream
1 teaspoon lemon
juice
1 clove garlic, crushed
paprika
chopped chives

Cook the cauliflower in boiling salted water for 2 minutes; drain and leave to cool completely. Place in a bowl with the mushrooms, avocado and almonds.

Mix the dressing ingredients together, adding salt and paprika to taste. Pour over the vegetables and toss thoroughly. Transfer to a serving dish and sprinkle with the chives.
Serves 6 to 8

FENNEL AND LEMON SALAD

2 bulbs of fennel
3 tablespoons
chopped parsley
2 tablespoons lemon
juice
2 tablespoons olive
oil
salt and pepper

Trim the stalks, base and tough outer leaves from the fennel. Cut the bulbs in half, then shred very finely. Place in a salad bowl with the remaining ingredients, adding salt and pepper to taste, and toss thoroughly. Leave to marinate for 1 hour. Toss again before serving.
Serves 4

MUSHROOM VINAIGRETTE

250 g (8 oz) button
mushrooms
4 spring onions,
chopped
6 tablespoons
Vinaigrette
Dressing (see
page 93)

Trim the mushroom stalks level with the caps. Wipe the mushrooms with a damp cloth, cut into thin slices and place in a salad bowl with the onion. Pour over the dressing and toss until well coated. Leave to stand for 30 minutes, stirring occasionally.
Serves 4

ABOVE: *Cauliflower and Mushroom Salad*
RIGHT: *Mushroom Vinaigrette; French Bean Vinaigrette; Watermelon Vinaigrette*

FRENCH BEAN VINAIGRETTE

250 g (8 oz) French beans, topped and tailed
salt
75 g (3 oz) streaky bacon, derinded and chopped
2 tablespoons Vinaigrette Dressing (see page 93)
few radicchio leaves

Place the beans in a pan of boiling salted water and simmer for 8 minutes. Drain and leave to cool.

Fry the bacon in its own fat until crisp. Place in a bowl with the beans, pour over the dressing and toss thoroughly.

Arrange the radicchio leaves on a serving dish and spoon the salad into the centre.
Serves 4

APPLE AND WALNUT SALAD

3 red-skinned dessert apples, quartered and cored
6 tablespoons Lemon Vinaigrette Dressing (see page 93)
1 small head of celery, sliced
1 bunch of watercress, divided into sprigs
25 g (1 oz) walnut pieces

Slice the apples into a small bowl, pour over the dressing and toss well. Add the celery, watercress and walnuts, mix well, then transfer to a salad bowl.
Serves 6 to 8

WATERMELON VINAIGRETTE

1 kg (2 lb) watermelon, cut into wedges
1 tablespoon chopped mint
1 Spanish onion, thinly sliced
3 tablespoons Lemon Vinaigrette (see page 93)

Pick out the seeds from the watermelon and discard. Slice the watermelon wedges diagonally into strips. Place in a bowl and sprinkle with the mint.

Mix the onion and dressing together in another bowl and leave for 1 hour, stirring occasionally.

Mix the onion and dressing with the watermelon before serving.
Serves 4 to 6

SWEDISH CUCUMBER SALAD

1 cucumber
salt
DRESSING:
1 tablespoon clear honey
1 tablespoon water
2 tablespoons chopped dill or fennel
4 tablespoons white wine vinegar

Slice the cucumber very thinly and place in a colander. Sprinkle liberally with salt and leave to drain for 30 minutes.

Meanwhile, mix the dressing ingredients together in a screw-topped jar. Shake well and leave for 30 minutes.

Dry the cucumber thoroughly on kitchen paper. Arrange the cucumber slices overlapping in a shallow dish and pour over the dressing.
Serves 4 to 6

WALDORF SALAD

150 ml (¼ pint) Quick Mayonnaise (see page 93)
2 tablespoons natural yogurt
3 dessert apples, cored and chopped
4 sticks of celery, chopped
25 g (1 oz) walnut pieces
chopped parsley

Mix the mayonnaise and yogurt together in a bowl. Add the apples, celery and walnuts and toss well to coat with mayonnaise.

Pile the salad onto a shallow serving dish and sprinkle with the parsley.
Serves 6 to 8

ABOVE: *Swedish Cucumber Salad; Waldorf Salad*
RIGHT: *Cottage Cheese Salad; Greek Salad; Tomato and Mozzarella Salad*

COTTAGE CHEESE SALAD

1 × 340 g (12 oz)
  carton cottage
  cheese
3 tomatoes, skinned,
  seeded and
  chopped
¼ cucumber, chopped
salt and pepper
few curly endive
  leaves

Place the cheese, tomatoes and
cucumber in a bowl and mix well,
seasoning with salt and pepper to
taste.
   Arrange the endive leaves on
4 individual serving dishes and spoon
the salad into the centre.
Serves 4

GREEK SALAD

6 tomatoes, cut into
  wedges
½ cucumber, diced
1 small onion, sliced
1 small green pepper,
  cored, seeded and
  roughly chopped
3 tablespoons olive
  oil
1 tablespoon wine
  vinegar
175 g (6 oz) feta
  cheese, cubed
125 g (4 oz) black
  olives
1 teaspoon dried
  oregano

Place the tomatoes, cucumber, onion
and green peppers in a bowl and
mix well. Pour over the oil and
vinegar, and toss thoroughly.
   Transfer the salad to a bowl and
cover with the cheese and olives.
Sprinkle with the oregano to serve.
Serves 4

TOMATO
AND MOZZARELLA SALAD

500 g (1 lb)
  tomatoes, sliced
salt and pepper
250 g (8 oz)
  Mozzarella
  cheese, sliced
3 tablespoons olive
  oil
4 tablespoons
  chopped parsley

Layer the tomatoes in a shallow
serving dish, sprinkling each layer
with salt and pepper. Arrange the
Mozzarella in overlapping layers on
top of the tomatoes. Pour over the
oil and sprinkle with the parsley.
   Serve with a green salad, salami if
liked, and granary bread.
Serves 4

TABBOULEH

75 g (3 oz) bulgur
 wheat
1 teacup chopped
 parsley
3 tablespoons
 chopped mint
4 spring onions,
 chopped
½ cucumber, diced
2 tablespoons olive oil
juice of 1 lemon

Soak the bulgur wheat in cold water for 1 hour. Line a sieve with muslin and tip the wheat into it. Lift out the muslin and squeeze out as much moisture as possible.

Place the wheat in a bowl and add the remaining ingredients, seasoning with salt and pepper to taste. Toss thoroughly, then transfer to a shallow dish to serve.

Serves 4

ADUKI BEAN SALAD

250 g (8 oz) aduki
 beans, soaked
 overnight
4 tablespoons Ginger
 Dressing (see
 page 91)
6 spring onions,
 chopped
4 tomatoes, chopped
3 celery sticks, sliced
2 tablespoons
 chopped parsley

Drain the beans, place in a pan of boiling water and boil rapidly for 10 minutes. Cover and cook for 30 to 35 minutes or until tender. Drain well and mix with the dressing while still warm. Leave to cool.

Add the remaining ingredients, seasoning with salt and pepper to taste. Mix thoroughly and transfer to a shallow dish to serve.

Serves 6

BUCKWHEAT AND CORN SALAD

75 g (3 oz) toasted
 buckwheat
4 tablespoons Ginger
 Dressing (see
 page 91)
1 × 198 g (7 oz) can
 sweetcorn
1 green pepper, cored
 and chopped
3 tomatoes, chopped
2 tablespoons
 chopped parsley
25 g (1 oz) toasted
 sunflower seeds

Place the buckwheat in a pan of boiling water, cover and simmer gently for 15 minutes. Drain thoroughly and place in a bowl with the dressing.

Add the remaining ingredients and toss thoroughly. Transfer to a shallow dish to serve.

Serves 4–6

NOTE: Buckwheat is available from healthfood stores.

TOMATO AND YOGURT SALAD

A delicious refreshing salad accompaniment to serve in the summer – perfect for 'al fresco' meals.

300 g natural yogurt
2 tablespoons chopped basil
salt and pepper
500 g (1 lb) tomatoes, skinned and cut into wedges

Place the yogurt in a bowl, add the chopped basil, and salt and pepper to taste and mix well. Stir in the tomatoes, then transfer to a shallow serving dish.

Chill in the refrigerator for about 30 minutes before serving.
Serves 4 to 6

Variation: If basil is unobtainable, replace it with 1 tablespoon chopped fresh coriander leaves. This salad makes an excellent accompaniment to serve with curries.

LEFT: *Tabbouleh; Aduki Bean Salad; Buckwheat and Corn Salad*
ABOVE: *Spring Cabbage and Pepper Salad; Artichoke Vinaigrette; Tomato and Yogurt Salad*

SPRING CABBAGE AND PEPPER SALAD

250 g (8 oz) spring cabbage, shredded
4 tablespoons Soy Sauce Dressing
3 celery sticks, sliced
4 spring onions, chopped
1 red pepper, diced

Place the spring cabbage in a bowl with the dressing, toss thoroughly and leave to marinate for 1 hour. Add the remaining ingredients and toss thoroughly. Transfer to a salad bowl to serve.
Serves 4 to 6

ARTICHOKE VINAIGRETTE

500 g (1 lb) Jerusalem artichokes
3 tablespoons French Dressing
1 tablespoon chopped parsley
1 tablespoon pumpkin seeds

Grate the artichokes coarsely and place in a mixing bowl with the remaining ingredients. Toss thoroughly and leave for 1 hour. Transfer to a shallow serving dish to serve.
Serves 4 to 6

ASPARAGUS VINAIGRETTE

500 g (1 lb)
  asparagus
salt
4 tablespoons French
  Dressing (see
  page 91)
1 hard-boiled egg
1 tablespoon chopped
  parsley

Cut the asparagus stalks all the same length, tie in bundles and place upright in a deep pan of boiling salted water. Make a lid with foil and dome it over the tips so that the heads cook in the steam. Small asparagus will take 15 minutes to cook; large stems up to 30 minutes. Drain very carefully, then arrange on a serving dish and leave to cool.

Spoon the dressing over the asparagus. Chop the egg white finely and sprinkle over the asparagus. Sieve the egg yolk over the top and sprinkle with the parsley.
Serves 4

SALADE DE FLAGEOLETS

250 g (8 oz)
  flageolet beans,
  soaked overnight
salt
6 tablespoons Garlic
  Dressing (see
  page 91)
50 g (2 oz) salami,
  cut into 5 mm
  ($\frac{1}{4}$ inch) squares
4 spring onions,
  sliced

Drain the beans, place in a pan and cover with cold water. Bring to the boil, boil for 10 minutes, cover and simmer for $1\frac{1}{4}$ to $1\frac{1}{2}$ hours, until tender, adding a little salt towards the end of cooking. Drain thoroughly and place in a bowl. Pour over the dressing and mix well while still warm. Leave to cool.

Add the salami and spring onions to the beans. Toss well to serve.
Serves 4 to 6

ENDIVE AND AVOCADO SALAD

$\frac{1}{2}$ head of curly
  endive
1 bunch of watercress
2 avocado pears,
  halved and stoned
6 tablespoons French
  Dressing (see
  page 91)

Tear the endive into pieces and separate the watercress into sprigs; place in a salad bowl.

Peel the avocados and slice into a bowl. Pour over the dressing and toss until completely coated. Add to the endive and watercress and toss.
Serves 6

SPICED RICE SALAD

75 g (3 oz) dried
  apricots, chopped
125 g (4 oz) long-
  grain brown rice
salt
1 tablespoon corn oil
50 g (2 oz) split
  almonds
1 teaspoon grated
  nutmeg
3 celery sticks, diced
4 spring onions,
  sliced
1 tablespoon chopped
  coriander
4 tablespoons French
  Dressing (see
  page 91)

Cover the apricots with boiling water, leave to soak for 1 hour, then drain well.

Place the rice in a pan of boiling salted water and simmer for 35 to 40 minutes, until tender. Rinse thoroughly, drain and leave to cool slightly.

Heat the oil in a small pan, add the almonds and fry until pale golden. Add the nutmeg and fry for a few seconds.

Place the warm rice in a salad bowl with the apricots. Add the spiced almonds with their oil. Mix in the celery, spring onions and coriander. Pour the dressing over the salad and toss thoroughly before serving.
Serves 4

Variation: Use stoned and chopped dates instead of the dried apricots; these will not require pre-soaking.

ABOVE: *Salade de Flageolets*
RIGHT: *Black Bean Salad; Chick Pea Salad; Bean and Mushroom Salad*

BLACK BEAN SALAD

175 g (6 oz) black beans, soaked overnight
6 tablespoons Garlic Dressing (see page 91)
75 g (3 oz) thick-cut streaky bacon, cut into strips
1 red pepper, cored, seeded and sliced
3 celery sticks, sliced

Drain the beans, place in a pan and cover with cold water. Bring to the boil, boil for 10 minutes, cover and simmer for 1½ to 2 hours, until tender, adding a little salt.

Drain the beans thoroughly and place in a bowl. Pour over the dressing and toss while still warm.

Fry the bacon in its own fat until crisp. Stir into the beans and cool.

Stir in the red pepper and celery.
Serves 6 to 8

CHICK PEA SALAD

250 g (8 oz) chick peas, soaked overnight
4 tablespoons Ginger Dressing (see page 91)
1 small onion, chopped
1 red pepper, cored, seeded and diced
2 tablespoons chopped parsley

Drain the chick peas, place in a pan and cover with cold water. Bring to the boil and simmer for 1½ to 2 hours or until softened, adding a little salt towards the end of cooking.

Drain thoroughly and place in a bowl. Pour over the dressing and toss well while still warm. Cool.

Add the remaining ingredients, toss thoroughly and transfer to a serving dish.
Serves 6

BEAN AND MUSHROOM SALAD

175 g (6 oz) black-eyed beans, soaked overnight
salt
125 g (4 oz) button mushrooms, sliced
4 tablespoons French Dressing (see page 91)
1 small red pepper, cored and sliced
2 tablespoons chopped parsley

Drain the beans, place in a pan and cover with cold water. Bring to the boil, cover and simmer for 40 to 45 minutes until tender, adding a little salt towards the end of cooking.

Drain thoroughly and place in a bowl with the mushrooms. Pour over the dressing and toss well while still warm. Leave to cool.

Add the red pepper and parsley, toss thoroughly and transfer to a salad bowl.
Serves 6

Potato and Egg Salad

POTATO AND EGG SALAD

500 g (1 lb) waxy
(salad) potatoes
2 tablespoons French
Dressing (see
page 91)
4 spring onions,
sliced
4 hard-boiled eggs,
chopped
2 dill pickles,
chopped
3 tablespoons Quick
Mayonnaise
(see page 93)
3 tablespoons natural
yogurt
fennel to garnish

Cook the potatoes in their skins in
boiling salted water until tender.
Drain well, chop roughly and place
in a bowl. Pour over the dressing
while still warm, toss thoroughly and
leave to cool. Add the spring onions,
eggs and dill pickles.

Mix together and mayonnaise,
yogurt and 2 tablespons juice from
the dill pickles until smooth. Pour
over the salad and mix thoroughly.
Transfer to a shallow dish and
sprinkle with the fennel to serve.
Serves 4

PEPERONATA

2 large red peppers
2 large green peppers
4 tablespoons olive
oil
1 onion, sliced
2 cloves garlic,
crushed
4 tomatoes, skinned,
seeded and
shredded
salt and pepper

Halve the peppers, discard the cores
and seeds, and slice thinly. Heat the
oil in a pan, add the onion and fry
for 5 minutes, until softened. Add
the garlic and peppers, cover and
cook gently for 10 to 15 minutes.

Add the tomatoes, and salt and
pepper to taste. Cook for a further
10 minutes, stirring occasionally.
Leave to cool. Serve in individual
dishes.
Serves 6

AUBERGINE SALAD

2 aubergines
salt and pepper
4 tablespoons olive
oil
1 onion, chopped
2 cloves garlic, finely
chopped
4 tomatoes, skinned,
seeded and
chopped
2 tablespoons
chopped parsley
1 tablespoon lemon
juice
few lettuce leaves

Cut the aubergines into 1 cm
($\frac{1}{2}$ inch) cubes. Place in a colander,
sprinkle with salt and leave for
30 minutes. Rinse and dry.

Heat the oil in a frying pan, add
the onion and aubergine and fry for
10 to 15 minutes, stirring
occasionally, until golden. Add the
garlic and tomatoes and fry for 2 to
3 minutes.

Leave to cool, then mix with the
parsley, lemon juice, and pepper.
Arrange the lettuce leaves in a dish
and spoon the salad into the centre.
Serves 4 to 6

RATATOUILLE SALAD

6 tablespoons olive
oil
1 small aubergine,
sliced
250 g (8 oz)
courgettes, sliced
1 green pepper,
cored, seeded and
sliced
2 cloves garlic, crushed
4 tomatoes, skinned
and sliced

Heat half the oil in a frying pan, add
the aubergine and fry on both sides
until light golden brown, adding more
oil if necessary. Place in a bowl.

Add the remaining oil to the pan
and fry the courgettes and pepper for
8 to 10 minutes, stirring occasionally,
until softened. Add the garlic, and
salt and pepper to taste and fry for
2 minutes. Add to the aubergines
with the tomatoes and toss.
Serves 4 to 6

POTATO AND MINT VINAIGRETTE

500 g (1 lb) new potatoes
salt
3 tablespoons French Dressing (see page 91)
3 tablespoons chopped mint
1 bunch radishes, thinly sliced

Cook the potatoes in their skins in boiling salted water until tender. Drain well and mix with the dressing while still warm, then leave to cool.

Add the chopped mint and radishes and mix well. Transfer to a salad bowl to serve.

Serves 4

Potato and Onion Vinaigrette: Omit the mint and radishes. Substitute with 6 chopped spring onions.

Potato and Mint Vinaigrette

FRENCH DRESSING

170 ml (6 fl oz) olive oil
4 tablespoons wine vinegar
1 teaspoon French mustard
1 clove garlic, crushed
1 teaspoon clear honey
salt and pepper

Put all the ingredients in a screw-topped jar, adding salt and pepper to taste. Shake well to blend before serving.

Makes 250 ml (8 fl oz)

Mustard Dressing: Add 2 tablespoons Meaux mustard.
Garlic Dressing: Crush 4 cloves garlic and add to the ingredients.

HONEY AND LEMON DRESSING

4 tablespoons lemon juice
2 tablespoons clear honey
3 tablespoons olive oil
salt and pepper

Put all the ingredients in a screw-topped jar, adding salt and pepper to taste. Shake well to blend before serving.

Makes 150 ml ($\frac{1}{4}$ pint)

ROQUEFORT DRESSING

50 g (2 oz) Roquefort cheese
142 ml (5 fl oz) single cream
1 tablespoon chopped chives

Mash the cheese with a fork and gradually add the cream to form a smooth paste. Mix in the chives. Store in an airtight container in the refrigerator.

Makes 250 ml (8 fl oz)

SOY SAUCE DRESSING

170 ml (6 fl oz) sunflower oil
4 tablespoons soy sauce
2 tablespoons lemon juice
1 clove garlic, crushed
salt and pepper

Put all the ingredients in a screw-topped jar, adding salt and pepper to taste. Shake well to blend.

Makes 300 ml ($\frac{1}{2}$ pint)

Ginger Dressing: Add a 2.5 cm (1 inch) piece chopped root ginger.
Chilli Dressing: Add 1 seeded and finely chopped green chilli.

SOURED CREAM DRESSING

142 ml (5 fl oz)
  soured cream
1 tablespoon lemon
  juice
1 clove garlic,
  crushed
1 teaspoon clear
  honey
salt and pepper
little milk (optional)

Place all the ingredients in a bowl, adding salt and pepper to taste, and mix thoroughly with a fork. Add milk to thin if necessary.
Makes 150 ml ($\frac{1}{4}$ pint)

Avocado Dressing: Place 1 peeled and chopped avocado pear, 5 tablespoons single cream and 1 teaspoon Worcestershire sauce in an electric blender or food processor. Blend until smooth, then mix with the soured cream dressing.
Makes 350 ml (12 fl oz)

QUICK MAYONNAISE

1 egg
$\frac{1}{2}$ teaspoon salt
$\frac{1}{2}$ teaspoon pepper
$\frac{1}{2}$ teaspoon mustard
  powder
2 teaspoons wine
  vinegar
150 ml ($\frac{1}{4}$ pint) olive
  oil
150 ml ($\frac{1}{4}$ pint)
  sunflower oil

Place the egg, seasonings and vinegar in an electric blender or food processor and blend on medium speed for a few seconds. Still on medium speed, add the oils drop by drop to begin with, through the lid, then in a thin stream as the mixture thickens.

Store in an airtight container in the refrigerator for up to 10 days.
Makes about 300 ml ($\frac{1}{2}$ pint)

Tomato Mayonnaise: Skin, seed and chop 2 tomatoes and place in the blender with 1 crushed clove garlic, $\frac{1}{2}$ teaspoon brown sugar and 2 teaspoons tomato purée. Blend on maximum speed for 30 seconds, then stir into half the mayonnaise.

Traditional Method Mayonnaise: Replace the 1 egg with 2 egg yolks. Beat the egg yolks and seasonings in a bowl. Add the oils drop by drop beating constantly. As the mixture thickens, add the oils in a steady stream. Mix in the vinegar.

Avocado Dressing; Herb Dressing; Quick Mayonnaise

VINAIGRETTE DRESSING

170 ml (6 fl oz)
  olive oil
4 tablespoons cider
  vinegar
1 teaspoon clear
  honey
1 clove garlic,
  crushed
2 tablespoons
  chopped mixed
  herbs
salt and pepper

Put all the ingredients in a screw-topped jar, adding salt and pepper to taste. Shake well to blend before using.
Makes 250 ml (8 fl oz)

Lemon or Lime Vinaigrette: Use 4 tablespoons fresh lemon or lime juice in place of the cider vinegar.

YOGURT DRESSING

150 g (5 oz) natural
  yogurt
1 clove garlic,
  crushed
1 tablespoon cider
  vinegar
1 teaspoon clear
  honey
salt and pepper

Place all the ingredients in a bowl, adding salt and pepper to taste, and mix thoroughly with a fork.
Makes about 150 ml ($\frac{1}{4}$ pint)

Herb Dressing: Place the above ingredients in an electric blender or food processor with 15 g ($\frac{1}{2}$ oz) parsley and 15 g ($\frac{1}{2}$ oz) mixed mint and chives. Blend on maximum speed for 1 to 2 minutes. Chill until required. Shake well before using.
Makes 250 ml (8 fl oz)

SALAD DRESSINGS

During the summer months when salad time really reaches its peak it is worth making a few dressings in bulk that store well in the refrigerator.

To make a good all-purpose French-style oil and vinegar dressing: Place 200 ml (7 fl oz) salad oil in a screw-topped jar with 100 ml ($3\frac{1}{2}$ fl oz) vinegar, $\frac{1}{2}$–1 teaspoon made mustard and salt and pepper to taste. Flavour, if liked, with a crushed clove of garlic, a few sprigs of herbs or a strip of citrus rind. Shake well and store for up to 6 weeks.

A good all-round yogurt dressing can be made by mixing 350 ml (12 fl oz) natural yogurt with 4 tablespoons lemon juice and salt and pepper to taste. Add crushed garlic, herbs and other seasonings. Store for up to 4 days.

A refreshing light tomato juice dressing, that keeps well for up to 1 week, can be made by mixing 300 ml ($\frac{1}{2}$ pint) tomato juice with 1 tablespoon tarragon vinegar, a few mixed dried herbs and salt and pepper to taste.

VEGETABLES

From Winter celery, root vegetables, Brussels sprouts and cabbage; Spring spinach, chicory, fennel and watercress; Summer salad greenery, tomatoes, peppers, beans and courgettes; to golden Autumn corn, marrow, aubergines and onions – there is a vegetable at its best for every month of the year. These wholefood recipes are designed to bring out the full natural flavour of vegetables, to create imaginative, tasty and nutritious dishes.

Endlessly versatile they can be steamed plain for a main course accompaniment; stuffed fit-to-burst for a hearty supper dish; chopped, sliced or slivered for adding to a curry or stir-fry mixture for a quick lunch idea; used as a wrapping for a savoury concoction to delight guests at dinner; or baked with wholegrains, fruit and nuts for a vegetarian feast.

Thanks to the good range of home-grown and imported vegetables available today from garden or field-picked peas to flown-in fennel, there is a vegetable suitable for serving at any meal whether it be simple or sumptuous. But choose and select with care – remember that the guidelines for quality include freshness, crispness, good colour and small not over-blown size. Your nose and eyes will be your best guides and your purse will reflect the best in season for economy. Thrifty cooks will freeze away extra produce when prices are low and quality is high.

Preserve all that nature intended by preparing vegetables for recipes in this section just before needed and remove skins only if necessary.

Don't overcook vegetables – or you'll lose flavour and nutritional value and if possible use cooking water for stocks and sauces.

Stir-Fried Vegetables with Tofu

STIR-FRIED VEGETABLES WITH TOFU

3 tablespoons soy
sauce
3 tablespoons dry
sherry
1 cm ($\frac{1}{2}$ inch) piece
fresh root ginger,
peeled and finely
chopped
2 cloves garlic, crushed
250 g (8 oz) firm
tofu, cubed
about 2 tablespoons
sesame oil
1 large onion, sliced
175 g (6 oz) mange-
tout, topped, tailed
and halved
1 red pepper, cored,
seeded and sliced
175 g (6 oz) button
mushrooms, sliced
500 g (1 lb) bean
shoots
2 tablespoons sesame
seeds, toasted

Mix the soy sauce, sherry, chopped ginger and garlic together in a bowl. Cut the tofu into cubes and add to the bowl, stirring to coat completely. Leave to marinate for 1 hour, then drain, reserving the marinade.

Heat the oil in a large wok, add the tofu cubes and stir-fry for about 2 minutes, until beginning to brown on all sides. Remove with a slotted spoon and keep warm.

Reheat the oil, adding a little more if necessary. Add the onion and stir-fry for 2 minutes. Add the mangetout and red pepper and stir-fry for 2 minutes. Add the mushrooms, beanshoots and reserved marinade and stir-fry for 2 minutes, until heated through.

Lightly stir in the tofu, then turn onto a warmed serving dish. Sprinkle with the sesame seeds.
Serves 4

BRAISED RED CABBAGE

1 red cabbage,
shredded
50 g (2 oz) butter
1 large onion, sliced
1 large cooking
apple, sliced
1 tablespoon light
soft brown sugar
2 tablespoons wine
vinegar
salt and pepper

Blanch the cabbage in a large pan of boiling water for about 5 minutes, then drain.

Melt half the butter in a pan, add the onion and apple and cook for about 5 minutes, until soft.

Spread about one third of the cabbage in a well greased ovenproof dish. Cover with one third of the onion and apple and sprinkle with a little sugar, vinegar, salt and pepper. Repeat the layers twice more.

Dot the remaining butter on top, cover with greaseproof paper, then with a lid or foil. Bake in a preheated moderate oven, 160°C (325°F), Gas Mark 3, for about 2 hours, stirring from time to time.
Serves 6

SWEDE WITH BACON

1 medium swede, cut
into 2.5 cm
(1 inch) cubes
salt
4 rashers streaky
bacon, derinded
and chopped
grated nutmeg
freshly ground
pepper
2 tablespoons milk or
single cream

Cook the swede in boiling salted water for about 30 minutes or until tender. Drain thoroughly.

Meanwhile, fry the bacon in its own fat until crisp.

Return the swede to the saucepan, add the fat from the bacon and mash to a pulp. Stir in the bacon and season with plenty of freshly ground pepper and nutmeg. Stir in the milk or cream and heat through. This dish is delicious with roast pork.
Serves 4

POMMES DUCHESSE

1 kg (2 lb) potatoes
salt and pepper
50 g (2 oz) butter
1 egg, beaten
TO SERVE:
1 small egg, beaten
parsley sprigs

Simmer the potatoes in boiling salted water until tender, then drain and mash. Add the butter and beat until smooth. Beat in the egg and season well with salt and pepper. Cool.

Pipe in small whirls on a baking sheet. Brush with beaten egg and bake in a preheated moderately hot oven, 200°C (400°F), Gas Mark 6, for about 30 minutes, until browned. Garnish with parsley.
Serves 4 to 6

CAULIFLOWER CRUMBLE

1 cauliflower, broken
*   into florets*
salt
2 tablespoons oil
4 tablespoons
*   wholemeal flour*
350 ml (12 fl oz)
*   milk*
1 × 326 g (11½ oz)
*   can sweetcorn,*
*   drained*
2 tablespoons
*   chopped parsley*
125 g (4 oz)
*   matured Cheddar*
*   cheese, grated*
TOPPING:
50 g (2 oz)
*   wholemeal flour*
25 g (1 oz)
*   margarine*
25 g (1 oz) porridge
*   oats*
25 g (1 oz) chopped
*   almonds*

Cook the cauliflower in boiling salted water for 5 minutes. Drain, reserving the water.

Heat the oil in the same pan and stir in the flour. Remove from the heat, add the milk, stirring until blended. Add 150 ml (¼ pint) of the reserved cooking liquid, bring to the boil and cook for 3 minutes, until thickened. Stir in the sweetcorn, parsley and half the cheese. Gently fold in the cauliflower and turn into a 1.5 litre (2½ pint) ovenproof dish.

For the topping, place the flour in a bowl and rub in the margarine until the mixture resembles fine breadcrumbs. Add the oats, almonds and remaining cheese. Sprinkle over the vegetable mixture and bake in a preheated moderately hot oven, 190°C (375°F), Gas Mark 5, for 30 minutes, until golden brown and crisp.
Serves 4

AUBERGINES WITH CHILLI AND GINGER

oil for shallow-frying
4 spring onions,
*   sliced*
4 cloves garlic, sliced
1 piece fresh root
*   ginger, shredded*
2 large aubergines,
*   cut into 5 cm*
*   (2 inch) long strips*
2 tablespoons soy
*   sauce*
2 tablespoons dry
*   sherry*
2 teaspoons chilli
*   sauce*
chopped red and
*   green chillies to*
*   garnish*

Heat 2 tablespoons oil in a wok or deep frying pan. Add the spring onions, garlic and ginger and stir-fry for about 30 seconds. Remove from the pan and set aside. Increase the heat, add the aubergine strips and fry until browned, adding more oil to the pan as necessary. Remove from the pan and drain on kitchen paper.

Pour off the oil from the pan. Return the spring onions, garlic, ginger and aubergine strips to the pan. Pour over the soy sauce, sherry and chilli sauce, stir well and cook for 2 minutes.

Spoon into a warmed serving dish, sprinkle with chillies and serve immediately.
Serves 4 to 6

Cauliflower Crumble

MUSHROOMS WITH WINE

8 large flat
    mushrooms
50 g (2 oz) butter
1 slice wholemeal
    bread, crusts
    removed
1 tablespoon chopped
    parsley
1 clove garlic,
    crushed
4 shallots, chopped
salt and pepper
4 tablespoons dry
    white wine

Remove the mushroom stalks and chop them finely. Melt half the butter in a pan, add the mushroom caps and cook for 5 minutes. Remove.

Soak the bread in water for a few minutes, then squeeze almost dry.

Melt the remaining butter in the pan, add the chopped mushroom stalks, parsley, garlic and shallots and cook for 5 minutes. Season with salt and pepper to taste and pour in the wine. Increase the heat and cook for 2 minutes. Stir into the bread.

Arrange the mushroom caps in an ovenproof dish and fill with the mixture. Cover and cook in a preheated moderate oven, 180°C (350°F), Gas Mark 4, for 20 minutes.
Serves 4

WALNUT-STUFFED AUBERGINES

2 large aubergines
2 tablespoons olive
    oil
1 onion, chopped
3 celery sticks,
    chopped
175 g (6 oz)
    mushrooms,
    chopped
6 tablespoons brown
    rice, cooked
50 g (2 oz) walnuts,
    ground
1 tablespoon tomato
    purée
2 tablespoons
    chopped parsley
salt and pepper
75 g (3 oz) Cheddar
    cheese, grated

Prick the aubergines all over, cut in half and place cut side down on a greased baking sheet. Bake in a preheated moderately hot oven, 190°C (375°F), Gas Mark 5, for 30 minutes.

Meanwhile, heat the oil in a pan, add the onion and fry until softened. Add the garlic and celery and fry for 5 minutes. Add the mushrooms and cook, stirring, for 3 minutes. Stir in rice, walnuts, tomato purée, parsley, and seasoning. Turn off the heat.

Scoop the flesh from the aubergines, without breaking the skins, chop finely and mix with the fried mixture. Pile into the aubergine skins, sprinkle with the cheese and heat under a hot grill.
Serves 4

*Curried Vegburgers; Walnut-Stuffed Aubergines;
Mushroom Plait*

CURRIED VEGBURGERS

2 tablespoons oil
2 onions, chopped
1 clove garlic, crushed
2 carrots, chopped
2 celery sticks,
    chopped
2 teaspoons curry
    powder
2 tablespoons
    chopped parsley
500 g (1 lb)
    potatoes, boiled
    and mashed
salt and pepper
wholemeal
    breadcrumbs
oil for shallow-frying

Heat the oil in a pan, add the onions and fry until softened. Add the garlic, carrots and celery and fry for 5 minutes, stirring. Mix in the curry powder and cook for 1 minute.

Add the fried vegetables and parsley to the potato and season with salt and pepper to taste. Divide the mixture into 8 pieces, shape into rounds, and coat with breadcrumbs. Press to flatten slightly and fry for 2 minutes on each side until golden. Serve with Piquant Sauce (page 21).
Serves 4

MUSHROOM PLAIT

3 tablespoons oil
1 onion, chopped
500 g (1 lb) frozen
    chopped spinach,
    half-thawed
pinch of grated
    nutmeg
salt and pepper
250 g (8 oz) button
    mushrooms, sliced
2 cloves garlic,
    crushed
wholemeal shortcrust
    pastry, made with
    350 g (12 oz)
    flour (see Spanish
    Lattice Flan, page
    37)
beaten egg to glaze
1 tablespoon sesame
    seeds

Heat 1 tablespoon oil in a pan, add the onion and fry until softened. Add the spinach, nutmeg, and salt and pepper to taste and cook for 5 minutes. Cool.

Wipe out the pan and heat the remaining oil. Add the mushrooms and garlic and fry until softened.

Roll out the pastry on a floured surface 20 × 30 cm (12 × 14 inches). Mark into 3 sections lengthways. Moisten the edges with water. Make diagonal slits along the outer sections, 2.5 cm (1 inch) apart and 7.5 cm (3 inches) long.

Spread half the spinach mixture over the centre section of the dough, place the mushrooms on top, then cover with remaining spinach. Fold the cut pastry strips over the spinach. Press to seal. Carefully lift onto a baking sheet and chill for 20 minutes.

Brush with egg and sprinkle with sesame seeds. Bake in a preheated moderately hot oven, 200°C (400°F), Gas Mark 6, for 30 to 35 minutes.
Serves 4 to 6

MINTED COURGETTES WITH PEAS AND CORN

175 g (6 oz)
  courgettes, thinly
  sliced
salt
50 g (2 oz) frozen
  peas
50 g (2 oz) frozen
  sweetcorn
2 mint sprigs
15 g ($\frac{1}{2}$ oz) butter
2 teaspoons chopped
  chives

Place the courgettes in a pan of boiling salted water. Add the peas, sweetcorn and mint. Cover and simmer for 5 to 6 minutes until the vegetables are just tender. Drain, remove the mint and return the vegetables to the pan.

Add the butter and chives and toss over a low heat for 1 minute. Transfer to a warmed serving dish. Serve hot.
Serves 2

Minted Courgettes with Peas and Corn

STIR-FRIED SUMMER VEGETABLES

2 tablespoons oil
2 spring onions,
  sliced
1 piece fresh root
  ginger, sliced
2 cloves garlic, sliced
2 chillies, seeded and
  chopped
50 g (2 oz) button
  mushrooms
125 g (4 oz) baby
  carrots
125 g (4 oz) mange-
  tout
125 g (4 oz) French
  beans
50 g (2 oz) bean
  sprouts
1 red pepper, cored,
  seeded and sliced
2 celery sticks, sliced
few cauliflower
  florets
4 tablespoons light
  soy sauce
2 tablespoons dry
  sherry
1 teaspoon sesame
  seed oil

Heat the oil in a wok or deep frying pan, add the spring onions, ginger and garlic and stir-fry for about 30 seconds. Add the chillies and all the vegetables. Toss well and cook, stirring, for 2 minutes. Stir in the soy sauce and sherry and cook for 2 minutes.

Sprinkle over the sesame seed oil, pile into a warmed serving dish and serve immediately.
Serves 4 to 6

GLAZED ONIONS

8 cloves
8 medium onions,
  peeled
300 ml ($\frac{1}{2}$ pint) beef
  stock
salt and pepper
25 g (1 oz) butter,
  melted
8 teaspoons light soft
  brown sugar

Push a clove into the base of each onion. Place in a greased ovenproof dish and spoon over the stock. Season with salt and pepper to taste and spoon over the butter. Bake in a preheated moderate oven, 160°C (325°F), Gas Mark 3, for 1$\frac{1}{4}$ to 1$\frac{1}{2}$ hours until tender.

Sprinkle a little sugar on each onion. Cook under a preheated hot grill until the sugar is caramelized. Serve hot, with roast or grilled meat.
Serves 4

VEGETABLE CURRY

2 tablespoons oil
1 onion, sliced
2 teaspoons ground
   coriander
2 teaspoons ground
   cumin
2 cloves garlic, crushed
5 cm (2 inch) piece
   of fresh root
   ginger, chopped
1 × 397 g (14 oz)
   can chopped
   tomatoes
1 green chilli, finely
   chopped
2 potatoes, diced
2 carrots, sliced
175 g (6 oz) okra,
   chopped
250 g (8 oz)
   cauliflower,
   broken into florets
salt and pepper
2 tablespoons
   chopped fresh
   coriander

ACCOMPANIMENTS:
DAHL:
2 tablespoons oil
1 onion, chopped
2 cloves garlic,
   chopped
2 teaspoons garam
   masala
1 teaspoon turmeric
175 g (6 oz) red
   lentils
600 ml (1 pint)
   water
1 tablespoon chopped
   coriander

CUCUMBER RAITA:
¼ cucumber
150 g (5 oz) natural
   yogurt
paprika

Heat the oil in a large pan, add the onion and fry until softened. Add the ground coriander, cumin, garlic and ginger and fry for 1 minute, stirring constantly. Add the tomatoes, 150 ml (¼ pint) water, chilli, potatoes, carrots, okra, cauliflower and salt and pepper to taste. Mix to coat the vegetables with the sauce. Cover and cook gently for 20 minutes, until tender. Stir in the chopped coriander.

Serve on a bed of brown rice with the following accompaniments.

Poppadums: Fry in deep hot oil for a few seconds.

Dahl: Heat the oil in a pan, add the onion and fry until softened. Add the garlic and spices and fry for 1 minute. Add the remaining ingredients, bring to the boil and simmer for 20 minutes, stirring occasionally. Serve hot.

Cucumber raita: Grate the cucumber and drain off any juices. Mix with the yogurt, and salt to taste. Turn into a serving bowl and sprinkle with paprika.

Onion relish: Mix thinly sliced onion rings with lemon juice, peppers and salt to taste until well coated. Leave to stand for 1 hour, then turn into a serving dish and sprinkle with paprika.

Serves 4

Vegetable Curry with accompaniments

SPINACH PANCAKE LAYER

PANCAKE BATTER:
125 g (4 oz)
  wholemeal flour
1 egg, beaten
300 ml (½ pint) milk
1 tablespoon oil
FILLING:
750 g (1½ lb) fresh
  spinach
salt and pepper
1 × 227 g (8 oz)
  carton cottage
  cheese
1 egg, beaten
grated nutmeg
TO FINISH:
50 g (2 oz) Cheddar
  cheese, grated

Place the flour in a bowl and make a well in the centre. Add the egg, then gradually stir in half the milk and the oil. Beat thoroughly until smooth. Add the remaining milk.

Heat a 15 cm (6 inch) omelette pan and add a few drops of oil. Pour in 1 tablespoon of the batter and tilt the pan to coat the bottom evenly. Cook until the underside is brown, then turn over and cook for a further 10 seconds. Turn onto a warmed plate. Repeat with the remaining batter.

Cook the spinach for 5 minutes in a large pan with just the water clinging to the leaves after washing and a pinch of salt; drain thoroughly. Chop finely and put in a bowl. Add the cottage cheese, egg, and salt, pepper and nutmeg to taste; mix.

Place a pancake on a heatproof plate, spread with some of the filling and cover with another pancake. Continue layering in this way, finishing with a pancake. Sprinkle with the cheese and cook in a preheated moderately hot oven, 190°C (375°F), Gas Mark 5, for 30 to 40 minutes. Serve immediately.
Serves 4

LAYERED POTATOES WITH SOUR CREAM

350 g (12 oz)
  potatoes, thinly
  sliced
1 small onion, finely
  chopped
4 tablespoons fresh
  sour cream
salt and pepper
40 g (1½ oz) butter
4 tablespoons milk
chopped chives to
  garnish

Line the base of a greased 600 ml (1 pint) ovenproof dish with potato slices. Add a little of the onion and sour cream. Sprinkle liberally with salt and pepper. Repeat the layers until all these ingredients are used, finishing with a layer of potato.

Melt 25 g (1 oz) of the butter in a saucepan, stir in the milk and pour over the potatoes. Dot the remaining butter on top.

Cover and cook in a preheated moderately hot oven, 190°C (375°F), Gas Mark 5, for 45 minutes. Uncover and cook for a further 20 minutes or until the potatoes are golden brown.

Garnish and serve hot with lamb chops or sausages and bacon.
Serves 2

POTATO CAKE

500 g (1 lb)
  potatoes, grated
1 onion, chopped
2 tablespoons
  chopped parsley
1 egg, beaten
salt and pepper
2 tablespoons olive
  oil

Place the potatoes in a bowl with the onion, parsley, egg and salt and pepper to taste. Mix thoroughly.

Heat the oil in a 20 to 23 cm (8 to 9 inch) heavy frying pan. Add the potato mixture and pat lightly into a cake. Fry gently for 5 to 7 minutes until the underside is brown.

Slide onto a plate, then invert back into the pan and fry the other side for 5 to 7 minutes until crisp and brown. Cut into wedges and serve.
Serves 4

SWEDE AND APPLE CASSEROLE

750 g (1½ lb) swede, cubed
salt and pepper
1 large cooking apple, peeled, cored and sliced
50 g (2 oz) light soft brown sugar
25 g (1 oz) butter
3 to 4 tablespoons medium sherry (optional)

Cook the swede in boiling salted water for 20 to 30 minutes or until just tender. Drain well.

Put half the swede in a greased casserole and cover with half the apple slices. Sprinkle over half the brown sugar and salt and pepper to taste. Dot with half the butter. Repeat the layers. Sprinkle over the sherry, if using.

Cover and cook in a preheated moderate oven, 180°C (350°F), Gas Mark 4, for 30 minutes.
Serves 4

MARROW, ONION AND TOMATO GRATIN

1 medium marrow
15 g (½ oz) butter
1 large onion, sliced
1 clove garlic, crushed
1 × 397 g (14 oz) can tomatoes
1 teaspoon each dried basil and oregano
salt and pepper
75 g (3 oz) Cheddar cheese, grated
25 g (1 oz) Gruyère cheese, grated
75 g (3 oz) fresh wholemeal breadcrumbs

Peel the marrow, halve lengthways and remove the seeds. Cut the flesh into 2.5 cm (1 inch) pieces.

Melt the butter in a large pan, add the onion and garlic and fry until soft. Add the marrow, tomatoes with their juice, basil, oregano, and salt and pepper to taste. Bring to the boil, cover and simmer for 30 to 35 minutes or until the marrow is soft. Pour into a shallow, heatproof dish.

Mix together the cheeses and breadcrumbs. Sprinkle over the vegetables and place under a preheated moderate grill for 2 to 3 minutes until the topping is golden brown. Serve immediately.
Serves 4

LEFT: *Layered Potatoes with Sour Cream*
RIGHT: *Swede and Apple Casserole; Pineapple Parsnips*

PINEAPPLE PARSNIPS

1 kg (2 lb) parsnips, quartered lengthways
150 ml (¼ pint) unsweetened pineapple juice
1 teaspoon light soft brown sugar
salt and pepper
40 g (1½ oz) butter

Cut the cores from the parsnips, then place in a greased baking dish. Mix together the pineapple juice, sugar and salt and pepper to taste and pour over the parsnips. Dot with the butter. Cover and cook in a preheated moderate oven, 180°C (350°F), Gas Mark 4, for 1 hour or until the parsnips are tender.
Serves 4

PEPPERS WITH TOMATOES

4 tablespoons oil
250 g (8 oz) onions, chopped
2 cloves garlic, crushed
2 bay leaves
6 large green peppers, halved, cored and seeded
500 g (1 lb) tomatoes, skinned and chopped
salt and pepper

Heat the oil in a wide pan, add the onions, garlic and bay leaves and fry gently for 5 minutes, stirring.

Cut the peppers into 1 cm (½ inch) strips and add to the pan. Stir lightly, then cover and cook for 10 minutes.

Add the tomatoes and a little salt and pepper and cook uncovered, stirring frequently, until most of the liquid has evaporated and the mixture is fairly thick. Remove the bay leaves and check the seasoning.
Serves 4

CAMEMBERT LEEKS

750 g (1½ lb) leeks
salt and pepper
25 g (1 oz) butter
1 tablespoon finely chopped onion
25 g (1 oz) plain wholemeal flour
300 ml (½ pint) milk
125 g (4 oz) Camembert cheese, derinded and chopped
1 hard-boiled egg, finely chopped
chopped parsley to garnish

Cut the leeks in half lengthways and wash thoroughly. Cook in boiling salted water for 8 minutes, or until tender. Drain and place in a shallow heatproof dish; keep warm.

Melt the butter in a pan, add the onion and fry until soft. Stir in the flour and cook for 1 minute. Gradually blend in the milk. Heat, stirring, until the sauce thickens. Add the cheese, egg, and salt and pepper to taste. Heat gently, then pour over the leeks.

Garnish with parsley and serve immediately.
Serves 4

CAREFUL PREPARATION

Most vegetables when bought are bursting with vitamins and minerals essential for good health. Ensure that you retain as many as possible by preparing your vegetables carefully.

Choose vegetables that are crisp and firm and wash thoroughly, scrubbing if necessary, before use. Do not soak the vegetables at any stage of their preparation since many vitamins and minerals are water soluble and so may be lost. And, since the most nutritious part of many vegetables lies just under the skin, peel only if absolutely necessary. Scraping the vegetables lightly is often preferable.

BROAD BEANS WITH WALNUTS

1 kg (2 lb) fresh broad beans, shelled
salt and pepper
25 g (1 oz) butter
1 small onion, finely chopped
150 ml (¼ pint) chicken stock
250 g (8 oz) Cheddar cheese, grated
1½ teaspoons French mustard
125 g (4 oz) walnuts, chopped

Cook the beans in boiling salted water for 5 minutes. Drain well.

Melt the butter in a clean saucepan. Add the onion and fry until softened. Stir in the stock and bring to the boil. Add the cheese, stir until melted, then mix in the mustard and salt and pepper to taste. Fold in the walnuts and beans.

Turn into a greased casserole. Cook in a preheated moderate oven, 180°C (350°F), Gas Mark 4, for 30 minutes.
Serves 4

TUSCAN BAKED FENNEL

625 g (1¼ lb) fennel bulbs
salt and pepper
1 thick slice lemon
1 tablespoon oil
25 g (1 oz) butter
25 g (1 oz) grated Parmesan cheese
fennel leaves to garnish (optional)

Trim the fennel bulbs and remove any discoloured skin with a potato peeler. Cut vertically into 2 cm (¾ inch) thick pieces. Place in a pan with a pinch of salt, the lemon and oil and add sufficient boiling water to cover. Cook for 20 minutes or until just tender. Drain well.

Melt the butter in a gratin dish or shallow flameproof casserole, add the fennel and turn to coat. Season to taste with pepper and sprinkle with cheese.

Place under a preheated grill until lightly browned. Serve immediately, garnished with fennel leaves if liked.
Serves 4

Spiced Cauliflower; Crispy Vegetables

SPICED CAULIFLOWER

2 tablespoons oil
1 teaspoon ground
  ginger
2 teaspoons ground
  coriander
1 teaspoon ground
  turmeric
1 cauliflower, broken
  into florets
2 carrots, sliced
1 onion, sliced
2 celery sticks, sliced
120 ml (4 fl oz) stock
150 g (5 oz) natural
  yogurt
1 tablespoon chopped
  coriander or
  parsley

Heat the oil in a pan, add the spices and fry gently for 1 minute. Add the vegetables and cook gently for a further 3 minutes, stirring occasionally. Add the stock, and salt and pepper to taste.

Cover and simmer for 10 minutes until the vegetables are just tender. Stir in the yogurt, sprinkle with the coriander or parsley and serve immediately.

Serves 4

CRISPY VEGETABLES

2 tablespoons oil
1 large onion, sliced
2 carrots, cut into
  thin strips
2 celery sticks, sliced
1 green pepper, cored
  and sliced
2 teaspoons chopped
  root ginger
125 g (4 oz)
  mushrooms, sliced
250 g (8 oz) bean
  shoots
1 clove garlic, crushed
2 tablespoons sherry
2 tablespoons soy
  sauce
salt and pepper

Heat the oil in a wok or deep frying pan. Add the onion, carrots, celery, pepper and ginger and fry briskly for 5 minutes, stirring constantly.

Add the mushrooms, beanshoots and garlic and stir-fry for a further 2 minutes.

Add the sherry, soy sauce, and salt and pepper to taste. Stir-fry for about 3 minutes. Serve immediately.

Serves 4

POTATOES WITH ONIONS

*4 medium onions,
thinly sliced into
rings
salt and pepper
4–6 medium
potatoes, cut into
5 mm ($\frac{1}{4}$ inch)
slices*

Cover the bottom of a small roasting pan with enough boiling water to reach a depth of about 2.5 cm (1 inch).

Arrange the onion rings in the bottom of the pan and sprinkle with pepper and a little salt.

Arrange the potato slices on top, season again, cover with foil and simmer over a low heat for 20 to 30 minutes until the vegetables are tender.

This Scottish dish is delicious served as a snack with crusty bread, or as an accompaniment to roast beef.

Serves 4

CREAMED CAULIFLOWER

*1 medium
cauliflower,
broken into florets
salt and pepper
25 g (1 oz) butter
25 g (1 oz)
wholemeal flour
300 ml ($\frac{1}{2}$ pint) milk
grated nutmeg*

Cook the cauliflower in lightly salted boiling water for about 10 to 15 minutes, or until tender. Drain well.

Meanwhile, melt the butter in a small pan and stir in the flour. Cook, stirring, for 1 minute, then gradually stir in the milk. Bring to the boil, stirring constantly, then season to taste with salt, pepper and nutmeg. Cook, stirring, for 2 minutes.

Return the cauliflower to the saucepan and mash down with a potato masher or a wooden spoon. Pour in the white sauce and beat into the cauliflower until smooth. Pile into a vegetable dish and sprinkle with a little more nutmeg.

Serves 4

BUTTERED LEEKS

*4–6 leeks, sliced
salt
50 g (2 oz) butter
grated nutmeg
freshly ground
pepper*

Cook the leeks in a pan of boiling salted water for 10 minutes. Drain well. Melt the butter in the saucepan and return the leeks to the pan. Toss well and sprinkle with plenty of nutmeg and freshly ground pepper.

Serves 4

LEFT: *Potatoes with Onions; Creamed Cauliflower; Buttered Leeks*
RIGHT: *Aubergine Pie; Courgette and Tomato Bake; Indian-Style Vegetables*

AUBERGINE PIE

1 kg (2 lb)
  aubergines
salt and pepper
200 ml (⅓ pint) olive
  oil
1 onion, chopped
1 clove garlic,
  crushed
500 g (1 lb)
  tomatoes, skinned
  and chopped
150 g (5 oz) natural
  yogurt
1 × 113 g (4 oz)
  carton cottage
  cheese
25 g (1 oz) grated
  Parmesan cheese

Slice the aubergines, sprinkle with salt and leave in a colander for 1 hour. Rinse, drain and pat dry.

Heat 2 tablespoons of the oil in a pan, add the onion and fry until softened. Add the garlic and tomatoes and simmer, uncovered, for 5 minutes.

Mix the yogurt and cottage cheese together, adding seasoning to taste.

Heat the remaining oil in a frying pan and cook the aubergines on both sides until golden. Drain.

Arrange a third of the aubergines in an ovenproof dish. Cover with half the tomato mixture, then top with half the yogurt mixture. Repeat the layers, finishing with aubergines.

Sprinkle with the Parmesan and cook in a preheated moderate oven, 180°C (350°F), Gas Mark 4, for 35 to 40 minutes. Serve immediately.
Serves 4

COURGETTE AND TOMATO BAKE

3 tablespoons olive
  oil
2 onions, sliced
750 g (1½ lb)
  courgettes, sliced
2 cloves garlic, crushed
6 tomatoes, skinned
  and chopped
1 tablespoon tomato
  purée
salt and pepper
TOPPING:
750 g (1½ lb)
  potatoes, boiled
  and mashed
4 spring onions,
  finely chopped
2 tablespoons olive
  oil
4 tablespoons milk

Heat the oil in a pan, add the onions and courgettes and fry for 10 minutes, stirring occasionally. Add the garlic, tomatoes, tomato purée, and salt and pepper to taste. Cover and simmer for 5 minutes, then turn into a 1.5 litre (2½ pint) ovenproof dish.

Beat the potatoes with the spring onions, oil, milk, and salt and pepper to taste. Spoon over the courgette mixture to cover. Cook in a preheated moderately hot oven, 200°C (400°F), Gas Mark 6, for 30 to 40 minutes until golden. Serve immediately, as a main dish.
Serves 4

INDIAN-STYLE VEGETABLES

4 tablespoons oil
2 onions, sliced
2 teaspoons each
  ground coriander
  and turmeric
1 teaspoon curry
  powder
2.5 cm (1 inch) piece
  of fresh root
  ginger, chopped
2 cloves garlic, crushed
4 carrots, sliced
350 g (12 oz)
  courgettes, sliced
300 ml (½ pint) stock
1 small cauliflower
50 g (2 oz) cashew
  nuts, roasted
150 g (5 oz) natural
  yogurt

Heat the oil in a large pan, add the onions and fry until softened. Add the spices and garlic and cook for a further 1 minute. Add the carrots and courgettes and fry for 2 to 3 minutes, stirring. Add the stock and salt and pepper to taste.

Cover and simmer for 10 minutes. Break the cauliflower into florets, add to the pan and cook for a further 10 minutes.

Stir in the nuts and yogurt and heat through gently. Serve with brown rice as a main dish, or as an accompaniment.
Serves 4 to 6

COURGETTES
WITH TOMATOES

50 g (2 oz) butter or
margarine
2 tablespoons olive
oil
4 large courgettes,
sliced
4 large tomatoes,
chopped
2 cloves garlic,
crushed (optional)
salt and pepper

Heat the butter or margarine and oil
in a large frying pan and fry the
courgette slices on one side until
golden brown. Turn them over and
add the tomatoes to the pan just as
the courgettes are beginning to
brown on the second side. Mix well,
add the garlic, if using, season to
taste with salt and pepper and
continue cooking until the tomatoes
are tender.
Serves 4

Courgettes with Tomatoes; Glazed Carrots

GLAZED CARROTS

500 g (1 lb) carrots
salt
1 tablespoon light
soft brown sugar
50 g (2 oz) butter or
margarine
chopped parsley to
garnish (optional)

Leave the carrots whole if small and
tender, otherwise slice into rings. Put
in a saucepan with just enough
lightly salted water to come up to
the level of the carrots.

Bring to the boil and add the
remaining ingredients. Cover and
cook for about 20 minutes, then
remove the lid and continue cooking
for a further 10 to 15 minutes or
until the carrots are cooked and the
water has nearly boiled away.

Drain and serve sprinkled with
parsley if liked.
Serves 4

POTATO PATTIES

tablespoon oil
onion, chopped
clove garlic, crushed
250 g (8 oz) frozen
   chopped spinach,
   thawed
500 g (1 lb)
   potatoes, boiled
   and mashed
¼ teaspoon ground
   nutmeg
125 g (4 oz)
   Cheddar cheese,
   grated
wholemeal flour
oil for shallow-frying

Heat the oil in a pan, add the onion and garlic and fry until softened. Squeeze the spinach dry and add to the pan with the potato, nutmeg, cheese, and salt and pepper to taste: mix thoroughly. Shape the mixture into 8 balls, using dampened hands, and flatten slightly.

Place some flour in a polythene bag, add the patties one at a time and shake to coat completely.

Fry in hot shallow oil for 2 minutes on each side, until golden brown.

Serves 3 to 4

STUFFED SPINACH LEAVES

12 large spinach
   leaves, stalks
   removed
salt and pepper
1 tablespoon oil
1 onion, chopped
2 cloves garlic,
   crushed
250 g (8 oz)
   mushrooms,
   chopped
75 g (3 oz)
   wholemeal
   breadcrumbs
1 tablespoon chopped
   mixed herbs, e.g.
   parsley, thyme
   and marjoram
1 egg, beaten
SAUCE:
2 egg yolks
1 tablespoon lemon
   juice

Put the spinach in a large pan with 300 ml (½ pint) salted water and boil for 2 minutes. Drain, reserving the liquid. Rinse and pat dry.

Heat the oil in a pan, add the onion and fry until softened. Add the garlic and mushrooms and cook for 5 minutes. Stir in the breadcrumbs, herbs, egg, and salt and pepper.

Place 1 tablespoon of the mixture in the centre of each spinach leaf, fold in both sides and roll up.

Lay the spinach rolls in a shallow ovenproof dish and pour over 150 ml (¼ pint) of the reserved liquid. Cover with foil and bake in a preheated moderately hot oven, 190°C (375°F), Gas Mark 5, for 45 minutes. Strain and reserve the juices.

For the sauce, whisk the egg yolks with the lemon juice in a heatproof bowl over a pan of simmering water. Add the reserved juices and stir for about 5 minutes, until thickened. Season and pour over the rolls.

Serves 4

Potato Patties; Stuffed Spinach Leaves

STUFFED GREEN PEPPERS

1 tablespoon oil
1 clove garlic,
    crushed
1 piece fresh root
    ginger, finely
    chopped
250 g (8 oz) minced
    pork
1 spring onion,
    chopped
1 celery stick, finely
    chopped
grated rind of
    1 lemon
4 green peppers

Heat the oil in a wok or frying pan, add the garlic and fry until lightly browned. Lower the heat, add the ginger and pork and cook for 2 minutes. Stir in the spring onion, celery and lemon rind, mix well and cook for 30 seconds. Cool slightly.

Cut the peppers into quarters and remove the core and seeds. Divide the mixture between the pepper quarters, pressing it well into the cavity.

Arrange the pepper quarters in an oiled ovenproof dish. Cook in a preheated modeately hot oven, 200°C (400°F), Gas Mark 6, for 20 to 25 minutes, until tender. Transfer to a warmed serving dish and serve immediately.
Serves 4 to 6

Baked Filled Tomatoes; Stuffed Green Peppers

BAKED FILLED TOMATOES

3 dried Chinese
    mushrooms
1 tablespoon oil
1 large onion, finely
    chopped
500 g (1 lb) minced
    beef or pork
50 g (2 oz) canned
    water chestnuts,
    drained and
    chopped
2 tablespoons soy
    sauce
2 tablespoons dry
    sherry
8 large tomatoes
1 tablespoon
    cornflour, blended
    with 2 tablespoons
    water
fresh coriander leaves
    to garnish

Soak the mushrooms in warm water for 15 minutes. Squeeze dry, discard the hard stalks and chop the caps.

Heat the oil in a wok or deep frying pan, add the onion and fry until browned. Add the meat and cook, stirring, for 5 minutes until evenly browned. Stir in the mushrooms, water chestnuts, soy sauce and sherry and cook for 2 minutes.

Cut the tomatoes in half, scoop out the flesh and add to the pan, discarding the seeds. Stir in the cornflour and cook for 1 minute.

Cool slightly, then spoon the mixture into the tomato halves. Arrange in a baking dish and cook in a preheated moderate oven, 180°C (350°F), Gas Mark 4, for 15 to 25 minutes, until tender.

Garnish and serve immediately.
Serves 4 to 8

BRAISED WHITE CABBAGE

1 large Chinese
   cabbage
250 g (8 oz) spinach
125 g (4 oz) spring
   greens
2 tablespoons oil
4 spring onions,
   chopped
1 tablespoon light
   soy sauce
2 teaspoons dry
   sherry
50 g (2 oz) peeled
   prawns

Cut the cabbage into 4 cm (2 inch) slices. Chop the spinach and greens.

Heat the oil in a wok or deep frying pan, add the spring onions and stir-fry for 1 minute. Add the cabbage, spinach and greens and stir over a medium heat for 2 minutes. Pour over the soy sauce and sherry and cook for 2 minutes. Add the prawns and cook for 1 minute.

Spoon into a warmed serving dish and serve immediately.
Serves 4 to 6

COURGETTE CASSEROLE

1 kg (2 lb) courgettes
salt and pepper
½ teaspoon dried
   oregano
125 g (4 oz) mature
   Double Gloucester
   cheese, grated
50 g (2 oz) blanched
   almonds, chopped
25 g (1 oz) butter,
   melted

Steam the courgettes until just tender. Cut into 1 cm (½ inch) slices and layer a quarter of these in a greased casserole. Sprinkle with salt and pepper and a quarter of the oregano. Cover with a quarter of the cheese. Continue making layers in this way, ending with cheese.

Mix together the nuts and butter and scatter over the top. Cook in a preheated moderate oven, 180°C (350°F), Gas Mark 4, for 20 minutes.
Serves 4 to 6

FRIED LETTUCE AND PRAWNS

3 tablespoons oil
3 spring onions,
   chopped
1 piece fresh root
   ginger, shredded
125 g (4 oz) peeled
   prawns
1 large Cos lettuce
1 tablespoon dry
   sherry

Heat the oil in a wok or deep frying pan, add the spring onions and stir-fry for 30 seconds until lightly browned. Add the ginger and prawns and cook for 1 minute. Separate the lettuce into leaves and add to the pan with the sherry and salt to taste. Stir quickly for 1 to 2 minutes.
Serves 4 to 6

FRENCH-STYLE GREEN BEANS

100 g (3½ oz) butter
2 bunches spring
   onions, cut into
   5 cm (2 inch)
   lengths
1 kg (2 lb) small
   French beans,
   topped and tailed
salt and pepper
1 crisp lettuce,
   quartered
1 bunch of mixed
   herbs (including
   parsley and
   chervil), tied
   together

Melt the butter in a pan, add the spring onions and cook for 2 minutes. Add the beans and cook for 20 minutes. Season with salt and pepper to taste. Add the lettuce and herbs and cook for 5 minutes.

Remove the herbs and transfer to a warmed serving dish. Serve immediately.
Serves 4

CHARLOTTE D'AUBERGINES

1 kg (2 lb)
   aubergines, sliced
salt
50 g (2 oz) butter
1 large onion, sliced
2 cloves garlic,
   crushed
500 g (1 lb)
   tomatoes, skinned
   and chopped
4 tablespoons oil
300 g (10 oz)
   natural yogurt
150 ml (¼ pint)
   chicken stock

Sprinkle the aubergine slices with salt and leave to stand for 30 minutes. Rinse under cold water and dry well.

Melt the butter in a pan, add the onion and garlic and fry until lightly browned. Stir in the tomatoes and cook for 20 to 25 minutes, until thickened.

Heat the oil in another pan and fry the aubergine slices until browned on both sides. Drain.

Line the base and sides of a 1.5 litre (2½ pint) charlotte mould with aubergine slices. Fill with layers of tomato mixture, yogurt and aubergines, finishing with aubergines.

Cover with foil and cook in a preheated moderate oven, 180°C (350°F), Gas Mark 4, for 40 to 45 minutes, until tender. Leave for 10 minutes, then turn out onto a warmed serving dish.

Heat any remaining tomato sauce with the stock and spoon around the charlotte. Serve immediately.
Serves 4 to 6

RICE, PASTA AND PULSES

Long-grain, short-grain, wild, brown or white; stranded, folded into nests, pressed into shells, bows, wheels or twists; and green, plain, wholemeal or tomato-flavoured – few foods other than rice or pasta come in such a variety of shapes, sizes and guises. Mixed and matched with a whole host of peas, beans and lentils from black bean to pearl barley and black-eyed or butter bean to haricot or pinto there are the makings of many a hearty feast to satisfy man-sized appetites.

Fun to cook and tasty to eat they are also the high-energy foods that provide the body with much needed heat and energy – although they offer more than calories alone since their high values of protein, vitamins and fibre makes them prized ingredients in any diet.

Combine them with fresh vegetables for long slow-cooking casseroles, hot pots and stews; simmer them with stock and flavourings for soothing and sustaining soups, savoury risottos and pilaffs; bake them with cheese, eggs and vegetables in countless crispy gratins, golden bakes and savoury quiches; or mix and fry into crisp rissoles and tasty croquettes.

Many of the dishes featured here will make admirable vegetarian main course meals and some like Lentil Rissoles, Provençale Bean Stew and Mixed Bean Casserole are special enough for entertaining. Others are so speedy to cook like Macaroni Cheese with Sour Cream, Fruit and Nut Pilaff and Chick Pea Curry that they make ideal quick meals for appetites that won't wait.

CHICK PEA CURRY

500 g (1 lb) chick
peas, soaked
overnight
3 tablespoons oil
2 onions, chopped
1 teaspoon chilli
powder
2 teaspoons ground
cumin
1 teaspoon ground
coriander
2 teaspoons chopped
root ginger
4 cardamoms
2 cloves garlic, crushed
500 g (1 lb)
tomatoes, skinned
and chopped
2 tablespoons tomato
purée
salt and pepper
1 tablespoon chopped
coriander or
parsley

Drain the chick peas, place in a pan
and cover with cold water. Bring to
the boil, boil for 10 minutes, then
simmer for 2 hours. Drain and
reserve the liquid.

Heat the oil in a large pan, add
the onions and fry until softened.
Add the spices and garlic and cook
for a further 2 minutes. Add the
tomatoes, tomato purée, chick peas,
300 ml ($\frac{1}{2}$ pint) of the reserved liquid,
and salt and pepper to taste.

Cover and simmer gently for
1 hour or until the peas are tender.
Sprinkle with the coriander or
parsley. Serve as a main dish or
accompaniment.
Serves 6

LENTIL RISSOLES

2 tablespoons oil
1 onion, chopped
2 celery sticks,
chopped
2 carrots, chopped
250 g (8 oz) red
lentils
600 ml (1 pint)
water
1 teaspoon ground
coriander
2 tablespoons
chopped parsley
175 g (6 oz) whole-
meal breadcrumbs
2 tablespoons
wholemeal flour
1 egg, beaten
YOGURT SAUCE:
300 g (10 oz)
natural yogurt
chopped parsley
1 clove garlic, crushed

Heat the oil in a pan, add the onion,
celery and carrots and fry until
softened. Add the lentils, water,
coriander, and salt and pepper to
taste. Bring to the boil, cover and
simmer for 50 minutes to 1 hour,
stirring occasionally. Mix in the
parsley and one third of the
breadcrumbs. Turn onto a plate.

Using floured hands, shape the
mixture into rissoles and coat with
the flour. Dip into the beaten egg
and coat with the remaining
breadcrumbs.

Pour the oil into a frying pan to a
depth of 5 mm ($\frac{1}{4}$ inch) and place
over moderate heat. When hot, add
the rissoles and fry until crisp and
golden brown, turning.

To make the sauce, mix the
yogurt, parsley and garlic together.
Serve the rissoles with the sauce.
Serves 4

LENTIL STEW

3 tablespoons oil
2 onions, chopped
4 carrots, sliced
4 celery sticks, sliced
500 g (1 lb)
tomatoes
1 clove garlic, crushed
1 bay leaf
300 ml ($\frac{1}{2}$ pint)
tomato juice
900 ml (1$\frac{1}{2}$ pints)
water
300 g (10 oz) red
lentils
2 tablespoons
chopped parsley
salt and pepper
chopped parsley

Heat the oil in a large pan, add the
onions, carrots and celery and fry for
10 minutes until softened.

Skin the tomatoes and cut into
quarters. Add to the pan with the
remaining ingredients, seasoning
with salt and pepper to taste. Cover
and simmer for 50 minutes to
1 hour, stirring occasionally, until the
lentils are tender.

Sprinkle with chopped parsley.
Serve as a main dish with crusty
wholemeal bread, or as an
accompaniment.
Serves 4 to 6

LEFT: *Chick Pea Curry; Lentil Rissoles; Lentil Stew*

BLACK BEAN CASSEROLE

350 g (12 oz) black
  beans, soaked
  overnight
2 tablespoons olive
  oil
2 onions, sliced
2 celery sticks, sliced
2 carrots, sliced
2 cloves garlic, crushed
500 g (1 lb)
  frankfurter
  sausages, sliced
1 tablespoon tomato
  purée
1 bay leaf
500 g (1 lb)
  tomatoes, skinned
  and chopped
salt and pepper
chopped parsley

Drain the beans, place in a pan and cover with cold water. Bring to the boil, boil for 10 minutes, then simmer gently for 1 hour. Drain and reserve 450 ml ($\frac{3}{4}$ pint) of the liquid.

Heat the oil in a flameproof casserole, add the onions and fry for 5 to 10 minutes until transparent. Add the celery, carrots and garlic and fry for 3 to 4 minutes.

Add the remaining ingredients, with the beans, reserved liquid, and salt and pepper to taste. Cover and cook in a preheated moderate oven, 180°C (350°F), Gas Mark 4, for 1 to 1½ hours until the beans are soft. Sprinkle with the parsley and serve immediately.
Serves 4

PUCHERO

350 g (12 oz) pinto
  beans, soaked
  overnight
250 g (8 oz) salt
  pork
2 tablespoons olive
  oil
1 large onion, sliced
1 red and 1 green
  pepper, cored,
  seeded and sliced
2 cloves garlic, crushed
2 teaspoons tomato
  purée
4 tomatoes, skinned
  and quartered
250 g (8 oz) chorizo
  or garlic sausage,
  thickly sliced
salt and pepper
chopped parsley

Drain the beans, place in a pan and cover with cold water. Bring to the boil, boil for 10 minutes, then simmer for 50 to 60 minutes. Drain and reserve 450 ml ($\frac{3}{4}$ pint) of the liquid.

Cover the pork with cold water, bring to the boil and simmer for 30 minutes. Drain and cut into

RIGHT: *Black Bean Casserole; Puchero*

FETTUCINE CASSEROLE

250 g (8 oz) green
   noodles (fettucine
   verde)
salt and pepper
2 tablespoons olive
   oil
1 onion, chopped
1 clove garlic,
   crushed (optional)
125 g (4 oz)
   mushrooms, sliced
250 g (8 oz) Italian
   garlic sausage,
   finely chopped
250 g (8 oz) Ricotta
   or curd cheese
1 egg
125 g (4 oz)
   Mozzarella or
   Gruyère cheese,
   shredded

Cook the noodles in boiling salted water until just tender.

Meanwhile, heat the oil in a frying pan, add the onion and garlic (if using) and fry until softened. Add the mushrooms and fry for a further 3 minutes, then stir in the sausage. Remove from the heat.

Drain the noodles and fold into the sausage mixture. Beat the Ricotta cheese and egg together and stir into the sausage mixture with salt and pepper to taste. Turn into a casserole and top with the Mozzarella cheese. Bake in a preheated moderate oven, 160°C (325°F), Gas Mark 3, for 35 minutes.
Serves 4

MACARONI CHEESE WITH SOUR CREAM

250 g (8 oz)
   macaroni
salt and pepper
25 g (1 oz) butter,
   melted
125 g (4 oz) mature
   Cheddar cheese,
   grated
142 ml (5 fl oz)
   fresh sour cream
4 tablespoons milk
1 egg, beaten
pinch of paprika

Cook the macaroni in boiling salted water. Drain well, then mix with the butter and salt and pepper to taste. Make alternate layers of macaroni and cheese in a casserole, reserving 2 tablespoons of cheese.

Mix together the sour cream, milk, egg, paprika and salt and pepper to taste. Pour over the macaroni and scatter the remaining cheese on top. Cook in a preheated moderately hot oven, 200°C (400°F), Gas Mark 6, for about 20 minutes.
Serves 4

SPAGHETTI WITH BABY VEGETABLES

3 tablespoons dry
   white wine
1 tablespoon chopped
   chervil
2 tablespoons double
   cream
175 g (6 oz) butter
125 g (4 oz)
   mushrooms, sliced
2 tomatoes, skinned,
   seeded and chopped
salt and pepper
1 teaspoon lemon
   juice
2 tablespoons olive
   oil
150 g (5 oz)
   cauliflower florets
1 courgette, sliced
50 g (2 oz)
   mangetout
4 canned artichoke
   hearts, quartered
50 g (2 oz) peas
350 g (12 oz) whole-
   wheat spaghetti

Put the wine and chervil in a pan, bring to the boil and boil steadily until reduced by half. Add the cream, 150 g (5 oz) of the butter in small pieces, the mushrooms and tomatoes. Season well with salt and pepper. Bring to the boil and boil for 30 seconds. Stir in the lemon juice.

Heat the olive oil in a large frying pan or wok, add all the remaining vegetables and stir-fry for 2 to 3 minutes.

Meanwhile, cook the spaghetti until *al dente*. Drain well and toss in the remaining butter. Spoon over the mushroom sauce and toss well.

Transfer to a warmed serving plate, surround with the vegetables and serve immediately.
Serves 4

HARICOT BEAN AND SWEETCORN CASSEROLE

250 g (8 oz) dried haricot beans, soaked overnight
1 × 326 g (11½ oz) can sweetcorn, drained
1 × 397 g (14 oz) can tomatoes, drained
salt and pepper
1 tablespoon light soft brown sugar
1 tablespoon grated onion
50 g (2 oz) browned wholemeal breadcrumbs

Drain the beans and place in a saucepan. Cover with fresh water, bring to the boil, boil for 10 minutes, then simmer for 45 minutes or until tender.

Drain the beans and mix with the sweetcorn, tomatoes, salt and pepper to taste, sugar and onion. Turn into a greased casserole and sprinkle the breadcrumbs over the top. Cook in a preheated moderate oven, 180°C (350°F), Gas Mark 4, for 45 minutes.
Serves 4

FRUIT AND NUT PILAFF

75 g (3 oz) sultanas
175 g (6 oz) dried fruit (apricots, apples, pears, etc.)
1 tablespoon sweet sherry
75 g (3 oz) butter
1 onion, finely chopped
250 g (8 oz) brown rice, cooked
¼ teaspoon ground allspice
salt and pepper
50 g (2 oz) flaked almonds

Put the sultanas and dried fruit in a bowl, sprinkle with the sherry and cover with water. Leave to soak for 4 hours. Drain and chop the apricots, apples or pears.

Melt the butter in a frying pan, add the onion and fry until softened. Stir in the rice and allspice, then add salt and pepper to taste and mix well.

Fold in the fruit and almonds, then turn the mixture into a greased casserole. Bake in a preheated moderately hot oven, 190°C (375°F), Gas Mark 5, for 30 minutes.
Serves 6

LEFT: *Spaghetti with Baby Vegetables*
RIGHT: *Haricot Bean and Sweetcorn Casserole; Fruit and Nut Pilaff*

BEANY CHEESE CRUNCH

75 g (3 oz) red
　kidney beans
75 g (3 oz) black-
　eyed beans
75 g (3 oz) butter
　beans
1 large onion
2 celery sticks
50 g (2 oz) bacon,
　derinded
2 tablespoons oil
1 clove garlic,
　crushed
1 × 397 g (14 oz)
　can tomatoes
150 ml (¼ pint) light
　stock
¼ teaspoon chilli
　powder
salt and pepper
75 g (3 oz)
　wholemeal
　breadcrumbs
125 g (4 oz)
　matured Cheddar
　cheese, grated

Soak the kidney, black-eyed and butter beans in cold water overnight. Drain and place in a saucepan. Cover with cold water, bring to the boil and boil rapidly for 10 minutes. Lower the heat, cover and simmer for 30 to 35 minutes or until tender. Drain and rinse under cold water.

Chop the onion, celery and bacon finely. Heat the oil in a pan, add the onion, garlic, celery and bacon and fry until soft. Add the tomatoes with their juice and the stock. Stir in the chilli powder, beans, and salt and pepper to taste. Bring to the boil, cover and simmer for 20 minutes. Transfer to a heatproof 1.2 litre (2 pint) dish.

Mix together the breadcrumbs and cheese and spoon over the bean mixture. Place under a preheated moderate grill until the topping is golden brown. Serve immediately.
Serves 4

ITALIAN BAKED BEANS

500 g (1 lb) dried
　white haricot
　beans, soaked
　overnight
125 g (4 oz) Italian
　garlic sausage,
　chopped
2 cloves garlic,
　crushed
2 teaspoons dried
　oregano
salt and pepper
4 tablespoons tomato
　purée
600 ml (1 pint)
　water
　(approximately)

Drain the beans and mix with the sausage, garlic, oregano, and salt and pepper to taste. Mix the tomato purée with the water.

Put the bean mixture in a flameproof casserole and stir in enough water to just cover the beans. Bring to the boil and boil for 10 minutes.

Cover and cook in a preheated cool oven, 140°C (275°F), Gas Mark 1, for 3 to 3½ hours or until the beans are tender. If necessary, add a little more water to the casserole during cooking.
Serves 6

BEAN AND EGG CURRY

50 g (2 oz) haricot
　beans
15 g (½ oz) butter
2 rashers streaky
　bacon, derinded
　and chopped
1 onion, chopped
1 celery stick,
　chopped
½–1 teaspoon curry
　powder
¼ teaspoon ground
　ginger
1 tablespoon
　wholemeal flour
150 ml (¼ pint) light
　stock
1 × 227 g (8 oz) can
　tomatoes
salt and pepper
4 hard-boiled eggs
chopped parsley to
　garnish

Place the beans in a bowl, cover with cold water and leave to soak overnight.

Drain, rinse and place in a saucepan. Cover with fresh cold water, bring to the boil, boil for 10 minutes, simmer for 45 minutes or until tender, then drain.

Melt the butter in a saucepan, add the bacon, onion and celery and fry until soft. Add the curry powder, ginger and flour and continue to cook for 1 minute. Gradually blend in the stock and the tomatoes with their juice. Heat, stirring until thickened. Add the beans and salt and pepper to taste.

Cut the eggs in half lengthways and add to the curry. Cover and simmer for about 20 minutes. Transfer to a warmed serving dish and garnish with parsley. Serve immediately.
Serves 4

LEFT: *Beany Cheese Crunch*
RIGHT: *Spiced Vegetables and Rice*

RICE WITH PARSLEY AND CHEESE

350 g (12 oz)
  cooked brown rice
6 spring onions,
  finely chopped
40 g (1½ oz)
  chopped parsley
3 eggs, beaten
4 tablespoons milk
125 g (4 oz)
  Cheddar cheese,
  grated
salt and pepper

Mix together the rice, spring onions and parsley. Combine the remaining ingredients with salt and pepper to taste and add to the rice mixture. Blend well, then turn into a greased casserole. Cook in a preheated moderate oven, 180°C (350°F), Gas Mark 4, for 30 minutes or until just set.
Serves 4

PEARL BARLEY CASSEROLE

50 g (2 oz) butter
2 medium leeks,
  thinly sliced
1 green pepper,
  cored, seeded and
  chopped
200 g (7 oz) pearl
  barley, soaked
  overnight
50 g (2 oz) cooked
  ham, diced
  (optional)
1 × 326 g (11½ oz)
  can sweetcorn,
  drained
300 ml (½ pint)
  chicken stock
salt and pepper

Melt the butter in a flameproof casserole. Add the leeks and green pepper and fry until softened. Drain the barley and add to the casserole. Stir in the remaining ingredients with salt and pepper to taste.
  Cover and cook in a preheated moderate oven, 160°C (325°F), Gas Mark 3, for 40 minutes or until the barley is tender and all the liquid absorbed.
Serves 4

SPICED VEGETABLES AND RICE

1 tablespoon oil
1 leek, sliced
1 carrot, thinly sliced
1 onion, sliced
½ dessert apple, cored
  and chopped
¼ teaspoon cumin
  seeds
¼ teaspoon ground
  coriander
pinch of cayenne
  pepper
salt and pepper
4–5 tablespoons stock
½ cup brown rice
chopped parsley to
  garnish

Heat the oil in a saucepan, add the leek, carrot, onion and apple and cook gently, stirring, for 3 minutes. Add the cumin, coriander, cayenne, and salt and pepper to taste. Continue to cook for 3 minutes, then stir in the stock. Cover and simmer for 10 to 15 minutes until the vegetables are tender but not soft.
  Cook the rice in plenty of boiling salted water for 45 to 50 minutes or until tender. Drain and rinse with boiling water.
  Stir the rice into the vegetables and heat gently for 5 minutes. Transfer to a warmed serving dish and garnish with parsley. Serve hot.
Serves 2

VEGETARIAN HOTPOT

25 g (1 oz) dried
  chick peas
25 g (1 oz) dried
  haricot beans
25 g (1 oz) dried
  black-eyed beans
25 g (1 oz) dried red
  kidney beans
15 g (½ oz) butter
1 small onion,
  chopped
1 carrot, sliced
1 celery stick,
  chopped
1 clove garlic,
  crushed
1 × 227 g (8 oz) can
  tomatoes
½ teaspoon dried
  mixed herbs
salt and pepper
75 g (3 oz) Cheddar
  cheese, grated

Place the chick peas, haricot beans and black-eyed beans in a bowl and cover with cold water. Place the kidney beans in a separate bowl and cover with water. Soak overnight.

Drain and place the chick peas, haricot beans and black-eyed beans in a saucepan; put the kidney beans in a separate pan (to avoid tinting the others pink). Cover the pulses with fresh cold water. Bring to the boil, boil for 10 minutes, then cover and simmer for 40 minutes or until tender. Drain, rinse under cold water, then drain thoroughly.

Melt the butter in a saucepan, add the onion, carrot and celery and fry until soft. Stir in the garlic, pulses, tomatoes with their juice, herbs, and salt and pepper to taste.

Bring to the boil, cover and simmer for 1 to 1¼ hours, adding a little water if the mixture becomes too dry. Check the seasoning. Transfer to a warmed serving dish. Sprinkle with the cheese.
Serves 2

FISH STUFFED PEPPERS

500 g (1 lb) cod
  fillets
300 ml (½ pint)
  boiling water
bouquet garni
½ onion
salt and pepper
1 tablespoon
  sunflower oil
1 onion, chopped
2 celery sticks,
  chopped
125 g (4 oz) brown
  rice
1 × 227 g (8 oz) can
  tomatoes
1 bay leaf
1 teaspoon chopped
  marjoram
150 ml (¼ pint) cold
  water
125 g (4 oz) frozen
  peeled prawns,
  thawed
4 tablespoons frozen
  sweetcorn
4 green peppers
TO GARNISH:
marjoram sprigs
whole prawns in
  shell

Place the fish in a pan with the boiling water, bouquet garni, half-onion, and season. Cover and simmer for 10 to 15 minutes.

Remove with a slotted spoon, remove any skin and bones and flake the fish into chunks. Set aside.

Heat the oil in a frying pan, add the chopped onion and celery and fry for 2 minutes. Add the rice and fry for a further 3 minutes.

Stir in the tomatoes, with their juice, bay leaf, marjoram, and salt and pepper to taste. Pour in the cold water, bring to the boil, cover and simmer for 40 minutes, until rice is tender and liquid absorbed. Remove from the heat and stir in the flaked fish, prawns and sweetcorn.

Remove the top from each pepper and reserve. Remove the core and seeds, and trim the base to level. Blanch in a pan of boiling water for 2 minutes, drain and plunge into cold water. Drain well.

Divide the rice and fish mixture between the 4 peppers. Arrange in an ovenproof dish and replace the tops. Cook in a preheated moderate oven, 180°C (350°F), Gas Mark 4, for 15 minutes. Garnish with marjoram sprigs and prawns.
Serves 4

Vegetarian Hotpot

GOOD COMPANIONS

Boiled rice is a traditional and time-honoured main course accompaniment to curries, stews and casseroles as well as being the major ingredient in dishes like paella and risotto. Try mixing in a few well-chosen wholefood grains.

To make a good well-balanced rice and grain mixture for adding to dishes like risotto or for serving as an accompaniment, mix about 25% long grain brown rice with a 75% mixture of oats, bulgar, rye, buckwheat, barley and seeds. Cook in boiling water (you will probably need a little more than usual) for 30–40 minutes.

LENTIL AND TOMATO QUICHE

cheese pastry made
with 175 g (6 oz)
flour (see Broccoli
and Cheese Flan,
page 38)
2 tablespoons oil
2 onions, chopped
2 celery sticks,
chopped
1 clove garlic, crushed
175 g (6 oz) green
lentils
1 × 397 g (14 oz)
can tomatoes
250 ml (8 fl oz)
water
3 tablespoons
chopped parsley
75 g (3 oz) Cheddar
cheese, grated
1 tablespoon sesame
seeds

Roll out the pastry on a lightly floured surface and use to line a 20 cm (8 inch) flan dish. Prick the base with a fork and chill.

Bake 'blind' in a preheated moderately hot oven, 200°C (400°F), Gas Mark 6, for 10 to 20 minutes. Remove the foil and beans and return to the oven for 5 minutes.

Meanwhile, heat the oil in a pan, add the onions, celery and garlic and fry until softened. Add the lentils, tomatoes with their juice, water and salt and pepper to taste. Cover and simmer for 1 hour, stirring occasionally, until the lentils are tender. Stir in the parsley and turn into the flan case. Sprinkle with the cheese and sesame seeds and return to the oven for 10 to 15 minutes, until the cheese is brown and bubbling.
Serves 4

Lentil and Tomato Quiche; Lentil and Mushroom Gratin

LENTIL AND MUSHROOM GRATIN

2 tablespoons oil
1 onion, chopped
1 carrot, chopped
2 celery sticks,
chopped
1 clove garlic, crushed
250 g (8 oz) red
lentils
600 ml (1 pint)
water
2 tablespoons soy
sauce
salt and pepper
MUSHROOM FILLING:
25 g (1 oz)
margarine
250 g (8 oz) flat
mushrooms, sliced
2 cloves garlic,
crushed
3 tablespoons
chopped parsley
75 g (3 oz) Cheddar
cheese, grated

Heat the oil in a pan, add the onion, carrot and celery and fry gently for 10 minutes, until softened. Add the remaining ingredients, with salt and pepper to taste. Cover and simmer for 50 minutes to 1 hour, stirring occasionally, until the lentils are tender.

Meanwhile, prepare the filling. Melt the margarine in a frying pan, add the mushrooms and fry for 2 minutes, stirring. Add the garlic, parsley, and salt and pepper to taste and mix well.

Place half the lentil mixture in an oiled shallow ovenproof dish. Spread the mushrooms over the top, then cover with the remaining lentil mixture. Top with the cheese and bake in a preheated moderately hot oven, 190°C (375°F), Gas Mark 5, for 20 to 25 minutes until golden.

Serve with salad and crusty bread.
Serves 4

LENTIL MOUSSAKA

150 ml (¼ pint) oil
1 onion, chopped
4 celery sticks,
    chopped
1 clove garlic,
    crushed
1 × 397 g (14 oz)
    can tomatoes
250 g (8 oz) green
    lentils
2 tablespoons soy
    sauce
¼ teaspoon pepper
900 ml (1½ pints)
    water
500 g (1 lb)
    aubergines
salt
TOPPING:
2 eggs, beaten
150 ml (¼ pint)
    fromage blanc
TO FINISH:
2 tablespoons grated
    Parmesan cheese

Heat 1 tablespoon of the oil in a pan, add the onion and cook until softened. Add the celery, garlic, tomatoes with their juice, lentils, soy sauce, pepper and water. Cover and simmer for 50 minutes, until cooked.

Slice the aubergines, sprinkle with salt and leave in a colander for 1 hour. Drain and pat dry.

Heat some of the remaining oil in a frying pan, add the aubergines in batches and cook on both sides until golden. Drain on kitchen paper.

Cover the base of a shallow ovenproof dish with the lentil mixture and arrange a layer of aubergine slices on top. Repeat the layers, finishing with aubergines.

Mix the topping ingredients and pour over the aubergines. Top with the cheese and bake in a preheated moderate oven, 180°C (350°F), Gas Mark 4, for 30 to 40 minutes, until golden.
Serves 4

CHEESE AND LENTIL GRATIN

1 tablespoon oil
1 onion, chopped
1 carrot, chopped
1 celery stick,
    chopped
175 g (6 oz) red
    lentils
450 ml (¾ pint)
    water
1 clove garlic, crushed
salt and pepper
2 tablespoons fresh
    wholemeal
    breadcrumbs
125 g (4 oz)
    Cheddar cheese,
    grated
2 tablespoons chopped
    parsley
1 egg, beaten
2 tablespoons sesame
    seeds
parsley sprigs

Heat the oil in a pan, add the onion and fry until softened. Add the carrot, celery, lentils, water, garlic, and salt and pepper to taste. Cover, bring to the boil, then lower the heat and simmer gently for about 20 minutes, until all the water is absorbed.

Add the breadcrumbs, three quarters of the cheese, the parsley and egg to the lentil mixture. Stir until thoroughly mixed. Spoon the mixture into a 1 litre (1½ pint) shallow ovenproof dish and smooth the top.

Sprinkle the sesame seeds and remaining cheese over the top. Bake in a preheated moderate oven, 180°C (350°F), Gas Mark 4, for 45 minutes, until the topping is crisp and golden brown.
Serves 6

Cheese and Lentil Gratin

FOR PERFECT RESULTS

Rice and pasta make wonderful fast-food meals and they couldn't be simpler to cook.

To cook dry pasta, just pop it into a saucepan of boiling, lightly salted water for the time recommended on the packet, then drain. Cooking times given by manufacturers are usually very specific since they aim for pasta that is cooked, as the Italians say, 'al dente' – which means that the pasta is tender but still has a bite to it. Fresh pasta, very popular and increasingly available, needs very little cooking – only about 3–5 minutes – in the same way as dry pasta.

Long-grain rice is also easy to cook and many people have their own favourite method for achieving the best results. A good method involves placing the rice in a pan with a pinch of salt and double its volume in water. Bring to the boil, reduce the heat and simmer for 45 minutes, keeping the lid of the pan firmly in position. By the end of the cooking time the rice grains will have absorbed all the water and be dry and separate. To serve, simply fluff with a fork.

PROVENÇALE BEAN STEW

*350 g (12 oz)
haricot beans or
pinto beans,
soaked overnight*
salt and pepper
*2 tablespoons olive
oil*
2 onions, sliced
*1 red pepper, cored,
seeded and sliced*
*1 green pepper,
cored, seeded and
sliced*
*2 cloves garlic,
crushed*
*1 × 397 g (14 oz)
can chopped
tomatoes*
*2 tablespoons tomato
paste*
*50 g (2 oz) black
olives, halved and
stoned*
*2 tablespoons
chopped parsley*

Drain the beans, place in a pan and
cover with cold water. Bring to the
boil, boil for 10 minutes, then cover
and simmer for 1 to 1¼ hours, until
almost tender, adding a pinch of salt
towards the end of cooking. Drain,
reserving 300 ml (½ pint) of the
liquid.

Heat the oil in a pan, add the
onions and fry until softened. Add
the peppers and garlic and fry gently
for 10 minutes. Add the tomatoes
with their juice, tomato paste, beans,
reserved liquid, and salt and pepper
to taste. Cover and simmer for
45 minutes, adding the olives and
parsley 5 minutes before the end of
the cooking time. Remove the
bouquet garni.

Serve with garlic bread and salad.

Serves 4

FASOLIA

*4 tablespoons olive
oil*
*1 large onion,
chopped*
*1 clove garlic,
crushed*
*250 g (8 oz) haricot
beans, soaked
overnight*
1 bouquet garni
*1 tablespoon tomato
paste*
*4 tomatoes, skinned
and chopped*
*600 ml (1 pint)
water*
salt and pepper
*2 teaspoons lemon
juice*
TO FINISH:
*thinly sliced onion
rings*
chopped parsley

Heat the oil in a pan, add the onion
and fry until pale golden. Add the
garlic, drained beans, bouquet garni,
tomato purée and tomatoes, then
pour over the water. Bring to the
boil, boil for 10 minutes, then cover
and simmer for 1¾ hours or until the
beans are tender, adding salt and
pepper to taste towards the end of
the cooking time; the liquid should
be the consistency of a thick sauce.
Remove the bouquet garni.

Add the lemon juice and turn into
a warmed serving dish. Garnish with
the onion rings and parsley.

Serves 4

ABOVE: *Provençale Bean Stew; Fasolia*

BLACK BEAN CURRY

500 g (1 lb) black
beans, soaked
overnight
3 tablespoons oil
2 onions, sliced
2 teaspoons ground
cumin
2 teaspoons ground
coriander
1 teaspoon garam
masala
1 teaspoon chilli
powder
1 cm (½ inch) piece
root ginger, chopped
4 cloves garlic, crushed
1 × 397 g (14 oz)
can tomatoes
3 celery sticks, sliced
1 teaspoon cardamom
seeds
chopped coriander

Drain the beans, place in a pan and cover with cold water. Bring to the boil, boil for 10 minutes, then cover and simmer for 1½ hours, until almost tender, adding a pinch of salt towards the end of cooking. Drain, reserving 300 ml (½ pint) of the liquid.

Heat the oil in a pan, add the onions and fry until softened. Add the cumin, ground coriander, garam masala, chilli powder, ginger and garlic and fry for 1 minute, stirring constantly. Add the reserved liquid, beans, tomatoes with their juice, celery, cardamom seeds, and salt to taste. Cover and simmer for 45 minutes, then stir in the chopped coriander. Serve with brown rice and Cucumber Raita (see page 101).
Serves 4

Black Bean Curry; Mixed Bean Casserole; Tandoori Cutlets

TANDOORI CUTLETS

250 g (8 oz) black-
eyed beans, soaked
overnight
1 tablespoon soy sauce
2 teaspoons tandoori
spice mixture
2 tablespoons
chopped coriander
8 spring onions,
chopped
2 carrots, grated
COATING:
1 teaspoon tandoori
spice mixture
50 g (2 oz)
wholemeal
breadcrumbs

Drain the beans, place in a pan and cover with cold water. Bring to the boil, boil for 10 minutes, then cover and simmer for 25 minutes, until tender. Drain well, then mash.

Add the remaining ingredients.

Shape into 8 ovals and flatten to about 1 cm (½ inch) thick. Mix the tandoori spice mixture with the breadcrumbs and use to coat the cutlets completely. Fry in hot shallow oil for 4 minutes on each side.
Serves 4

MIXED BEAN CASSEROLE

175 g (6oz) red
kidney beans,
soaked overnight
175 g (6 oz) butter
beans, soaked
overnight
2 tablespoons oil
2 onions, sliced
2 celery sticks, sliced
2 carrots, sliced
1 tablespoon
wholemeal flour
1 × 397 g (14 oz)
can tomatoes
1 tablespoon tomato
purée
1 bouquet garni
1 small wholemeal
French stick
50 g (2 oz)
margarine
1 clove garlic, crushed
1 tablespoon chopped
parsley
1 tablespoon sesame
seeds

Drain the beans, place in separate pans and cover with cold water. Bring to the boil, boil for 10 minutes, then cover and simmer for 1 hour, or until tender. Drain and reserve 150 ml (¼ pint) of the liquid.

Heat the oil in a flameproof casserole, add the onions and fry until softened. Add the celery and carrots and fry for 3 to 4 minutes. Stir in the flour. Add the remaining ingredients, with the beans, reserved liquid, salt and pepper to taste. Cover and cook in a preheated moderate oven, 180°C (350°F), Gas Mark 4, for 1 hour. Discard the bouquet garni. Increase the temperature to 200°C (400°F), Gas Mark 6.

Cut the French stick into 1 cm (½ inch) diagonal slices. Mix together the margarine, garlic, parsley, and seasoning and spread on the bread.

Arrange plain side down to cover the casserole. Sprinkle with sesame seeds. Cook for 20 minutes.
Serves 4

WALNUT AND LENTIL LOAF

1 tablespoon oil
1 onion, chopped
2 celery sticks, sliced
175 g (6 oz) green
    lentils
450 ml ($\frac{3}{4}$ pint)
    water
125 g (4 oz)
    walnuts, ground
50 g (2 oz)
    wholemeal
    breadcrumbs
2 tablespoons
    chopped parsley
1 tablespoon soy
    sauce
1 egg, beaten
salt and pepper

Heat the oil in a pan, add the onion and fry until softened. Add the celery, lentils and water and bring to the boil. Cover and simmer gently for 50 to 60 minutes, until the lentils are tender, stirring. Remove the lid for the last 10 minutes to allow the moisture to evaporate.

Mix in the ground walnuts, bread-crumbs, parsley, soy sauce, egg, and salt and pepper to taste, and mix.

Line a 500 g (1 lb) loaf tin with foil to cover the bottom and long sides. Brush with oil. Spoon the mixture into the tin, cover with foil and bake in a preheated moderately hot oven, 190°C (375°F), Gas Mark 5, for 45 to 50 minutes.

Leave in the tin for 2 minutes, before turning onto a dish.
Serves 6

HAZELNUT LOAF

2 tablespoons oil
1 onion, chopped
2 celery sticks
    chopped
1 tablespoon
    wholemeal flour
170 ml (6 fl oz)
    tomato juice
125 g (4 oz)
    hazelnuts, ground
    and browned
125 g (4 oz)
    wholemeal
    breadcrumbs
2 carrots, grated
1 tablespoon soy
    sauce
2 tablespoons
    chopped parsley
1 egg, beaten

Heat the oil in a pan, add the onion and fry until softened. Add the celery and fry for 5 minutes, stirring occasionally. Mix in the flour, then stir in the tomato juice until thickened.

Place the remaining ingredients, with salt and pepper to taste, in a bowl and add the tomato mixture, stirring until blended.

Turn into a lined and greased 500 g (1 lb) loaf tin, cover with foil and bake in a preheated moderate oven, 180°C (350°F), Gas Mark 4, for 1 hour.

Turn out onto a warmed serving dish and serve hot.
Serves 4

Walnut and Lentil Loaf; Hazelnut Loaf

Curried Rice

NUT CROQUETTES

1 tablespoon oil
1 onion, chopped
1 celery stick,
  chopped
1 clove garlic, crushed
75 g (3 oz)
  mushrooms,
  chopped
2 teaspoons ground
  coriander
2 tablespoons
  wholemeal flour
150 ml (¼ pint)
  water
1 tablespoon soy sauce
125 g (4 oz) cashew
  nuts, ground
125 g (4 oz)
  wholemeal
  breadcrumbs
2 tablespoons
  chopped parsley
wholemeal flour to
  coat

Heat the oil in a pan, add the onion and fry until softened. Add the celery, garlic and mushrooms and fry for 5 minutes, stirring occasionally. Add the coriander and fry for 1 minute, then stir in the flour. Remove from the heat and stir in the water and soy sauce until thickened. Add the cashew nuts, breadcrumbs and parsley, and salt and pepper to taste and mix well. Divide the mixture into 8 pieces, using dampened hands, then shape into croquettes.

Place the flour in a plastic bag, add the croquettes one at a time and shake until well coated. Fry in hot oil for 2 minutes on each side, until golden brown and crisp. Serve with a tomato sauce.
Serves 4

CURRIED RICE

250 g (8 oz) brown
  rice
1 litre (1¾ pints)
  water
1 onion, finely
  chopped
2 celery sticks,
  coarsely chopped
250 g (8 oz)
  tomatoes, skinned
  and chopped
1½ teaspoons salt
1½ teaspoons mild
  curry powder (or
  more to taste)
50 g (2 oz) butter,
  melted

Put the rice in a casserole and pour over the water. Leave to soak for 45 minutes.

Stir the remaining ingredients into the rice. Cook in a preheated moderate oven, 180°C (350°F), Gas Mark 4, for 1½ hours or until the rice is tender and all the liquid has been absorbed.
Serves 6

NOODLES WITH BROCCOLI AND SHELLFISH

1 head of broccoli
2 tablespoons olive
  oil
2 cloves garlic, sliced
125 g (4 oz) button
  mushrooms, sliced
250 g (8 oz) scallops
175 g (6 oz) cooked,
  peeled prawns
150 ml (¼ pint) dry
  sherry
284 ml (½ pint)
  double cream
1 tablespoon parsley
salt and pepper
500 g (1 lb)
  wholemeal
  tagliatelle

Break the broccoli into florets and cook for 1 minute; leave to cool.

Heat the oil in a wok or large frying pan, add the garlic and brown lightly. Stir in the mushrooms, scallops and prawns. Pour over the sherry. Boil rapidly until the liquid has reduced to about 2 tablespoons. Add the cream, parsley, and salt and pepper to taste.

Meanwhile, cook the tagliatelle until *al dente*; drain thoroughly.

Add the broccoli to the sauce, and heat through.

Transfer the tagliatelle to a warmed serving dish, pour over the sauce and serve immediately.
Serves 4 to 6

VEGETABLE RISOTTO

4 tablespoons oil
1 onion, chopped
175 g (6 oz) brown
  rice
3 cloves garlic, crushed
600 ml (1 pint)
  water
1 teaspoon salt
2 celery sticks, sliced
1 red pepper, cored,
  seeded and diced
250 g (8 oz) button
  mushrooms, sliced
1 × 425 g (15 oz)
  can red kidney
  beans, drained
3 tablespoons
  chopped parsley
1 tablespoon soy
  sauce
50 g (2 oz) roasted
  cashew nuts
chopped parsley

Heat 2 tablespoons of the oil in a pan, add the onion and fry until softened. Add the rice and 2 cloves garlic and cook, stirring, for 2 minutes. Add the water and salt and bring to the boil, stirring. Cover and simmer gently for 35 to 40 minutes, until all the water has been absorbed.

Heat the remaining oil in a frying pan, add the celery and red pepper and fry for 5 minutes, until softened. Add the mushrooms and remaining garlic and fry for 3 minutes.

Add the cooked rice, kidney beans, parsley, soy sauce and nuts. Cook, stirring to mix, until the beans are heated through. Serve garnished with parsley, and accompanied by a green salad.

Serves 4

TIAN

3 tablespoons olive
  oil
1 onion, chopped
2 cloves garlic, crushed
500 g (1 lb)
  courgettes, chopped
250 g (8 oz)
  spinach, cooked,
  drained and
  chopped
4 tablespoons brown
  rice, cooked
3 eggs, beaten
50 g (2 oz) Gruyère
  cheese, grated
salt and pepper
1 tablespoon fresh
  wholemeal
  breadcrumbs
1 tablespoon grated
  Parmesan cheese

Heat the oil in a frying pan, add the onion and cook until softened. Add the garlic and courgettes and cook for 5 minutes, stirring occasionally. Stir in the spinach, rice, eggs, Gruyère cheese, and salt and pepper to taste and mix well.

Turn into a greased 1.2 litre (2 pint) earthenware gratin dish and sprinkle with the breadcrumbs and Parmesan cheese.

Bake in a preheated moderate oven, 180°C (350°F), Gas Mark 4, for 35 minutes, until golden.

Serve with salad and wholemeal bread.

Serves 4

Vegetable Risotto; Tian

SPANISH RICE CASSEROLE

5 tablespoons olive oil
1 onion, finely
    chopped
1 clove garlic,
    crushed
250 g (8 oz) brown
    rice
1 tablespoon chilli
    powder (or to
    taste)
salt and pepper
125 g (4 oz) chorizo
    or garlic sausage,
    diced
125 g (4 oz) small
    button mushrooms
600 ml (1 pint)
    boiling stock
    (approximately)

Heat the oil in a flameproof casserole, add the onion and garlic and fry until softened. Stir in the rice, chilli powder, and salt and pepper to taste. Cook, stirring, until the rice is golden. Add the chorizo or garlic sausage and mushrooms and mix well. Add enough stock to come about 2.5 cm (1 inch) above the level of the rice; stir thoroughly.

Cover tightly and cook in a preheated moderate oven, 180°C (350°F), Gas Mark 4, for 40 minutes or until the rice is tender and the liquid absorbed.

Serves 4

PEANUT ROAST

3 tablespoons oil
1 onion, chopped
2 celery sticks,
    chopped
2 cloves garlic,
    crushed
250 g (8 oz)
    peanuts, ground
125 g (4 oz)
    wholemeal
    breadcrumbs
250 g (8 oz) potato,
    boiled and mashed
1 size 1 egg, beaten
1 tablespoon soy
    sauce
1 tablespoon tomato
    purée
2 tablespoons
    chopped parsley
salt and pepper
250 g (8 oz)
    mushrooms, sliced
coriander leaves to
    garnish

Heat 1 tablespoon of the oil in a pan, add the onion, celery and garlic and fry until softened.

Mix the peanuts and breadcrumbs together in a bowl. Add the fried vegetables, potato, egg, soy sauce, tomato purée, parsley, and salt and pepper to taste and mix thoroughly.

Heat the remaining oil in a pan, add the mushrooms and fry for 2 minutes, stirring.

Grease a 1 kg (2 lb) loaf tin and press in half the nut mixture. Cover with the mushrooms, then press the remaining nut mixture on top.

Cover with foil and bake in a preheated moderate oven, 180°C (350°F), Gas Mark 4, for about 1 hour.

Leave in the tin for 5 minutes, then turn out onto a warmed serving dish. Garnish with coriander and serve with a mushroom sauce.

Serves 4 to 6

LAYERED LENTIL CASSEROLE

500 g (1 lb) green
    lentils, soaked
    overnight
1 bay leaf
6 slices cooked ham
    or gammon, cut
    into strips
1 teaspoon dried
    thyme
salt and pepper
350 g (12 oz)
    cooked chicken
    meat, cut into
    strips
300 ml ($\frac{1}{2}$ pint)
    chicken stock
    (approximately)
25 g (1 oz)
    Parmesan cheese,
    grated
25 g (1 oz) dry
    wholemeal
    breadcrumbs

Drain the lentils and put into a saucepan with the bay leaf. Add fresh water to cover and bring to the boil. Simmer gently for about 1 hour or until tender. Drain the lentils, discarding the bay leaf.

Put about one third of the lentils in a greased casserole. Cover with the ham and sprinkle with half the thyme and salt and pepper to taste. Cover with another third of the lentils, then add the chicken. Sprinkle with the rest of the thyme and salt and pepper to taste.

Top with the remaining lentils and pour in the stock. Cover and cook in a preheated moderate oven, 180°C (350°F), Gas Mark 4, for 30 minutes.

Mix together the cheese and breadcrumbs and sprinkle over the top. Cook, uncovered, for 15 minutes until golden brown.

Serves 4 to 6

TORTELLINI WITH RICOTTA AND SPINACH SAUCE

125 g (4 oz) butter
250 g (8 oz) frozen
  leaf spinach,
  thawed and
  chopped
salt and pepper
500 g (1 lb) fresh
  tortellini
125 g (4 oz) Ricotta
  or curd cheese
50 g (2 oz)
  Parmesan cheese,
  grated

Heat half the butter in a large frying pan, add the spinach and toss thoroughly. Season well with salt and pepper. Sauté the spinach for 2 minutes, stirring constantly.

Cook the tortellini until *al dente*. Drain thoroughly and toss in the remaining butter.

Stir the Ricotta cheese and half of the Parmesan into the spinach mixture, then stir in the pasta. Transfer to a warmed serving dish, sprinkle with the remaining Parmesan and serve immediately.
Serves 4

BOSTON BAKED BEANS

500 g (1 lb) dried
  haricot beans,
  soaked overnight
2 litres (3½ pints)
  water
salt and pepper
75 g (3 oz) dark
  brown sugar
1 teaspoon dry
  mustard
6 tablespoons dark
  treacle
125 g (4 oz) salt
  pork, chopped
1 medium onion,
  chopped

Drain the beans and put in a saucepan with the water and ½ teaspoon salt. Bring to the boil, boil for 10 minutes, then cover and simmer for about 1 hour or until the beans are tender. Drain, reserving the liquid.

Mix together the sugar, mustard, treacle, 600 ml (1 pint) of the reserved cooking liquid, and salt and pepper to taste. Put the beans, salt pork and onion in a casserole and stir in the treacle mixture.

Cover and cook in a preheated cool oven, 150°C (300°F), Gas Mark 2, for 4 hours, stirring occasionally and adding more of the reserved cooking liquid if necessary, during cooking.
Serves 6 to 8

LEFT: *Peanut Roast*
RIGHT: *Garlic Noodles*

GARLIC NOODLES

2 tablespoons oil
75 g (3 oz) butter
1 large onion, chopped
500 g (1 lb) boneless
  chicken breasts
2–3 garlic bulbs,
  broken into cloves
300 ml (½ pint) dry
  white wine
1 teaspoon chopped
  tarragon
125 g (4 oz) button
  mushrooms, sliced
4 tablespoons
  chopped parsley
500 g (1 lb) fresh
  tagliatelle verde or
  noodles
25 g (1 oz) dried
  wholemeal
  breadcrumbs
25 g (1 oz)
  Parmesan cheese,
  grated
tarragon sprigs

Heat the oil and 50 g (2 oz) of the butter in a pan, add the onion and cook for 2 minutes, until transparent.

Cut the chicken into 5 cm (2 inch) pieces, add to the pan and brown on all sides. Add the garlic, wine, tarragon, and salt and pepper to taste, bring to the boil, cover and simmer for 30 minutes. Remove the garlic, stir in the mushrooms and cook for 2 minutes. Stir in the parsley.

Cook the pasta until *al dente*; drain thoroughly and toss in the remaining butter.

Mix the sauce and noodles together, spoon into a buttered ovenproof dish, and sprinkle with the breadcrumbs and Parmesan cheese. Bake in a preheated moderately hot oven, 200°C (400°F), Gas Mark 6, for 20 to 25 minutes, until hot and golden brown.

Garnish with tarragon, and serve immediately.
Serves 4 to 6

PUDDINGS AND DESSERTS

Dried and fresh fruit salads in glistening syrups; light, feathery mousses flavoured with cream, yogurt and honey; crisp-baked crumbles or stuffed and baked fruit; shimmering jellies or super tall-scooped ice creams – the full range of wholefood puddings and desserts is a sweet-toothed and indulgent delight.

Fruity and refreshing like Kiwi and Ginger Salad and Blackberry and Apple Mousse or rich and sustaining like Apple and Pear Crumble, Plum Crumb Pudding and Apricot Pancakes there are puddings and desserts in this section to serve after both light and hearty main course offerings.

Light on calorie laden cream, sugar and refined flours they make the very best of fruits in season, nuts ripe from harvesting, yogurt fresh from the dairy and honey sticky from the hive. Most rely upon the natural flavour of fruit sugars, honey or fruit juices for their sweetness and taste all the better for it.

So many like Date and Apple Shortcake, Summer Pudding and Red Fruit Salad can be made well ahead of eating so make ideal puddings and desserts for entertaining. While others are so simple they can be sliced and served or whisked and blended in a trice like Nut Cream, Orange Honey Fluff and Fresh Fruit Salad.

Serve in pretty bowls, tall glasses or daintily decorated china with crisp dessert wafers or biscuits, a sprinkling of nuts and seeds or a swirl of special Yogurt Snow for special endings that are sure to please.

STRAWBERRY CHEESE WITH ALMOND FINGERS

ALMOND FINGERS:
125 g (4 oz) margarine
50 g (2 oz) dark soft brown sugar
125 g (4 oz) wholemeal flour
50 g (2 oz) ground almonds, toasted
25 g (1 oz) flaked almonds, chopped
STRAWBERRY CHEESE:
2 tablespoons clear honey
175 g (6 oz) strawberries
175 g (6 oz) curd cheese

Cream the margarine and sugar together until light and fluffy. Add the flour and ground almonds and stir until the mixture binds together.

Roll out the dough to an oblong and press into an 18 × 28 cm (7 × 11 inch) baking tin. Flatten with a palette knife and prick with a fork, then sprinkle with the chopped almonds and press in lightly. Bake in a preheated moderate oven, 180°C (350°F), Gas Mark 4, for 30 to 35 minutes until pale golden. Allow to cool slightly, then mark into 20 fingers. Cool completely before removing from the tin.

Place the honey and half of the strawberries in an electric blender or food processor and work to a purée. Beat the cheese until smooth, then fold in the fruit purée. Slice the remaining strawberries, set aside 4 slices for decoration and divide the rest between individual dishes.

Spoon the strawberry cheese into the dishes, decorate with the reserved strawberry slices and serve with the almond fingers.
Serves 4

BANANA AND APRICOT YOGURT

125 g (4 oz) dried apricots, chopped
300 g (10 oz) natural yogurt
1 banana
1 tablespoon flaked almonds, toasted

Place the apricots in a bowl with the yogurt. Mix well, then cover and leave in the refrigerator overnight.

Slice the banana and fold into the yogurt mixture. Spoon into individual glasses and sprinkle with the almonds to serve.
Serves 4

*Strawberry Cheese with Almond Fingers; Highland Cream;
Banana and Apricot Yogurt*

HIGHLAND CREAM

25 g (1 oz) flaked almonds, chopped
25 g (1 oz) medium oatmeal
25 g (1 oz) wholemeal breadcrumbs
142 ml (5 fl oz) double cream
3 tablespoons whisky
2 tablespoons clear honey
150 g (5 oz) natural yogurt

Mix together the almonds, oatmeal and breadcrumbs and place on a baking sheet. Place under a preheated hot grill until golden brown, stirring frequently. Leave to cool.

Whip the cream, whisky and honey together until soft peaks form, then fold in the yogurt and the almond mixture. Spoon into individual glasses and chill until required.
Serves 6

KIWI AND GINGER SALAD

1 Ogen melon, halved and seeded
2 kiwi fruit, thinly sliced
250 g (8 oz) green grapes, halved and pipped
pinch ground ginger
6 tablespoons apple juice

Scoop the flesh from the melon halves with a melon baller, or cut into cubes, and place in a bowl with the kiwi fruit and grapes.

Mix the ginger and apple juice together and pour over the fruit. Serve in individual dishes.
Serves 4

APPLE AND GRANOLA CRUNCH

500 g (1 lb) dessert apples, peeled, cored and chopped
125 g (4 oz) dates, chopped
300 ml (½ pint) apple juice
¼ teaspoon cinnamon
142 ml (5 fl oz) double cream, whipped
75 g (3 oz) Granola (see page 147)

Place the apples, dates, apple juice and cinnamon in a pan, cover and cook, until the apples are soft. Mash with a fork and leave to cool.

Spoon half the mixture into 4 glass serving dishes, top each with half the cream, then sprinkle with three quarters of the granola. Repeat the layers, finishing with granola.
Serves 4

FRUIT AND NUT CRUMBLE

175 g (6 oz) dried
    apricots
125 g (4 oz) dried
    pitted prunes
125 g (4 oz) dried
    figs
50 g (2 oz) dried
    apples
600 ml (1 pint)
    apple juice
175 g (6 oz)
    wholemeal flour
75 g (3 oz)
    margarine
50 g (2 oz) dark soft
    brown sugar,
    sifted
50 g (2 oz)
    hazelnuts,
    chopped

Place the dried fruits in a bowl with the apple juice and leave overnight. Transfer to a saucepan and simmer for 10 to 15 minutes, until softened. Turn into an ovenproof dish.

Place the flour in a bowl and rub in the margarine until the mixture resembles breadcrumbs. Stir in the sugar and hazelnuts, then sprinkle over the fruit.

Bake in a preheated moderately hot oven, 200°C (400°F), Gas Mark 6, for 25 to 30 minutes. Serve with Yogurt Snow (see page 137).
Serves 6

Variation: For the topping, replace the hazelnuts with toasted chopped almonds or grated coconut.

ORANGE HONEY FLUFF

25 g (1 oz) honey
grated rind and juice
    of 1 orange
2 teaspoons lemon
    juice
300 g (10 oz)
    natural yogurt
2 egg whites
few strips of orange
    rind to decorate

Blend the honey with the orange and lemon juice. Stir in the grated orange rind and yogurt.

Whisk the egg whites until stiff and fold into the mixture. Spoon into 4 sundae dishes and decorate with the orange rind. Serve chilled.
Serves 4

NOTE: Do not stand for more than 1 hour or the mixture will separate.

APRICOT PANCAKES

PANCAKE BATTER:
50 g (2 oz)
    buckwheat flour
50 g (2 oz) plain
    wholemeal flour
1 egg, beaten
300 ml ($\frac{1}{2}$ pint) milk
1 tablespoon oil
oil for frying
FILLING:
350 g (12 oz) dried
    apricots, chopped
    and soaked for
    2 hours
450 ml ($\frac{3}{4}$ pint)
    apple juice
TO FINISH:
2 tablespoons clear
    honey
25 g (1 oz) flaked
    almonds, toasted

Place the flours in a bowl and make a well in the centre. Add the egg, then gradually stir in half the milk and the oil. Beat thoroughly until smooth, then add the remaining milk.

Heat a 15 cm (6 inch) omelette pan and add 1 teaspoon oil. Pour in 1 tablespoon of the batter, tilting the pan to coat the bottom evenly. Cook until the underside is brown, then turn and cook for 10 seconds. Repeat with the remaining batter, stacking the pancakes as they are cooked.

To make the filling, place the apricots and apple juice in a pan, cover and cook gently for 10 minutes.

Place a little of the filling on each pancake, roll up and arrange in an ovenproof dish. Warm the honey and spoon over the pancakes to glaze. Bake in a preheated moderate oven, 180°C (350°F), Gas Mark 4, for 10 to 15 minutes, until heated through. Sprinkle with the almonds and serve with Yogurt Snow (see page 137).
Serves 4

LEFT: *Fruit and Nut Crumble*
RIGHT: *Apple and Raisin Pie; Date and Apple Shortcake*

APPLE AND RAISIN PIE

300 g (10 oz)
    wholemeal flour
150 g (5 oz)
    margarine
4–5 tablespoons iced
    water
FILLING:
750 g (1½ lb) dessert
    apples, peeled,
    cored and thinly
    sliced
2 tablespoons light
    soft brown sugar
1 teaspoon ground
    cinnamon
4 cloves
50 g (2 oz) raisins
TO FINISH:
1 tablespoon sesame
    seeds

Place the flour in a bowl and rub in the margarine until the mixture resembles fine breadcrumbs. Stir in enough water to mix to a dough.

Turn onto a floured surface, knead lightly until smooth, then divide in half. Roll out one piece thinly and use to line a shallow 20 cm (8 inch) pie dish.

Layer the apples with the sugar, spices and raisins in the pastry case. Brush the pastry rim with water.

Roll out the remaining pastry and use to cover the pie. Seal and pinch the edges well, then trim of any surplus pastry with a sharp knife. Make a hole in the centre of the pie and chill for 20 minutes.

Brush with water and sprinkle with the sesame seeds. Bake in a preheated moderately hot oven, 200°C (400°F), Gas Mark 6, for 30 to 40 minutes, until golden. Serve warm or cold with Yogurt Snow (see page 137).
Serves 6

DATE AND APPLE SHORTCAKE

NUT PASTRY:
75 g (3 oz)
    margarine
40 g (1½ oz) dark
    soft brown sugar
125 g (4 oz)
    wholemeal flour
75 g (3 oz) brazil
    nuts, ground
egg white
1 tablespoon chopped
    brazil nuts
FILLING:
3 tablespoons apple
    juice
500 g (1 lb) dessert
    apples, peeled
125 g (4 oz) dates,
    chopped
1 teaspoon ground
    cinnamon
142 ml (5 fl oz)
    double cream,
    whipped

Beat the margarine and sugar together until softened. Stir in the flour and ground nuts and mix to a firm dough. Turn onto a floured surface; knead lightly until smooth. Divide in half and roll each piece into a 20 cm (8 inch) round on a baking sheet. Brush one with egg white and sprinkle with the nuts.

Bake in a preheated moderately hot oven, 190°C (375°F), Gas Mark 5, for 10 to 15 minutes, until golden. Cut the nut-covered round into 8 sections while warm. Transfer both rounds to a wire rack to cool.

Place the apple juice in a pan and slice the apples into it. Cover and cook gently for about 10 minutes, stirring occasionally, until just soft. Add the dates and cinnamon. Cool.

Spread the apple filling over the whole shortcake round, cover with the cream and the cut top.
Serves 8

DRIED FRUIT SALAD

175 g (6 oz) dried
    apricots
125 g (4 oz) dried
    prunes
125 g (4 oz) dried
    figs
125 g (4 oz) dried
    apples
600 ml (1 pint)
    apple juice
2 tablespoons
    Calvados or
    brandy
25 g (1 oz) walnuts,
    coarsely chopped

Place the dried fruits in a bowl with the apple juice and leave to soak overnight.

Transfer to a saucepan and simmer for 10 to 15 minutes. Turn into a glass bowl and pour over the Calvados or brandy. Sprinkle with the walnuts. Serve immediately with natural yogurt.
Serves 6
NOTE: This fruit salad can alternatively be made in advance and served cold.

NUT CREAM

125 g (4 oz) cashew
    nuts
150 ml ($\frac{1}{4}$ pint) milk

Place the nuts and milk in an electric blender and blend until smooth. Chill and serve instead of cream.
Makes about 150 ml ($\frac{1}{4}$ pint)

APPLE TOFFEE DESSERT

1 medium cooking
    apple, peeled,
    cored and chopped
1 large dessert apple,
    peeled, cored and
    chopped
50 g (2 oz)
    demerara sugar
50 g (2 oz) butter
juice of $\frac{1}{2}$ lemon
2 slices stale
    wholemeal bread,
    crusts removed, cut
    into cubes
4 tablespoons double
    cream, whipped

Sprinkle the apples with the sugar and toss well to coat evenly.

Melt half the butter in a frying pan, add the apple and fry quickly until just soft. Transfer to a warmed serving dish, using a slotted spoon. Sprinkle with the lemon juice and keep warm.

Melt the remaining butter in the pan, add the bread cubes and fry, turning, until crisp and evenly golden.

Add the bread to the apple pieces and mix well. Serve immediately, topped with whipped cream.
Serves 4

STUFFED ORANGES

2 large oranges
1 dessert apple,
    peeled, cored and
    chopped
1 tablespoon raisins
1 tablespoon chopped
    dates
1 tablespoon
    hazelnuts, toasted
    and chopped
1 tablespoon light
    soft brown sugar
120 ml (4 fl oz)
    double cream
orange twists to
    decorate (optional)

Halve the oranges and scoop out the flesh, keeping the shells intact; set aside.

Chop the orange flesh, discarding all pith, and place in a bowl. Add the apple, raisins, dates, nuts and brown sugar. Mix well and pile into the orange halves.

Whip the cream until it forms soft peaks. Spoon on top of the oranges. Chill before serving, decorated with orange twists if liked.
Serves 4

ITALIAN FRUIT SALAD

600 ml (1 pint)
    orange juice
grated rind of
    2 lemons
6 tablespoons lemon
    juice
125 g (4 oz) black
    cherries
$\frac{1}{2}$ Galia melon
3 bananas
4 nectarines
1 mango
3 peaches
125 g (4 oz) apricots
4 green dessert apples
2 pears
125 g (4 oz) white
    seedless grapes
25–50 g (1–2 oz)
    light soft brown
    sugar
10 tablespoons
    Maraschino
    liqueur

Put the orange juice, lemon rind and juice in a large bowl.

Prepare the fruit, adding to the bowl as you do so; stone the cherries, scoop the melon into small balls using a melon baller; slice the bananas; stone and slice the nectarines, mango, peaches and apricots; core and slice the apples and pears. Add the grapes and stir well.

Sprinkle over the sugar to taste and the Maraschino and stir well. Cover and chill for 1 hour.
Serves 15

YOGURT SNOW

2 egg whites
3 tablespoons clear
  honey
300 g (10 oz)
  natural yogurt

Whisk the egg whites until stiff, then whisk in the honey and continue whisking until very thick. Carefully fold in the yogurt and serve immediately, instead of cream.
Makes about 450 ml ($\frac{3}{4}$ pint)

SUMMER PUDDING

500 g (1 lb) mixed
  blackberries and
  blackcurrants
3 tablespoons clear
  honey
125 g (4 oz)
  raspberries
125 g (4 oz)
  strawberries
8 slices wholemeal
  bread, crusts
  removed

Place the blackberries, blackcurrants and honey in a heavy-based pan and cook gently for 10 to 15 minutes until tender, stirring occasionally. Add the raspberries and strawberries and leave to cool. Strain the fruit, reserving the juice.

Cut 3 circles of bread to fit the base, middle and top of a 900 ml ($1\frac{1}{2}$ pint) pudding basin. Shape the remaining bread to fit round the side of the basin. Soak all the bread in the reserved fruit juice.

Line the bottom of the basin with the smallest circle of bread, then arrange the shaped bread around the side. Pour in half the fruit and place the middle sized circle of bread on top. Cover with the remaining fruit, then top with the largest bread circle. Fold over any bread protruding from the basin.

Cover with a saucer small enough to fit inside the basin and put a 500 g (1 lb) weight on top. Leave in the refrigerator overnight.

Turn onto a serving plate, pour over any remaining fruit juice and serve with whipped cream or Yogurt Snow (above).
Serves 8

Yogurt Snow; Summer Pudding; Nut Cream

ORANGE SALAD

6 large juicy oranges
2 tablespoons gin
125 g (4 oz) light
    soft brown sugar

Pare the rind from one orange and cut it into thin shreds. Peel the remaining oranges and remove the white pith from all six. Slice the oranges and put into a serving bowl. Sprinkle over the gin.

Put the sugar and shredded rind into a saucepan and heat gently, stirring until the sugar has melted. Continue heating until the syrup is golden brown and begins to bubble, then pour quickly over the oranges.

Leave for 30 minutes, then chill. Serve with single cream.

Serves 6

RED FRUIT SALAD

4 tablespoons clear
    honey
150 ml (¼ pint) red
    wine
150 ml (¼ pint)
    orange juice
250 g (8 oz)
    blackcurrants
250 g (8 oz)
    strawberries
250 g (8 oz)
    raspberries
1 tablespoon
    arrowroot

Place the honey, wine and orange juice in a pan. Add the blackcurrants, bring to the boil, cover and simmer for 10 minutes, until soft.

Strain the fruit, reserving the syrup. Place the blackcurrants in a bowl and add the remaining fruit.

Return the syrup to the pan and bring to the boil. Blend the arrowroot with a little cold water and stir into the boiling syrup. Cook, stirring, until the syrup is clear. Pour over the fruit, leave to cool then chill.

Serve with whipped cream.

Serves 8

Oatmeal and Yogurt Cream

PEARS EN COMPOTE

500 g (1 lb) fresh
    pears, peeled,
    cored and halved
300 ml (½ pint) red
    wine
150 ml (¼ pint)
    water
2 teaspoons ground
    cinnamon
50 g (2 oz) dates,
    chopped

Place the pears, wine, water and cinnamon in a pan. Bring to the boil, then lower the heat, cover and simmer for 10 minutes.

Add the dates, remove from the heat and leave to cool. Serve chilled, with cream if liked.

Serves 4

BAKED BANANAS

50 g (2 oz) butter
2 tablespoons light
    soft brown sugar
2 tablespoons lemon
    juice
4 bananas
2 tablespoons brandy

Put the butter, sugar and lemon juice in a shallow casserole. Place in a preheated moderate oven, 180°C (350°F), Gas Mark 4, for a few minutes until melted.

Cut the bananas into large pieces and arrange in the casserole, turning to coat with the sauce. Add the brandy, cover and return to the oven for 30 minutes.

Serve with single cream.

Serves 4

BLACKCURRANT ICE CREAM

1.5 kg (3 lb)
  blackcurrants
550 g (1 lb 2 oz)
  light soft brown
  sugar
900 ml (1½ pints)
  water
grated rind and juice
  of 1 lemon
1.25 litres (2¼ pints)
  double cream,
  lightly whipped

Place the blackcurrants in a large pan, with the sugar, water, lemon rind and juice. Bring to the boil, cover and simmer for 12 to 15 minutes, until the fruit is soft.

Leave to cool, then place the fruit and syrup in a food processor or an electric blender and work until smooth. Rub through a nylon sieve to remove pips. Fold the fruit purée into the cream.

Spoon the mixture into a rigid freezerproof container and freeze until firm. Remove from the freezer and whisk well. Refreeze for 2 hours, the whisk again. Return the ice cream to the container, cover, seal and freeze until firm.

Transfer to the refrigerator 30 minutes before serving to soften. Spoon into chilled dishes to serve.
Serves 12 to 16

Fresh Fruit Salad

OATMEAL AND YOGURT CREAM

40 g (1½ oz)
  blanched almonds,
  finely chopped
40 g (1½ oz)
  medium oatmeal
25 g (1 oz)
  muscovado sugar
grated rind and juice
  of ½ lemon
150 g (5 oz) natural
  yogurt
142 ml (5 fl oz)
  double cream,
  whipped
1 tablespoon flaked
  almonds, roasted

Mix together the chopped almonds and oatmeal. Spread on a baking sheet and place under a preheated hot grill for about 2 minutes, stirring frequently to brown evenly. Leave to cool.

Mix the sugar with the lemon rind and juice. Stir into the yogurt along with the almond mixture, then fold in the cream.

Spoon into individual glass dishes and chill until required. Decorate with the flaked almonds to serve.
Serves 4

FRESH FRUIT SALAD

2 tablespoons honey
120 ml (4 fl oz)
  water
thinly pared rind and
  juice of 1 lemon
1 red dessert apple,
  quartered and
  cored
1 pear, quartered and
  cored
1 banana
1 small pineapple
2 oranges
125 g (4 oz) black
  grapes, halved and
  seeded
125 g (4 oz)
  strawberries, sliced

Place the honey, water and lemon rind in a small pan. Bring to the boil, simmer for 2 minutes, then strain and leave to cool. Stir in the lemon juice.

Slice the apple, pear and banana into a bowl, pour over the lemon syrup and stir to coat the fruit.

Peel the pineapple with a sharp knife and cut the flesh into sections, discarding the central core.

Peel the oranges, removing all pith, and divide into segments. Add to the bowl with the pineapple, grapes and strawberries and mix.

Turn into a glass dish and chill until required.
Serves 8

FROZEN BUTTERSCOTCH MOUSSE

125 g (4 oz) light
  soft brown sugar
25 g (1 oz) butter
pinch of salt
120 ml (4 fl oz)
  water
4 egg yolks
250 ml (8 fl oz)
  double cream
1½ teaspoons vanilla
  essence

Put the sugar, butter and salt in a saucepan. Stir until the sugar has dissolved and the butter melted, then bring to the boil. Boil for 1 minute. Stir in the water and cook until the butterscotch mixture is smooth and syrupy.

Beat the egg yolks in a heatproof bowl. Gradually beat in the butterscotch syrup. Place the bowl over a pan of simmering water and heat, beating, until the mixture is light and fluffy. Cool.

Whip the cream with the vanilla essence until thick. Fold into the butterscotch mixture. Pour into a decorative freezerproof mould and freeze until firm.

Transfer the mousse to the refrigerator 30 minutes before serving. To turn out, dip the mould quickly into hot water and invert onto a serving plate; the mousse should slide out. Serve with fresh soft fruit.
Serves 6

BLACKCURRANT BRÛLÉE

500 g (1 lb)
  blackcurrants
1 tablespoon water
1 tablespoon honey
142 ml (5 fl oz)
  fresh sour cream
25 g (1 oz) light soft
  brown sugar
15 g (½ oz) flaked
  almonds

Remove the stalks from the blackcurrants and wash well. Place in a pan with the water and cook gently until soft. Add honey to taste.

Divide the fruit between 4 heatproof dishes, then place in the refrigerator to chill thoroughly.

Top with the cream and sprinkle with the sugar and almonds. Place under a preheated moderate grill until the sugar has melted and the almonds are brown. Serve immediately.
Serves 4

STUFFED GRAPEFRUIT

2 grapefruit
1 orange, peeled
1 tablespoon raisins
1 tablespoon chopped
  dates
1 tablespoon
  almonds, toasted
  and chopped
1 tablespoon clear
  honey
120 ml (4 fl oz)
  double cream
orange twists to
  decorate (optional)

Halve the grapefruit and scoop out the flesh, keeping the shells intact; set aside.

Chop the grapefruit and orange flesh, discarding all pith, and place in a bowl. Add the raisins, dates, nuts and clear honey. Mix well and pile into the grapefruit halves.

Whip the cream until it forms soft peaks. Spoon on top of the fruit. Chill before serving, decorated with orange twists if liked.
Serves 4

Frozen Butterscotch Mousse

STRAWBERRY MOULD

250 g (8 oz) cottage
  cheese, sieved
150 g (5 oz) natural
  yogurt
250 g (8 oz)
  strawberries,
  puréed
15 g (½ oz) gelatine
3 tablespoons water
a little honey
2 egg whites
125 g (4 oz) fresh
  sliced strawberries,
  to decorate

Mix together the cottage cheese, yogurt and strawberry purée.

Dissolve the gelatine in the water in a bowl over a pan of gently simmering water. Cool, then fold into the cheese mixture with a little honey to taste.

Whisk the egg whites until stiff and fold into the mixture. Pour into a 20 cm (8 inch) loose bottom flan tin. Chill until set.

Remove from the tin, place on a serving plate and decorate with the strawberries.

Serves 6

APRICOT AND BANANA COMPOTE

125 g (4 oz) dried
  apricots
2 bananas
2 teaspoons lemon
  juice
25 g (1 oz) raisins
150 g (5 oz) natural
  yogurt
grated nutmeg

Wash the apricots, place in a bowl and cover with cold water. Leave to soak overnight.

Slice the bananas and toss in the lemon juice. Place the apricots in a bowl with a little of the soaking liquid. Add the bananas and raisins, then divide the fruit between 4 glass serving dishes.

Spoon the yogurt over the fruit and sprinkle with grated nutmeg. Chill before serving.

Serves 4

CREAM TOPPINGS

Whipped cream, delicious and indulgent though it is, is wickedly high in fat. However, you can make a lighter more healthy topping for fruits, puddings, desserts and baked treats if you add the stiffly whisked white of an egg to about 300 ml (½ pint) whipped double cream. Alternatively, mix whipped double cream with about half as much again of set natural yogurt for a lower-fat cream topping that has a refreshing taste. For extra colour and flavour add a set fruit yogurt or a teaspoon of honey.

BLACKBERRY AND APPLE MOUSSE

250 g (8 oz)
  blackberries
250 g (8 oz) apples,
  peeled, cored and
  sliced
6 tablespoons water
a little honey
15 g (½ oz) gelatine
1 tablespoon lemon
  juice
2 egg whites
TO DECORATE:
120 ml (4 fl oz)
  whipping cream,
  whipped
  (optional)
few blackberries

Wash the blackberries and place in a pan with the apples and 2 tablespoons of the water. Cook gently until the fruit is soft, then add honey to taste. Leave to cool, then pass through a sieve to make a purée and remove the pips.

Dissolve the gelatine in the remaining water, in a bowl placed over a pan of gently simmering water. Stir in the lemon juice and leave to cool. Add the gelatine to the fruit and blend thoroughly.

Whisk the egg whites until stiff and fold into the mixture. Pour into 4 serving dishes and leave until set.

Decorate with the whipped cream, if using, and blackberries.

Serves 4

GOOSEBERRY MERINGUE

500 g (1 lb)
  gooseberries
1 tablespoon water
a little honey
2 egg whites
75 g (3 oz) light soft
  brown sugar

Top and tail the gooseberries and wash well. Place in a pan with the water. Cook gently until the fruit is soft, then add honey to taste. Spoon into a 900 ml (1½ pint) ovenproof dish.

Whisk the egg whites until stiff, then whisk in half the sugar. Fold in the remaining sugar with a metal spoon and pile or pipe the meringue over the gooseberries. Place in a preheated moderate oven, 180°C (350°F), Gas Mark 4, for 15 minutes or until the meringue is just turning brown. Serve hot or cold.

Serves 4

APPLE AND PEAR CRUMBLE

250 g (8 oz) apples,
peeled, cored and
sliced
250 g (8 oz) pears,
peeled, cored and
sliced
grated rind of
1 lemon
½ teaspoon ground
cinnamon
1 tablespoon water
1 tablespoon honey
TOPPING:
75 g (3 oz) Swiss-
style muesli
25 g (1 oz) porridge
oats

Place the apples and pears in a pan with the lemon rind, cinnamon, water and honey. Cook gently until the fruit is soft, but not pulpy. Spoon into a 1.2 litre (2 pint) ovenproof dish.

Mix together the muesli and porridge oats and pile on top of the fruit. Cook in a preheated moderately hot oven, 190°C (375°F), Gas Mark 5, for 15 minutes or until the topping is crisp. Serve hot.
Serves 4

CINNAMON PLUMS

250 g (8 oz) dessert
plums
1 teaspoon ground
cinnamon
2 egg yolks
300 g (10 oz)
natural yogurt
½ teaspoon vanilla
essence
1 tablespoon honey
25 g (1 oz)
cornflakes, crushed

Cut the plums in half, discard the stones and place in a 600 ml (1 pint) ovenproof dish or 4 individual dishes. Sprinkle the plums with ½ teaspoon cinnamon.

Beat the egg yolks with the yogurt, vanilla essence and honey and pour over the plums.

Place in a roasting pan and add water to come halfway up the dish(es). Cook in a preheated moderate oven, 180°C (350°F), Gas Mark 4, for 30 minutes or until set.

Mix the cornflakes with the remaining cinnamon and sprinkle over the custard. Serve hot or cold.
Serves 4

SOMERSET PEARS

200 ml (⅓ pint) dry
cider
2 teaspoons lemon
juice
½ teaspoon ground
cinnamon
pinch of grated
nutmeg
grated rind of
1 orange
4 dessert pears
1 tablespoon honey

Place the cider, lemon juice, cinnamon, nutmeg and orange rind in a pan. Bring to the boil, cover and simmer for 5 minutes.

Peel the pears, cut in half and remove and core. Place in the liquid and poach for 20 to 30 minutes or until soft. Add honey to taste.

Lift the pears into a serving dish and pour the liquid over. Serve hot or cold with natural yogurt or single cream.
Serves 4

LEFT: *Apple and Pear Crumble*
RIGHT: *Fruit Brulée*

CITRUS SORBET

2 grapefruit
  (preferably pink)
1 envelope gelatine,
  dissolved in
  2 tablespoons water
600 ml (1 pint)
  grapefruit juice
25 g (1 oz) light soft
  brown sugar
150 g (5.2 oz)
  natural yogurt
2 egg whites, stiffly
  beaten
8 mint sprigs to
  decorate

Finely grate the rind from both grapefruits. Place in a large bowl and add just enough boiling water to cover. Leave to soak for 5 minutes, then drain.

Cut the grapefruits in half and squeeze thoroughly so that the flesh comes out with the juice. Add to the soaked rind, together with the dissolved gelatine, grapefruit juice, sugar and yogurt. Stir well, then transfer to a rigid frezerproof container, cover with clingfilm and freeze for about 1 hour, until just beginning to freeze around the edge. Whisk, then fold in the egg whites. Partly freeze and whisk twice more. Cover, seal and freeze until firm.

Transfer to the refrigerator 10 minutes before serving to soften. Scoop into chilled glasses and decorate with mint sprigs.
Serves 8

PLUM CRUMB PUDDING

1 kg (2 lb) plums,
  stoned
25 g (1 oz) light soft
  brown sugar
300 ml ($\frac{1}{2}$ pint)
  water
175 g (6 oz)
  wholemeal
  breadcrumbs
50 g (2 oz)
  demerara sugar
50 g (2 oz) butter
TO SERVE:
142 ml (5 fl oz)
  double cream,
  whipped
15 g ($\frac{1}{2}$ oz) flaked
  almonds
  (optional)

Place the plums, sugar and water in a saucepan and cook until soft; cool. Mix the breadcrumbs and sugar together. Melt the butter in a pan, add the crumb mixture and fry until crisp; cool. Layer the plums and crumbs alternately in a pudding dish.

Cook in a preheated moderately hot oven, 190°C (375°F), Gas Mark 5, for 30 minutes. Cover the top thickly with whipped cream and decorate with almonds, if liked.
Serves 6

FRUIT BRÛLÉE

3 tablespoons light
  soft brown sugar
  (or to taste)
6 tablespoons water
1 tablespoon lemon
  juice
750 g–1 kg
  (1$\frac{1}{2}$–2 lb) mixed
  fruit in season
  (strawberries,
  peaches, bananas,
  apples, pears,
  grapes, etc.), cored
  and sliced
284 ml (10 fl oz)
  double cream
4 tablespoons dark
  soft brown sugar

Dissolve the light soft brown sugar in the water in a small saucepan. Stir in the lemon juice and remove from the heat.

Put the prepared fruit into a flameproof serving dish and stir in the sugar syrup. Press the fruit down to level the top. Whip the cream until stiff and spread over the fruit. Chill until just before serving.

To serve, sprinkle the cream with the dark, soft brown sugar and grill until the sugar melts. Serve immediately.
Serves 4 to 6

WHOLEGRAIN BAKING

Wholegrain baking – making the most of wholemeal flour, crunchy nuts and seeds, dried and fresh fruits, wholegrains, honey and natural unrefined sugar – is wholesome healthy baking that reflects all that is good for you.

Natural, light, crunchy or crumbly, the selection of cakes, biscuits, breads and savoury bakes found here have a special heartiness that shouldn't be confused in the slightest with heaviness.

Newcomers to this style of baking will notice at once the special golden colour and appearance of items baked the wholegrain way and will quickly appreciate the subtle sweetening power of molasses, honey, syrups and dried fruit instead of white refined sugar. The unmistakable nuttiness and delicious textures of these bakes comes from using wholegrain flours where the bran is retained for its valuable fibre.

Wholegrain baking isn't so very different from traditional white flour baking and follows more or less the same ground rules on preparation and baking. It is important to remember, however, if sifting flour to tip the bran back into the bowl from the sieve and that a little extra liquid may be required in mixing. As an added bonus storage times are often improved but there will be little need to hoard such delicious baked fare.

The selection presented here is comprehensive from plain breads to teabreads, biscuits to cookies and cakes to scones – but remember any recipe using white flour can almost invariably be given the wholemeal treatment, if in doubt make a gradual halfway start by replacing say half of the white flour with wholemeal and half of the white sugar with unrefined and a little extra liquid if necessary.

SESAME THINS

175 g (6 oz)
wholemeal flour
50 g (2 oz) medium
oatmeal
pinch of salt
1 teaspoon baking
powder
75 g (3 oz)
margarine
1 tablespoon malt
extract
2 tablespoons milk
25 g (1 oz) sesame
seeds

Place the flour, oatmeal and salt in a mixing bowl and sift in the baking powder; mix well. Rub in the margarine until the mixture resembles breadcrumbs.

Whisk the malt and milk together until blended, then add to the dry ingredients with the sesame seeds. Mix to a firm dough.

Turn onto a floured surface and roll out thinly. Cut into 6 cm (2½ inch) rounds with a plain cutter.

Place on a baking sheet and bake in a preheated moderately hot oven, 190°C (375°F), Gas Mark 5, for 12 to 15 minutes, until golden. Transfer to a wire rack to cool.
Makes 20 to 24

WHOLEMEAL BREAD

1.5 kg (3 lb)
wholemeal flour
1 tablespoon salt
25 g (1 oz) fresh
yeast
900 ml (1½ pints)
warm water
2 tablespoons malt
extract
2 tablespoons oil
1 tablespoon sesame
seeds

Mix the flour and salt together in a bowl. Mix the yeast with a little of the water and leave until frothy. Add to the flour with the remaining water, malt extract and oil. Mix to a dough.

Turn onto a floured surface and knead for 8 to 10 minutes, until smooth and elastic. Place in a clean bowl, cover with a damp cloth and leave to rise in a warm place for about 2 hours, until doubled in size.

Turn onto a floured surface, knead for a few minutes, then divide into 2 pieces. Shape and place in greased 1 kg (2 lb) loaf tins. Brush with water and sprinkle with the sesame seeds.

Cover and leave to rise in a warm place for about 30 minutes, until the dough just reaches the top of the tins. Bake in a preheated hot oven, 220°C (425°F), Gas Mark 7, for 15 minutes, then lower the temperature to 190°C (375°F), Gas Mark 5, and bake for a further 20 to 25 minutes, until the bread sounds hollow when tapped underneath. Turn onto a wire rack to cool.
Makes two 1 kg (2 lb) loaves

Wholemeal Baps: Use ½ quantity dough, replacing half the water with warm milk. Divide the risen dough into 12 equal pieces. Knead each piece into a ball, then roll into a 10 cm (4 inch) round and place on floured baking sheets. Sprinkle with sesame seeds or flour. Cover and leave to rise until doubled in size. Bake in a preheated hot oven, 220°C (425°F), Gas Mark 7, for 10 to 15 minutes. Cool on a wire rack.

LEFT: *Wholemeal Bread; Sesame Thins*
RIGHT: *Granola; Granary Loaf*

GRANOLA

120 ml (4 fl oz)
  safflower oil
6 tablespoons malt
  extract
6 tablespoons clear
  honey
250 g (8 oz) rolled
  oats
250 g (8 oz) jumbo
  oats (large oat
  flakes)
125 g (4 oz)
  hazelnuts
25 g (1 oz)
  desiccated coconut
50 g (2 oz)
  sunflower seeds
25 g (1 oz) sesame
  seeds

Place the oil, malt and honey in a large pan and heat gently until the malt is runny. Mix in the remaining ingredients and stir thoroughly.

Turn into a large roasting pan and bake in a preheated moderately hot oven, 190°C (375°F), Gas Mark 5, for 30 to 35 minutes, stirring occasionally. Leave to cool, then separate the pieces with your fingers.

Store in an airtight container. Serve with natural yogurt at breakfast time, or use as a topping for stewed fruits.
Makes 1 kg (2 lb)

GRANARY LOAF

250 g (8 oz)
  Granary flour
250 g (8 oz)
  wholemeal flour
1 teaspoon salt
15 g (½ oz) fresh
  yeast
300 ml (½ pint)
  warm water
1 tablespoon malt
  extract
1 tablespoon oil
cracked wheat for
  sprinkling

Mix the flours and salt together in a bowl. Cream the yeast with a little of the water and leave until frothy. Add to the flour with the remaining water, malt and oil and mix to a dough.

Turn onto a floured surface. Knead for 5 minutes, until smooth and elastic. Place in a clean bowl, cover with a damp cloth and leave to rise in a warm place until doubled in size.

Turn onto a floured surface and knead for a few minutes. Shape into an 18 cm (7 inch) round and flatten slightly. Place on a greased baking sheet. Brush with water and sprinkle with cracked wheat. Cover and leave to rise in a warm place for about 30 minutes, until doubled in size.

Bake in a preheated moderately hot oven, 220°C (425°F), Gas Mark 7, for 25 to 30 minutes. Cool on a wire rack.
Makes 1 granary loaf

RYE BREAD

350 g (12 oz) rye
  flour
500 g (1 lb)
  wholemeal flour
2 teaspoons salt
25 g (1 oz) fresh
  yeast
450–600 ml
  ($\frac{4}{3}$–1 pint) warm
  water
2 tablespoons black
  treacle
2 tablespoons oil
milk for brushing
1 teaspoon caraway
  seeds

Mix the flours and salt together in a bowl. Cream the yeast with a little of the water and leave until frothy. Add to the flour mixture with the remaining water, treacle and oil and mix thoroughly to a firm dough.

Turn onto a floured surface and knead for 5 minutes until smooth and elastic. Place in a clean bowl, cover with a damp cloth and leave to rise in a warm place for 2 hours, until doubled in size.

Turn onto a floured surface and knead for a few minutes. Shape into 2 oval loaves and place on greased baking sheets. Prick with a fork in 8 or 9 places. Leave to rise in a warm place for 1½ hours, until doubled in size.

Brush with milk and sprinkle with caraway seeds. Bake in a preheated hot oven, 220°C (425°F), Gas Mark 7, for 15 minutes. Lower the heat to 190°C (375°F), Gas Mark 5, and bake for a further 30 to 40 minutes. Cool on a wire rack.

Makes 2 loaves

ABOVE: *Rye Bread; Malted Wholemeal Loaf*

MALTED WHOLEMEAL LOAF

1.5 kg (3 lb)
  wholemeal flour
50 g (2 oz) fine
  oatmeal
1 tablespoon salt
25 g (1 oz) fresh
  yeast
900 ml–1.2 litres
  (1½–2 pints)
  warm water
2 tablespoons malt
  extract
2 tablespoons oil
2 tablespoons rolled
  oats

Mix the flour, oatmeal and salt together in a bowl.

Mix the yeast with a little of the water and leave until frothy. Add to the flour with the remaining water, malt extract and oil and mix to a smooth dough.

Turn onto a floured surface and knead for 8 to 10 minutes until smooth and elastic. Place in a clean bowl, cover with a damp cloth and leave to rise in a warm place for about 2 hours, until doubled in size.

Turn onto a floured surface, knead for a few minutes, then divide into 4 pieces. Shape and place in greased 500 g (1 lb) loaf tins. Brush with water and sprinkle with the oats.

Cover and leave to rise in a warm place for about 30 minutes, until the dough just reaches the top of the tins. Bake in a preheated hot oven, 220°C (425°F), Gas Mark 7, for 15 minutes.

Lower the temperature to 190°C (375°F), Gas Mark 5, and bake for a further 20 to 25 minutes. Turn onto a wire rack to cool.

Makes four 500 g (1 lb) loaves

WHOLEMEAL STICK

250 g (8 oz)
   Granary flour
250 g (8 oz)
   wholemeal flour
1 teaspoon salt
15 g (½ oz) fresh
   yeast
300 ml (½ pint)
   warm water
1 tablespoon malt
   extract
1 tablespoon oil
cracked wheat for
   sprinkling

Mix the flours and salt in a bowl.

Cream the yeast with a little of the water and leave until frothy. Add to the flour with the remaining water, malt extract and oil; mix to a soft dough.

Turn onto a floured surface and knead for 5 minutes until smooth and elastic. Place in a clean bowl, cover with a damp cloth and leave to rise in a warm place for about 1½ hours until doubled in size.

Turn onto a floured surface and knead for a few minutes. Shape into a long stick and place on a greased baking sheet. Make slits slantwise along the length of the stick. Brush with water and sprinkle with cracked wheat. Cover and leave to rise in a warm place for about 30 minutes until almost doubled in size.

Bake in a preheated hot oven, 220°C (425°F), Gas Mark 7, for 25 to 30 minutes or until it sounds hollow when tapped. Cool on a wire rack.
Makes 1 wholemeal stick

Wholemeal Stick; Herb and Onion Bread

HERB AND ONION BREAD

750 g (1½ lb)
   wholemeal flour
2 teaspoons salt
15 g (½ oz) fresh
   yeast
450 ml (¾ pint)
   water
1 large onion, minced
1 tablespoon each
   chopped parsley,
   thyme and sage
1 tablespoon oil
1 tablespoon sesame
   seeds

Mix the flour and salt together in a bowl. Cream the yeast with a little of the water and leave until frothy. Add to the flour with the remaining water, the onions, herbs and oil and mix to a dough.

Turn onto a floured surface and knead for 8 to 10 minutes until smooth and elastic. Place in a clean bowl, cover with a damp cloth and leave to rise in a warm place for about 1½ hours, until doubled in size.

Turn onto a floured surface and knead for a few minutes. Form into a fairly wide roll and place on a greased baking sheet. Brush with water and sprinkle with sesame seeds.

Cover and leave to rise in a warm place for about 30 minutes, until almost doubled in size.

Bake in a preheated hot oven, 220°C (425°F), Gas Mark 7, for 15 minutes. Lower the temperature to 190°C (375°F), Gas Mark 5, and bake for a further 20 to 25 minutes, until the bread sounds hollow when tapped. Turn onto a wire rack.
Makes 1 loaf

LIGHT RYE BREAD

250 g (8 oz) rye
  flour
500 g (1 lb)
  wholemeal flour
2 teaspoons fine sea
  salt
15 g (½ oz) fresh
  yeast
450 ml (¾ pint)
  warm water
2 tablespoons
  molasses
2 tablespoons oil
milk for brushing
1 teaspoon caraway
  seeds

Mix the flours and salt together in a bowl. Cream the yeast with a little of the water and leave until frothy. Add to the flour mixture with the remaining water, molasses and oil.

Turn onto a floured surface and knead for 5 minutes, until smooth and elastic. Place in a clean bowl, cover with a damp cloth and leave to rise in a warm place for about 2 hours, until doubled in size.

Turn onto a floured surface and knead for a few minutes. Shape into 2 oval loaves and place on greased baking sheets. Prick with a fork in 8 or 9 places, then leave to rise in a warm place for 30 minutes.

Brush with milk, sprinkle with the caraway seeds and bake in a preheated hot oven, 220°C (425°F), Gas Mark 7, for 10 minutes. Lower the heat to 190°C (375°F), Gas Mark 5, and bake for a further 25 to 30 minutes, until the loaves sound hollow when tapped underneath. Cool on a wire rack.

Makes 2 loaves

Buckwheat Plait: Use buckwheat flour and whole buckwheat instead of rye flour and caraway seeds.

To shape the plait, cut the dough in half, then cut each half into 3 equal pieces. Shape the pieces into long thin 'sausages'. Take 3 'sausages', moisten one end of each with water and press together; plait, dampening the ends to join. Repeat with the remaining 3 'sausages' to make 2 loaves.

Leave to rise in a warm place for 30 minutes, until doubled in size. Bake in a preheated hot oven, 220°C (425°F), Gas Mark 7, for 10 minutes, then lower the heat to 190°C (375°F), Gas Mark 5, and bake for a further 15 to 20 minutes. Cool on a rack.

Light Rye Bread; Buckwheat Plait

MUESLI CAKE

175 g (6 oz) muesli
125 g (4 oz)
  molasses sugar
175 g (6 oz)
  sultanas
2 tablespoons malt
  extract
250 ml (8 fl oz)
  apple juice
2 cooking apples,
  peeled and grated
175 g (6 oz)
  wholemeal flour
3 teaspoons baking
  powder
8 walnut halves

Place the muesli, sugar, sultanas, malt extract and apple juice in a mixing bowl and leave to soak for 30 minutes. Add the apple and flour, sift in the baking powder and mix together thoroughly.

Turn into a lined and greased 18 cm (7 inch) round cake tin and arrange the walnuts around the edge. Bake in a preheated moderate oven, 180°C (350°F), Gas Mark 4, for 1½ to 1¾ hours, or until a skewer inserted into the centre comes out clean. Leave in the tin for a few minutes, then turn onto a wire rack to cool.
Makes one 18 cm (7 inch) cake

NUTTY FLAPJACKS

125 g (4 oz)
  margarine
120 ml (4 fl oz)
  clear honey
75 g (3 oz)
  muscovado or dark
  soft brown sugar
250 g (8 oz) rolled
  oats
50 g (2 oz) walnuts,
  chopped

Melt the margarine with the honey and sugar in a pan. Stir in the oats and walnuts and mix thoroughly. Turn into a greased 18 × 28 cm (7 × 11 inch) shallow tin and smooth the top with a palette knife.

Bake in a preheated moderate oven, 180°C (350°F), Gas Mark 4, for 25 to 30 minutes.

Cool in the tin for 2 minutes, then cut into fingers. Cool completely before removing from the tin.
Makes 20

Muesli Cake; Nutty Flapjacks

Banana and Walnut Slices

MALTED CHOCOLATE CAKE

175 g (6 oz) molasses sugar
2 eggs
120 ml (4 fl oz) corn oil
120 ml (4 fl oz) milk
2 tablespoons malt extract
175 g (6 oz) wholemeal flour
25 g (1 oz) cocoa powder
2 teaspoons baking powder
125 g (4 oz) curd cheese
75 g (3 oz) plain chocolate

Place the sugar, eggs, oil, milk and malt extract in a bowl and mix thoroughly. Add the flour, sift in the cocoa and baking powder and beat until smooth.

Divide the mixture between two lined and greased 18 cm (7 inch) sandwich tins and smooth with a palette knife.

Bake in a preheated moderate oven, 160°C (325°F), Gas Mark 3, for 25 to 30 minutes until the cakes spring back when lightly pressed. Turn onto a wire rack to cool.

Beat the cheese in a bowl until smooth. Melt the chocolate in a basin over a pan of hot water, add to the cheese and beat thoroughly.

Use half the mixture to sandwich the cakes together. Spread the remainder over the top of the cake and mark a swirl pattern, using a palette knife.

Makes one 18 cm (7 inch) cake

BANANA AND WALNUT SLICES

125 g (4 oz) margarine or butter
125 g (4 oz) molasses sugar
2 eggs
125 g (4 oz) wholemeal flour
2 teaspoons baking powder
2 bananas, mashed
125 g (4 oz) walnuts, chopped

Cream the fat and molasses together until light and fluffy. Beat in the eggs, one at a time, adding a tablespoon of flour with the second egg. Fold in the remaining flour and baking powder with the bananas.

Spread the mixture evenly in a lined and greased 20 cm (8 inch) square shallow tin. Sprinkle with the walnuts and bake in a preheated moderately hot oven, 190°C (375°F), Gas Mark 5, for 20 to 25 minutes until the cake springs back when lightly pressed.

Leave in the tin for 2 minutes, then cut into 16 slices. Transfer to a wire rack to cool.

Makes 16 slices

CASHEW FINGERS

125 g (4 oz) margarine
90 ml (3 fl oz) clear honey
1 tablespoon malt extract
250 g (8 oz) rolled oats
50 g (2 oz) cashew nuts, chopped

Place the margarine, honey and malt extract in a pan and heat gently until melted. Remove from the heat, stir in the rolled oats and cashew nuts and mix thoroughly. Turn into a greased shallow 18 × 28 cm (7 × 11 inch) tin and smooth the top with a palette knife.

Bake in a preheated moderate oven, 180°C (350°F), Gas Mark 4, for 25 to 30 minutes.

Cool in the tin for 2 minutes, then cut into fingers. Allow to cool completely before removing the flapjacks from the tin.

Makes 20

RIGHT: *Sesame and Oat Biscuits; Sesame Snaps; Malted Oat Fingers*

SESAME AND OAT BISCUITS

75 g (3 oz) rolled
  oats
50 g (2 oz) medium
  oatmeal
2 tablespoons sesame
  seeds, toasted
75 g (3 oz) molasses
  sugar
120 ml (4 fl oz) oil
1 egg beaten

Place the oats, oatmeal, sesame seeds, sugar and oil in a mixing bowl. Stir well and leave to stand for 1 hour. Add the egg and mix thoroughly.

Place teaspoonfuls of the mixture well apart on a greased baking sheet and flatten with a palette knife.

Bake in a preheated moderate oven, 160°C (325°F), Gas Mark 3, for 15 to 20 minutes until golden brown. Leave to cool for 2 minutes then transfer to a wire rack to cool completely.

Makes about 25

SESAME SNAPS

175 g (6 oz)
  medium oatmeal
50 g (2 oz) sesame
  seeds, roasted
6 tablespoons clear
  honey
6 tablespoons oil
50 g (2 oz)
  muscovado or dark
  soft brown sugar

Place all the ingredients in a bowl and mix thoroughly. Press into a greased 20 × 30 cm (8 × 12 inch) Swiss roll tin and smooth the top with a palette knife.

Bake in a preheated moderate oven, 180°C (350°F), Gas Mark 4, for 20 to 25 minutes. Cool in the tin for 2 minutes, then cut into 24 squares. Cool completely before removing from the tin.

Makes 24

MALTED OAT FINGERS

120 ml (4 fl oz) oil
3 tablespoons malt
  extract
50 g (2 oz)
  muscovado or dark
  soft brown sugar
125 g (4 oz) jumbo
  oats
125 g (4 oz) rolled
  oats
2 tablespoons sesame
  seeds, roasted

Place the oil, malt extract and sugar in a saucepan and heat gently. Add the remaining ingredients and mix thoroughly. Press into a greased 20 cm (8 inch) square shallow cake tin and smooth the top with a knife.

Bake in a preheated moderate oven, 180°C (350°F), Gas Mark 4, for 30 minutes.

Cool in the tin for 2 minutes, then cut into 16 fingers. Cool completely before removing from the tin.

Makes 16

Digestive Biscuits

OAT CAKES

350 g (12 oz) fine
  oatmeal
1 teaspoon salt
pinch of bicarbonate
  of soda
40 g (1½ oz)
  margarine
150 ml (¼ pint)
  boiling water

Place the oatmeal, salt and bicarbonate of soda in a mixing bowl.

Cut the margarine into pieces and place in a separate bowl. Pour over the water and stir until the margarine is melted. Add to the oatmeal and mix to a dough.

Turn onto a surface sprinkled with oatmeal and knead lightly until smooth. Dust with oatmeal and roll out very thinly into two 25 cm (10 inch) rounds. Cut each round into 8 sections and place on greased baking sheets.

Bake in a preheated cool oven, 150°C (300°F), Gas Mark 2, for 1 hour until crisp. Transfer to a wire rack to cool.

Reheat to serve if preferred. Spread with butter or cream cheese.
Makes 16

MUESLI BISCUITS

125 g (4 oz) butter
  or margarine
90 ml (3 fl oz) clear
  honey
350 g (10 oz)
  muesli
2 tablespoons
  sunflower seeds

Place the butter or margarine and honey in a large pan and heat gently until melted. Remove from the heat, stir in the muesli and sunflower seeds and mix thoroughly.

Spoon mounds of the mixture onto lightly greased baking sheets, spacing them well apart and flatten with a palette knife.

Bake in a preheated moderately hot oven, 190°C (375°F), Gas Mark 5, for 10 to 12 minutes until golden brown. Leave for 3 minutes, then loosen the biscuits with a palette knife and leave on the baking sheets until completely cool.
Makes 16
NOTE: The sweetness of these delicious biscuits will depend on the type of muesli used. If you use an unsweetened variety, add 1 to 2 tablespoons raw sugar.

DIGESTIVE BISCUITS

175 g (6 oz)
  wholemeal flour
50 g (2 oz) fine
  oatmeal
½ teaspoon salt
1 teaspoon baking
  powder
75 g (3 oz)
  margarine
25 g (1 oz)
  muscovado or dark
  soft brown sugar
3–4 tablespoons milk
1 tablespoon sesame
  seeds

Mix the flour, oatmeal, salt and baking powder together. Rub in the margarine until the mixture resembles breadcrumbs, then stir in the sugar. Add the milk and mix to a firm dough.

Turn onto a floured surface and roll out thinly. Prick and cut into 6 cm (2½ inch) rounds. Brush with water and sprinkle with sesame seeds.

Place on a greased baking sheet and bake in a preheated moderately hot oven, 190°C (375°F), Gas Mark 5, for 15 to 20 minutes.
Makes 20 to 24

DATE AND WALNUT BREAD

125 g (4 oz)
  All-Bran
75 g (3 oz) molasses
  sugar
125 g (4 oz) dates,
  chopped
50 g (2 oz) walnuts,
  chopped
300 ml ($\frac{1}{2}$ pint) milk
125 g (4 oz)
  wholemeal flour
2 teaspoons baking
  powder

Put the 'Breakfast Bran', sugar, dates, walnuts and milk in a mixing bowl. Stir well and leave for 1 hour. Add the flour, sift in the baking powder and mix together thoroughly.

Turn into a lined and greased 500 g (1 lb) loaf tin and bake in a preheated moderate oven, 180°C (350°F), Gas Mark 4, for 55 minutes to 1 hour, or until a skewer inserted into the centre comes out clean. Turn out onto a wire rack to cool.
Makes one 500 g (1 lb) loaf

YOGURT SCONES

250 g (8 oz)
  wholemeal flour
$\frac{1}{2}$ teaspoon salt
$\frac{1}{2}$ teaspoon baking
  powder
50 g (2 oz)
  margarine or
  butter
1 tablespoon
  muscovado or dark
  soft brown sugar
150 g (5 oz) natural
  yogurt
milk for brushing
sesame seeds for
  sprinkling

Place the flour and salt in a mixing bowl and sift in the baking powder. Rub in the fat until the mixture resembles breadcrumbs, then stir in the sugar. Add the yogurt and mix to a soft dough.

Turn onto a floured surface, knead lightly and roll out to a 2 cm ($\frac{3}{4}$ inch) thickness. Cut into 5 cm (2 inch) rounds with a fluted cutter and place on a floured baking sheet. Brush with milk, sprinkle with sesame seeds and bake in a preheated hot oven, 220°C (425°F), Gas Mark 7, for 12 to 15 minutes. Transfer to a wire rack to cool.
Makes 12 to 14

Cheese and Sesame Scones: Sift in 1 teaspoon dry mustard and a pinch of cayenne pepper with the baking powder. Replace the sugar with 75 g (3 oz) grated cheese and 1 tablespoon sesame seeds.
Date and Nut Scones: Sift in $\frac{1}{2}$ teaspoon ground cinnamon with the baking powder. Mix in 25 g (1 oz) chopped dates and 25 g (1 oz) chopped walnuts with the sugar.

Date and Walnut Bread; Yogurt Scones

INDEX

ACKNOWLEDGEMENTS

The publishers would like to thank the following individuals who were involved in the preparation of material for this book:
Photography by Roger Phillips, Fred Mancini, Charlie Stebbings and Paul Williams

Photographic Stylist: Hilary Guy

Food for photography prepared by Allyson Birch

Designed by Patrick McLeavy